Ritual Healing in Suburban America

RITUAL

HEALING

IN

SUBURBAN

AMERICA

Meredith B. McGuire

with the assistance of Debra Kantor

89-972

RUTGERS UNIVERSITY PRESS
New Brunswick and London

Library of Congress Cataloging-in-Publication Data

McGuire, Meredith B.
    Ritual healing in suburban America / Meredith B. McGuire : with
the assistance of Debra Kantor.
       p.   cm.
    Includes index.
    ISBN 0-8135-1312-X   ISBN 0-8135-1313-8 (pbk.)
    1. Spiritual healing—United States—History—20th century.
2. Mental healing—United States—History—20th century.
3. Medicine, Magic, mystic, and spagiric—United States—
History—20th century.   4. United States—Religion—1960-
5. United States—Social life and customs—1971-   6. Spiritual
healing—New Jersey—History—20th century.   7. Mental healing—New
Jersey—History—20th century.   8. Medicine, Magic, mystic, and
spagiric—New Jersey—History—20th century.   9. New Jersey—
Religion.   10. New Jersey—Social life and customs.   I. Kantor,
Debra.   II. Title.
BL65.M4M4 1988
615.5—dc 19   88-1094
                                                                             CIP

British Cataloging-in-Publication
information available

Copyright © 1988 by Rutgers, The State University

With appreciation
to Daniel, Rachel, and Kieran McGuire
and
to Mark Kantor

CONTENTS

FIGURES

AND

TABLE

ACKNOWLEDGMENTS

In writing this book, I have received help from many people, whose assistance I gratefully acknowledge. Special thanks is due to the entire staff of the Alternative Healing Systems project: Pat Brown, Debra Kantor, Matt Krautheim, Kathy Lee, Linda Podhurst, and Valerie Simpson, and numerous student transcribers and coders. Two research associates, Debra Kantor and Linda Podhurst, worked on the data analysis long after grant funding ended. Debra Kantor drafted portions of Chapter Six, Chapter Seven, and Appendix A; Linda Podhurst also assisted in writing Appendix A. Their special efforts and exceptional research skills throughout this research project are particularly commended.

For thoughtful comments on earlier drafts, thanks to Steve Aulicino, Jim Beckford, Fred Bird, Virginia Black, Gail Ciecierski, Peter Conrad, Peter Freund, Harriet Klein, Laura Kramer, George Martin, Ted Mills, Deborah Offenbacher, Jim Richardson, Evelyn Savage, and Frances Westley. The advice and encouragement of my editor, Marlie Wasserman, and reviewers Arthur Parsons and William Sims Bainbridge are greatly appreciated. Thanks also to the staff of Montclair State College's interlibrary loan services; their help was invaluable.

This volume is based upon research made possible by NIMH grant #1RO 1MH33664, Meredith B. McGuire, Principal Investigator. Additional funding assistance was received from the Society for the Scientific Study of Religion, Montclair State College Alumni Association, and a grant of released time from Montclair State College.

Parts of Chapter Nine are included in Meredith McGuire, "Words of Power: Personal Empowerment and Healing," *Culture, Medicine and Psychiatry* 7: 221–240, copyright © 1983 by D. Reidel Publishing Company, reprinted by permission. Other parts of Chapter Nine are used, by permission, from Meredith McGuire, "Ritual, Symbolism and Healing," *Social Compass* (1988), published by Centre de Recherches Socio-Religieuses, Louvain, Belgium. Small portions of Chapters Three, Four, and Six were also used in Meredith McGuire and Debra Kantor, "Belief Systems and Illness Experiences: The Case of Nonmedical Healing Groups," in J. Roth and P. Conrad, eds., *Research in the Sociology of Health Care*, 6 (1987): 221–248, and are used with permission of JAI Press.

On behalf of the staff of the Alternative Healing Systems Research Project, I want to express our gratitude to the members of the various groups we have studied. They have given us much time, thoughtful interviews, and lots of basic kindness. While not endorsing any specific healing approaches, we hope we have rendered our respondents' beliefs and practices as faithfully and fairly as possible. We have been impressed by the sincerity and commitment of most persons involved in this study; they deserve to be taken seriously.

Meredith McGuire
Montclair, New Jersey
Fall 1987

Ritual Healing in Suburban America

MIDDLE-CLASS USE OF NONMEDICAL HEALING

Tuesday night finds a group of serious suburbanites sitting on the plush carpet of a darkened living room. Eight women and five men, mostly in their thirties, form a rough circle, holding hands, eyes gently closed in meditation. After nearly half an hour, they begin to stir and look about with quiet smiles and nods. They share their meditative experiences with each other, tell each other of their problems and needs, offer advice and sympathy, and mention articles on nutrition, exercise, and child psychology. Each person around the circle tells of some special problem or need anticipated in the coming week—chronic pain, a job interview, a rebellious teenager, a series of scheduled medical tests, recurring anxiety or fear. The three-hour session closes with another meditation for these particular needs. Some linger for refreshments before saying farewell until the next week's meeting. What is this group about? One of its main focuses is healing.

And this group is hardly unique. Elsewhere in the same upper-middle-class suburban town are numerous others for whom nonmedical healing is an important part of their lives. Some seek healing in churches and prayer meetings; others take classes to learn self-healing methods; some go out of their way to grow and prepare special foods required by their healing approach; yet others go to practitioners of various non-medical approaches. The acceptability of belief in alternative healing systems among middle-class persons belies the notion that marginal medicine is a characteristic of the lower classes, a remnant of folk culture that is waning as education and socioeconomic prospects increase.

"Alternative healing" refers to a wide range of beliefs and practices that adherents expect to affect health but that are not promulgated by medical personnel in the dominant biomedical system.[1] Examples of

4 MIDDLE-CLASS USE OF NONMEDICAL HEALING

alternative healing used by middle-class persons include: naturopathy, faith healing, Christian Science, psychic healing, Transcendental Meditation (TM) and other meditational systems, occult and New Age therapies, human potential therapeutic methods (such as Arica, est, and psychosynthesis), reflexology, iridology, and Native American healing methods.[2]

We have scant empirical data on how widespread alternative healing is in the United States and Europe. Homeopathy and naturopathy are more widely practiced in Europe than in America. Older forms of alternative healing—spiritualist and psychic healing, mesmerism, radionics, faith healing, and other nonmedical approaches—have been documented in various European countries (England, the Netherlands, Belgium, West Germany), Australia, New Zealand, and Canada, as well as the United States.[3]

Some indications of the extent of use of other alternative therapeutic approaches come from a 1976 Gallup poll, which found that 4 percent of those polled had engaged in Transcendental Meditation, another 3 percent practiced yoga, and a further one percent were involved in an Eastern religion. Projecting from this sample, these figures suggest that over ten million Americans are involved in just a few of these "alternatives."[4] A 1973 study in California found a predictably higher percentage of participants in the San Francisco Bay area: Approximately 8 percent had participated in yoga, 5 percent in TM, 3 percent in Zen, 1.5 percent in est, and 1.1 percent in Scientology. Furthermore, this study documented the fact there there were more respondents who considered getting to know the inner self and becoming aware of their own bodies important than there were respondents who attached importance to having a high-paying job, having a beautiful home, or belonging to a church or synagogue.[5]

A Sociological Approach

In interpreting this widespread phenomenon, we need to get beyond understanding only why individuals use alternative healing methods. Rather, we should ask: What does this suggest about society and the social location of these beliefs and practices? Of what larger social phenomenon is this an example?

Some common misconceptions about alternative healing interfere with an adequate sociological perspective on marginal medicine. One such misconception is that marginal medicine functions merely as an alternative healing technique to which people resort when all else fails. Although a few persons seek alternative healing as a last resort, most adherents are more deeply involved. This study found that only a tiny minority of adherents initially came to their alternative healing group or healer out of a need to heal a prior condition. Most adherents were initially attracted by the larger system of beliefs, of which health-illness related beliefs and practices are only one part.

For most adherents, therefore, the use of alternative healing typically involves a totally different definition of medical reality, an alternative etiology of illness, and a specific theory of health, deviance, and healing power. Thus, in order to fully understand the alternative healing practices of these suburban groups, it is necessary to delve into their root conceptions of health and illness and to explore all the functions of their healing practices and beliefs.

A second notion that must also be set aside is the assumption that the medical reality, as promulgated by the dominant health specialists in this culture, is necessarily the "true" reality. From a sociological perspective, this medical definition of reality must be seen as one among many competing conceptions of illness, its causes, and treatment. Medical reality, too, is socially constructed.[6]

This relativistic stance toward the "truth" of biomedicine means that it cannot be used to explain nonmedical healing. One paradigmatic system cannot really explain another, although the comparison may be useful as a legitimating device. For example, if faith healing has elements X, Y, and Z that are also present in psychotherapy, the parallel does not explain either faith healing or psychotherapy. Likewise, findings from current psychosomatic medicine cannot be used to "prove" or "disprove" alternative healing, although they do suggest that it is not so improbable in biomedical terms as some doctors think. Basically, biomedicine and alternative healing systems operate within totally different paradigms of health, illness, and healing.

One of the most commonly asked questions about alternative healing approaches is: Do they work? This question is based on the notion that alternative healing involves a series of techniques—discrete methods, devices, or even "tricks"—that could be used in place of medical techniques.[7] Much alternative healing, on the contrary, is not merely a technique, but rather entails an entire system of beliefs and practices. Thus, it "works" in several complex ways. Medical systems have many functions (i.e., ways in which they "work") beyond the healing practices per se, including construction of the illness experience, cognitive management of the illness experience (e.g., through categorization and explanation), and management of death.[8]

Much alternative healing works in all of these meaning-providing senses of the word. Indeed, part of the appeal of these medical systems is probably their lack of sharp dichotomies between the meaning-providing elements and the healing practices, in contrast with modern "scientific" medicine. Most contemporary Western physicians limit their help to the cure of *disease*—a biological disorder. They are generally unprepared to heal *illness*—the way the ill person experiences his or her disorder, in a given social and cultural context.[9] Alternative healing, by contrast, appears generally to address illness more than disease; the relative focus, however, varies among the different alternative medical systems.

Studying healing in other cultures or in U.S. subcultures, anthropologists have emphasized the ritual and symbolic significance of healing practices. Their findings suggest that healing beliefs and practices address not only the concrete condition of a person's body, but also sociocultural meanings and conditions in the larger social group. Healing is typically part of a larger system of beliefs and practices that deals with issues such as moral responsibility, social status, and family or community cohesion.[10] Is modern Western society so different that healing and healing beliefs and practices have no sociocultural referents? Data from this research show that American suburbanites, too, use health, illness, and healing as expressions of their concerns for meaning, moral order, and individual effectiveness and power in their social world.[11]

Unfortunately, many studies of marginal medicine in Western societies have assumed that these systems of belief and practice are characteristic of the lower classes and poorly educated people, that they are basically vestiges of earlier folk healing practices, and that they are likely to wane as education and socioeconomic levels in the society increase.[12]

Alternative healing is sometimes viewed as the poor persons' alternative to expensive medical care or as a psychological buffer against the precariousness of their socioeconomic predicament.[13] This study shows, however, the appeal of certain kinds of nonmedical healing to well-educated, economically comfortable, established denizens of middle- and upper-middle-class suburban communities.

Some historical perspective on the orthodox-medicine/alternative-healing dichotomy is helpful. What we know as "modern" medicine has itself evolved from a much more heterogeneous set of competing medical perspectives. In the twentieth century in America, one approach, allopathy, gained virtual monopoly over medical practice, education, and licensing. There have been several other important professional approaches, such as homeopathy, osteopathy, Thompsonism (an American form of herbalism), chiropractic, and naturopathy, each positing different interpretations of causes and treatments of illness. These approaches have, however, been effectively subordinated or suppressed by the monopoly of allopathic medicine. Persons who seek practitioners of these other forms of medicine constitute one segment of "marginal" medicine.[14]

As allopathic physicians consolidated their control and prestige, they also annexed and subordinated a number of potentially competing healing roles, such as nursing, pharmacy, and medical technology. Other competitors, such as midwives, herbalists, and bone-setters, were effectively driven out of practice and their functions taken over by the medical profession.[15] Anyone seeking these traditional forms of healing or health care outside of their medically controlled settings would represent another segment of alternative healing.

A third and perhaps more far-reaching part of the background of alternative healing is the extent of self-care or home health care. In "modern" Western societies, institutional specialization, professionalization, and medical dominance have created the impression that *health care* means "medical care." This conception obscures the reality that historically (and to a considerable extent, even today) most health care has been a function of the family.[16]

To keep these alternative healing groups' self-treatment in perspective, it is important to keep in mind that self-treatment of all kinds is prevalent in this society. One informed estimate suggests that between 67 and 80 percent of adult Americans self-treat and medicate themselves in any given thirty-six-hour period.[17] The respondents in this study may employ a wider range of self-treatment options than other Americans, but their decision to treat themselves is hardly unique.

"Scientific" medicine of the eighteenth and nineteenth centuries often employed "heroic" measures, such as bleeding, purging, or prescription of doses of known poisons. Self-medication with herbal or patent medicines or use of therapies such as mineral water baths was certainly more palatable and often just as effective as a doctor's treatment. Although some self-care has been necessitated by the unavailability of professional medicine (for example, in remote rural places), it has also been spurred on by populism—a recurrent theme in American culture.[18]

One small fringe of this background is what has been called "quackery" (i.e., pretending to heal, usually for the purpose of financial gain). Much of the labelling of quackery has, or course, been the effort of the medical profession to suppress competition with its professional dominance. The American Medical Association (AMA), for example, funds a Bureau of Investigation to trace "quacks" and aid in their legal control and prosecution.[19]

For the purposes of this study, a useful distinction is the intent of the healer(s). Does the healer actually intend to heal and believe he or she can heal? Few, if any, of the healers or groups studied here appear to be pretending to heal. All of the individuals in this study use their healing methods personally and devote considerable time and effort to these methods; this suggests that little, if any, of the alternative healing studied was being promoted cynically.

A further criterion also helps distinguish "quacks." What do they gain (especially financially) from offering their form of healing? The sale of fraudulent or misrepresented nostrums and devices can, indeed, be quite lucrative. For example, in 1950, Dudley J. LeBlanc, a former Louisiana state senator, grossed over twenty million dollars on sales of his tonic, Hadicol, for which he claimed therapeutic effects for virtually every human ailment, including asthma and cancer.[20]

In this study, the majority of persons engaged in healing had no financial interests whatsoever. Many healing situations were simply friends or fellow believers seeking healing for each other. A smaller number of persons engaged in healing sold their services but no products. Within this group, we can further distinguish between persons who received pay for teaching others self-healing methods and persons who received pay for performing healing services, such as massage. Since both of these approaches are labor-intensive and rarely covered by health insurance, they might provide a modest livelihood or side income but are not likely to produce "easy money." Although several persons engaged in healing recommended purchase of products (usually books or vitamins) to their students, clients, or friends, they themselves did not usually sell these products.[21]

The hegemony of biomedical definitions of reality in modern Western societies is related to the gap in our understanding of alternative beliefs and practices. Orthodox biomedicine is assumed to be the "modern" perspective. Accordingly, educated and acculturated members of "modern" societies are assumed to share biomedicine's general perspective. Does the root conception of health and illness held by middle-class, educated persons really resemble the officially promulgated one? It is probable that lay and professional conceptions are less similar than social scientists have assumed.

For this reason, it is difficult to say for certain whether coming to believe in a given alternative healing system represents a deviation from the world view into which persons were initially socialized. It is entirely possible that many middle-class, relatively well-educated persons were socialized into a set of medical conceptions that are neither "officially" acceptable nor internally consistent: a curious mixture of elements of folk beliefs, religious explanations, partially understood "scientific" and medical explanations, superstition, recipe-knowledge for everyday situations, mass media caricatures, and cocktail-party versions of "pop" therapeutic concepts.

Methodology

The healing groups and healers studied represent all types of nonmedical healing found in the suburban communities of western Essex County, New Jersey, and in nearby counties where groups draw adherents from Essex. Over 130 different groups or healers were identified. Some groups of each broad healing type were studied intensively by participant-observation for ten to eighteen months; other groups were visited only occasionally. A total of 255 group sessions in 31 different groups were observed and recorded in detail.

Three hundred thirteen interviews, lasting between one and three hours, were conducted with leaders, healers, adherents, and clients of the various forms of nonmedical healing. An additional forty-three interviews were conducted with a control group selected from comparable neighborhoods and matched for gender and age.

Interviews were conducted according to an open-ended schedule that elicited: the respondent's conception of healing, illness, health, and death; healing beliefs and practices, images of healing power, and personal experiences with healing; attitudes toward the dominant medical system, toward other alternative healing approaches, and toward related religious belief systems; information about the respondent's recruitment and degree of commitment to alternative healing systems and "career" as adherent; and relevant background information about the respondent. Verbatim transcripts of these interviews, together with extensive field notes of ethnographic material, provide the empirical base of these interpretations. Appendix A of this volume describes this methodology in detail, outlining working definitions, methodological judgments, and the advantages and limitations of these methodological approaches. Appendix B includes the interview schedules for adherents and control group respondents, respectively.

Middle-Class Adherents

This volume reports data from a study of middle-class suburbanites who practice and believe in various forms of alternative healing. A brief description of these adherents demonstrates how dramatically they differ from the stereotypical uneducated, poor, rural adherent of alternative healing. This description is a composite from all groups studied; some variations are reported in more detail in subsequent chapters.

Respondents in this study were economically comfortable. In 1982, when most of the interviewing was conducted, the median family income reported by respondents was about $30,000. Fifty percent of the respondents reported incomes between $20,000 and $40,000. Only 9 percent reported incomes under $10,000; all of these, however, were better off than their reported income indicates. For example, one was a retired widow, living in a substantial, unmortgaged home, who later mentioned that her sister lived with her eight months each year and contributed equally to the household's maintenance. Likewise, two respondents gave their own incomes as "under $10,000" but elsewhere noted that they lived with another person who virtually supported them. Slightly more than 22 percent of the respondents reported incomes between $10,000 and $20,000, and most of these were single, widowed, and/or retired. At the other end of the income spectrum were the more than 18 percent of the respondents who earned over $40,000 per year.

Occupations represented were consistently middle-class, too. Forty-four percent of the respondents were (or had been, before retirement) professionals, in such fields as teaching, nursing, and architecture. Another 16 percent were white-collar or business workers, including several self-employed persons. Pink-collar occupations (secretary, book-keeper) accounted for 13 percent of the respondents; under 4 percent were skilled blue-collar workers (plumber, telephone installer). Sixteen percent described themselves as "housewife"; those who worked part-time have been categorized according to their paid occupation, above. Fewer than one percent considered their primary occupation to be "student," although several were attending college or graduate school part-time. The remaining 6 percent fell into a residual category of artists, dancers, craftsmen, and musicians.

Consistent with these relatively high-level occupations, respondents' educational levels were quite high. Virtually all had completed high school,[22] and 86 percent had some college education. Fifty-six percent had achieved a B.A. or its equivalent, and 32 percent had some graduate or professional education beyond college. Several Ph.D.'s were represented among the respondents, and many respondents were currently taking graduate-level classes. These figures do not reflect the many additional non-degree courses taken by a large number of respondents —for example, courses on massage therapy, nutrition, art, dance, and so on. Indeed, several respondents told of first learning of alternative healing methods through adult education courses.

One notable feature of this sample is the low degree of residential mobility represented. Based upon their place of residence since age twenty-five, respondents were categorized for high, medium, or low mobility. Seventy-five percent of the respondents were of "low mobil-ity"—i.e., they had moved few times and only within the immediate tristate area of New York, New Jersey, and Pennsylvania. The number of persons who had lived in the same town all their lives was remarkable;

indeed, some respondents were living in the same house they were born in decades ago. Seventy percent of the respondents were born in the tristate area.

These mobility figures show clearly that our sample is hardly made up of ex-Californians who imported their "strange" practices to staid East Coast communities. Nor are we talking about recent immigrants; only about 6 percent of the respondents were foreign-born (most were from England and other Western European countries, two from Eastern Europe, and three from the Caribbean and Latin America). Most respondents in this study were at least three generations removed from "the old country."

Respondents in this study were largely middle-aged. Persons under thirty represented only 10 percent of the sample.[23] The modal age of respondents was thirty-eight, with 53 percent of the sample between thirty and fifty years of age. Another 20 percent was between fifty and sixty, and 17 percent was over sixty. These figures indicate that we are not observing a "youth culture" phenomenon; adherents to alternative healing studied are solidly middle-aged.

They are also established in their careers, marriages, child-rearing, home-owning, and other normative middle-age statuses. Fifty-eight percent of the sample described themselves as currently married, with another 13 percent divorced. Nearly 18 percent were single (almost all of these were under thirty-five or over sixty). Eleven percent were widowed. Most of those who were married, widowed, or divorced had children. Forty-five percent of the sample had one or two children; another 34 percent had three or more children.

Reflecting, in part, the composition of the communities in which these groups were located, the sample was largely white (95 percent). Just under 5 percent of the respondents were black, with a fraction of one percent Hispanic. Although a handful of Oriental persons belonged to two groups, no Orientals were interviewed.

The respondents in the sample were generally female (80 percent). Although women are disproportionately involved in alternative healing groups studied, they are slightly overrepresented in this sample, because we chose two all-female groups, among others, for intensive study.

There is nothing unusual about the religious backgrounds of respondents in this study. They were recruited to alternative healing from ordinary religious backgrounds; major religious groups are represented in roughly their proportion in communities studied. Episcopalians are slightly overrepresented among respondents because a largely Episcopalian healing movement was chosen for intensive study.

About 34 percent of respondents were from Roman or Eastern Catholic backgrounds. Jewish persons comprised 17 percent of the sample, while just under 3 percent described themselves as from nonreligious backgrounds. Eleven percent were from an Episcopalian background, and 19 percent were from other mainline Protestant denominations. Nearly 10 percent had been raised in fundamentalist or pentecostal traditions; several (less than 2 percent) had been raised Mormon, and an equal number had been raised in Christian Science. Unitarians and "other" religious backgrounds accounted for the remaining approximately 4 percent. Nearly half of these persons considered themselves still affiliated (in varying degrees of commitment) to these religious groups, but many others (especially Catholics) had utterly rejected the religion of their upbringing.

In general, then, the respondents depicted in this study hardly fit the stereotype of adherents to alternative healing. They are clearly middle-class, middle-aged, well-educated, socially, culturally, and residentially established suburbanites.

The Significance of Middle-Class Healing Movements

The significance of this research for a social scientific understanding of health and healing lies in the apparently widespread use of such alternative medical systems by middle-class persons and the value of looking at the meaning of healing beliefs and practices in these people's lives. It is not possible to document whether middle-class acceptance and utilization of such marginal medical practices are, in fact, growing, because we have no accurate clear data on what prior usage and belief were. It is possible to discover, however, the present extent of usage and belief. The diversity of types of marginal medicine appealing to middle-class persons suggests that the topic is complex, not traceable to a single social movement. The points of commonality among these diverse alternative healing approaches are, however, significant.

These data offer the opportunity to understand several aspects of alternative healing. They shed light on the complex help-seeking process and the use of nonprofessional resources in health referral, information, and treatment. The data also locate adherents' beliefs and practices in the context of their larger belief systems and social relationships. They give a clearer picture of how persons come to be attracted to and influenced by beliefs and practices other than those promulgated by the "official" health education system. By studying numerous groups in the same region, the extent of adherence to multiple alternatives can also be explored. In addition, these data yield interesting patterns of recruitment, "conversion," and commitment.

Other relevant aspects of the social setting of such alternative healing include the context of the actual healing practices. Are they done in a group setting, a practitioner-client relationship, face-to-face, or from a distance? What actually happens during healing practices? Are there ritual acts, a special physical setting, ritual objects, special words used? What is the meaning of the experience for the person being healed and for others involved? What kinds of evidence of healing are sought and found satisfying by adherents? What events or experiences are disconfirming of their beliefs? What kinds of legitimations are used to explain suffering, death, or therapeutic failures?

These data show that even the strangest, most difficult to understand healing beliefs and practices provide very important functions for their adherents: meaning, order, and a sense of personal empowerment in the face of upsetting or even traumatic experiences in life. Alternative healing systems are meeting some people's needs, which the dominant medical system does not address. Thus they highlight some of the limits of modern "scientific" medicine.

The Organization of This Volume

For descriptive purposes, the many groups studied are presented in five broad types. Chapter Two presents the general qualities of these types. For each type a brief ethnographic description of a representative group gives a flavor of that approach to healing. The fifth type, technique practitioners, was not comparable, because few adherents knew or cared about the ideals and beliefs underlying these forms of healing. Very few respondents used technique practitioners as their primary form of alternative healing. This fifth type is used mainly for comparison, as is the control group.

Chapters Three, Four, Five, and Six are detailed discussions of the belief systems of the four main types of healing studied. Each type of healing is analyzed according to:

> Ideals of health and wellness
> Notions of illness and healing
> Causes of illness
> Diagnostic approaches
> Source of healing power
> Healing and health practices
> Therapeutic success, therapeutic failure, and death

Chapter Seven describes the role of alternative healers (or of the entire healing group, when healing is done in the context of a group). This chapter explores the importance of key relationships—with a specialized healer or with other members of the group. Various patterns of healer-patient relationship are important (e.g., whether the healer is paid or volunteer, whether the healing is done in a group or one-to-one setting, sources of income for the leader and/or group, patterns of authority and prestige, degree of patient activity or passivity in the healing process). Use of alternative healing is related to adherents' attitudes toward orthodox medical practice and institutions. Chapter Eight describes these attitudes and adherents' help-seeking patterns. Contrary to the way the media and AMA portray alternative healing, very little of it is in direct conflict with orthodox medical practices, and virtually all adherents use both medical and alternative healing. Their criticism of doctors and medical institutions is acute; it helps explain their complex pattern of help-seeking and their qualified use of the dominant medical system.

At the same time, various developments in psychosomatic medicine point to some convergences between the forms of alternative healing studied and biomedical understanding. Psychosomatic medicine demonstrates the probable linkage of illness and disease with social conditions, such as ambiguity, stress, loss of control, helplessness, disorder, sense of things being out of control, emotional or social disequilibrium. This chapter presents an overview of this literature but argues that biomedical science is not an adequate vantage point for interpreting alternative healing.

In Chapter Nine, the special uses of metaphor, symbols, language, and ritual in alternative healing are described and interpreted. The groups studied used a rich variety of symbols and ritual practices. Often special ritual language marked their healing approaches. Imagery and visualization were a common part of the healing process. The use of metaphor, ritual, and symbolization is a key to understanding how alternative healing works. At one level, the body imagery used in each group reveals much about social relationships in that group and about individual members' senses of their bodies, illnesses, and selves.

Furthermore, these symbolic aspects of alternative healing systems are linked with the process of empowering adherents to combat their illnesses, to cope with them, and to deal with a wide range of normal problems in everyday life. Specifically, this volume proposes that alternative healing often works (both for social-emotional and physical problems) by empowering the individual to mobilize internal resources. Alternative healing groups also often provide very real networks of social and material support, thus strengthening their members in the face of illness or disease. By contrast, the dominant medical approach, while effectively tackling the disease entity, often diminishes the patient's sense of personal power and, unknowingly, reduces the patient's ability to mobilize personal resources against the disease/illness. Thus this research has a number of implications for evaluating both alternative and orthodox medical systems. Important differences in the ways groups used ritual imagery and visualization suggest differences in these groups' functions for linking the individual to the larger society.

Chapter Ten interprets alternative healing, somewhat speculatively, in terms of larger cultural and social structural issues. It argues that these healing movements may be related to a new mode of individualism, a new form of connection between the individual and society. This chapter explores adherents' dominant "world images," especially the significance of "holism" and the alternative notions of moral responsibility. Another important feature is the groups' healing rituals, collective but privately experienced enactments of self-transformation. Both the alternative world images and the healing rituals may represent a specifically middle-class assertion against the rationalization of several aspects of contemporary life.

Appendix A describes the methods used in this study. It includes details about the range of groups studied, and how they were located and sampled. It also describes the participant-observation method, its problems and advantages for this research. The structure of the interview instrument and the actual interviewing process are developed in detail. Appendix B contains the actual interview schedules.

2 FEATURES OF GROUPS STUDIED

This study covers five broad types of nonmedical healing (although several groups represent an overlap between types). This typology is based primarily upon the sources of groups' belief systems; further distinctions occur in their notions of the source of healing power and their relative emphasis on the individual. For descriptive purposes, however, it is helpful to conceive of the groups as falling into five belief-system types. They include: (1) Christian healing; (2) Eastern meditation and human potential groups; (3) traditional metaphysical groups; (4) psychic and occult groups; and (5) manipulation/technique practitioners. All of these forms of healing, but especially the first four, involve an alternative understanding of the nature and etiology of illness; healing power; and the essence of health.

Since it is impossible to describe in detail all of the many different types of alternative healing studied, five examples will be described, one of each major healing type. In subsequent chapters, examples from these and other groups or practitioners will be included to show some of the fascinating diversity among the groups.

Christian Groups

This type of group included several fundamentalist churches, pentecostal and neo-pentecostal groups, and healing cults within mainline churches, as well as nondenominational men's and women's groups, such as Women's Aglow and Full Gospel Businessmen's Association, in which healing has some significance. Pentecostal-style healing has typically been associated with lower-class religiosity, but in recent years it is relatively widespread among middle-class persons, as well. One factor is that some pentecostalists have retained their style of religiosity even as they moved into the middle classes. Another major factor is the development of charismatic movements within many middle-class churches in the last two decades. These movements have been prominent in the Roman Catholic, Episcopalian, and other mainline denominations; since the early 1970s these charismatic movements have emphasized faith healing as one of their foremost features.

Most of these groups base their healing emphasis primarily upon New Testament descriptions of Jesus' healing ministry and the place of healing in the early churches, although some groups also incorporate beliefs from medieval and modern saint cults. Generally, although these groups were middle-class, members were less well-to-do than in the other types studied. Far more women than men were active members in gender-mixed groups, but men were conspicuously predominant in number and influence among the leadership of all groups. Members were drawn from all age groups, but were mainly middle-aged (forty to sixty). Families were more likely than in other types of group to have three or more children. The groups studied were not racially mixed, and no middle-class black Christian healing group was found in the racially mixed suburban communities studied. Christian groups were highly sectarian in orientation—that is, extremely intolerant of non-Christian forms of healing.

Women's Aglow, International, is a very good example of these Christian groups. It is a nondenominational fellowship of pentecostal (Full Gospel) women. The movement began in 1967 in Seattle, eventually taking its name from a scripture verse admonishing Christians to "Be aglow and burning with the Spirit" (Romans 12:1). Since then, thirteen hundred local Women's Aglow fellowships have developed worldwide. The international organization publishes a sophisticated monthly magazine, provides Bible study guides, paperback books (with special emphasis on themes of interest to women), pamphlets, instructional and devotional tape cassettes, and television and radio series of programs.

Although the membership is essentially all female, the international organization requires that each chapter's advisors be men (since they believe that Scripture teaches that women should be submissive to men's authority). Furthermore, women need their husband's permission, as well as the approval of their local pastors and chapter advisors, to become officers of Aglow. The activities of Aglow are, for most members, only one—albeit a very important—aspect of their religiosity; most are also active in local churches and watch much religious programming on television. Very few of the members are employed full-time. Religious and child-rearing activities dominate their daytime lives. It is not uncommon for a member to spend three to four half-days a week on Aglow and other religious group activities.

Healing is an important focus of Women's Aglow, since healing is one of the "gifts of the Spirit" that pentecostal Christians believe is given them by God. Although members recognize the extraordinary healing ministries of faith healers, such as Kathryn Kuhlman and Oral Roberts, they also emphasize that the Spirit works through ordinary Christians. Thus regular prayer meetings usually include petitions for healing of members and their loved ones; study group members frequently lay hands on each other in healing prayer, and testimonies often recount stories of healings of body, mind, and spirit.

One typical weekly "prayer and share" meeting began with a brown bag lunch in a church basement. Conversation consisted of swapping advice about children's entertainment; members felt that too much children's television programming, games, and other influences were not "of the Lord." Members talked about how to control children's activities in the face of strong social pressures and other cultural influences.

After a leisurely lunch, members were joined upstairs in the church by others who came just for the prayer service. A lengthy period of gospel hymns opened the service. The opening blessing was led by the chapter president, who included prayers for several organizational needs, as well as the ritual invocation of the Spirit and exorcism of "other" spirits. There were Scripture readings, and more hymns, followed by three long (thirty- to forty-minute) prepared testimonies by members.

One woman emphasized how the Lord had helped her overcome difficulties in her marriage and adjust to the bad situation of a husband who was not born-again. Another talked about how frequently her husband had been transferred from one part of the country to another and how important her faith and local churches were in helping keep the family stable and in settling into unfamiliar towns. The third described a problem child and how his symptoms could be reinterpreted through the eye of faith.

After the testimonies there was a long period of praise, in which participants all engaged in prayers of praise—some in "tongues" (glossolalia) out loud and simultaneously. This style of prayer is common to most pentecostal groups and not peculiar to Aglow. One member also pronounced a prophecy in proficient tongues; a brief interpretation of the prophecy was "received" by another member: The Lord was reminding the group to "wait on" Him, even when it was not convenient in their busy lives; He was telling them that He never promised it would be easy to be a Christian—they had to sacrifice and use self-control.

After more Scripture reading and hymns, there was a period for petitions during which participants presented special needs for the prayers of the entire group. Sometimes they described these petitions in detail (such as going into a lengthy description of a woman who had lupus, her family, and their needs), but more often a simple sentence was sufficient. The service leader gathered the petitions, figuratively, with a fervent prayer for healing and a show of God's power. The vigorous delivery style of this prayer led to another period of prayers out loud by the entire group—this time with more glossolalia. As the prayers died down, the music leader played a few chords to introduce a favorite hymn. More hymns were requested by members of the audience. A brief final blessing and announcements ended the service.

There were several local chapters of Aglow in the region. A typical chapter held large monthly luncheon meetings at a restaurant; these attracted over one hundred paying members for an entire afternoon that typically featured national or international movement speakers. There were smaller weekly prayer meetings (attracting about fifty persons) in a Full Gospel church. Regular members typically also belong to Bible study/prayer groups of some eight to twenty persons, who met weekly in members' homes. The chapter organized a substantial "prayer-chain," which mobilized the prayers of members for anyone requesting prayers for a particular need—a forthcoming operation, a child's illness, recuperation after an accident.

Healing activities in this group, as in other Christian groups, were mainly in the form of prayer and laying-on-of-hands. Words of Scripture, too, were important in the healing process. While healing was seen as a very important "gift of the Spirit," it is not a primary reason for most members' belonging. Nevertheless, healing is a significant function in virtually every Aglow meeting, and it is an important part of the network of mutual support for these women.

Metaphysical Groups

For the purposes of this typology, metaphysical groups are those spawned by the early-twentieth-century metaphysical movement; they include Christian Science, Unity, and Religious Science. While these groups hold many beliefs in common with the psychic and occult type described later, they are organized more like denominations, maintain church buildings, and control religious teaching. They also emphasize their continuity with Christian traditions far more than eclectic and occult groups.

Metaphysical groups were quite varied, despite their denominationlike religious status; the groups studied were considerably more diverse than comparable Christian groups. Some groups had almost exclusively elderly members, whereas other groups attracted a range of ages, including numerous young adults. Some groups were all or mostly white; other groups, in the same community, were approximately half black. Women predominated in both membership and leadership in these groups (indeed, women have historically been leaders in the metaphysical movements). The membership pattern was characteristic of most denomination-type groups; members were not particularly sectarian about their beliefs, compared with the Christian healing groups, but they were not as eclectic as adherents of meditation, human potential, or occult beliefs.

Unity (or Unity School of Christianity) is a prime example of this type of group. Unity is one of many metaphysical movements emphasizing the transcendent nature of self rather than a distant deity. Accordingly, individuals have total control of their lives; there are no chance events. Indeed, things that appear to be chance or luck are known "intuitively" to be "the inner spirit, the activity of God." Every single moment of life is filled with meaning and lessons. One has only to become aware of them. Believers must "be true to this moment for a divine experience awaits us all." This emphasis on individual responsibility, control, and the here-and-now has appeal to this movement's largely middle-class following.

One Unity center with over 500 on its mailing list had an average attendance of 100–120 adherents at the Sunday services, with a much smaller number drawn to other activities. Services attracted a largely middle-aged, mostly female, racially integrated group. A second Unity center had an average attendance of 60 people. Its members were older, generally middle-aged to elderly, with few young adults. Women outnumbered men by a significant margin, but there were fewer minority members.

To become a "student of Truth," as Unity adherents call themselves, requires little commitment to the group itself. Members may simultaneously maintain membership in other religions; Unity membership requires no dues or obligations. Since anyone may attend any class or seminar, the main advantage to officially joining is voting privileges in center elections. One minister cautioned that membership is like "being part-owner in a corporation and shouldn't be taken lightly." Those who do join, thus, consider the center "theirs."

Each Unity center operates independently and may take on distinct characteristics as the result of its leadership or congregation composition. Nevertheless, centers are required to have all books used in study groups approved by the central headquarters (Unity of the Infinite Presence) in Michigan. Also, central headquarters supplies the weekly affirmation statements that are used in local Unity services.

A typical Unity meeting consisted of: a before-Service meditation; Opening Statement (containing the day's affirmation statement); the Lord's Prayer (in song); a period for welcome and announcements; Meditation hymn (often a solo performance); the Lesson; Blessing of Gifts (offertory); hymn; and a closing prayer. Thus, in many respects, Unity worship services resemble many Protestant denominational services. Lessons were typically delivered by the center's minister; occasionally, licensed Unity teachers were substitutes for the regular minister. Lesson themes were taken from biblical stories, popular psychology, metaphysics, or personal concerns such as inflation.

The two Unity centers studied differed in atmosphere. The smaller center was more personal, intimate, and oriented toward specifically Christian practices. The larger center was more individualistic and eclectic in its message. The larger Unity was not identified as a church either in title or in physical setting. Sunday services were held in a rented school auditorium to accommodate the large numbers who attend. The center's own building looks more like a modern office building than a church. The sign outside said only "Unity." Inside, there were no specifically religious objects or pictures, although there were friendly portraits of the Fillmores, Unity's founders.

The smaller Unity center, by contrast, was identified as the "Unity Church of Christ." A large framed portrait of Jesus hung on the wall behind the podium. This center used only regular religious hymns, whereas the larger Unity center frequently used popular and show tunes, as well as hymns. At the smaller center, affirmation statements were referred to as prayers.

Unity's emphasis on individuality is reinforced by the process of meditation, which, while performed in a group setting, is totally intro-spective, requiring no interaction among members. Meditations are led by the minister and are given in the first person—as one minister explained, "so as not to impinge on anyone's 'space.'" The goal of med-itation is to get in touch with one's true self, God within. The ultimate goal is to be able to say: "Order, harmony, perfect peace, are restored to my mind and heart." The lights are dimmed, the body relaxed, soft background music is provided. The leader's soft voice frequently evokes nature imagery to assist in one's becoming "still." A typical meditation contained the following images: "Visualize a quiet pool and the still waters of that scene. Take the time to get the image clear. [pause] Whisper into this scene: 'My mind is a quiet pool. My mind is stirred only by the ripples of God's inspiration. I am the keeper of my mind. No condition can agitate the quiet waters unless I permit it.'"

This introspective and mentalistic emphasis, combined with a lack of prescribed doctrine and commitment requirements, gives individuals a sense of control. At the same time, Unity's organizational structure is religious enough for those seeking the atmosphere of traditional Chris-tianity. Sunday services that include baptisms, hymns, biblical passages, and frequent references to God and Jesus demonstrate Unity's continuity with traditional religion.

It is possible to be involved in Unity's beliefs without ever actually attending a meeting. Initial introduction to Unity is often through non-personal media such as Eric Butterworth's radio program, a local Dial-A-Prayer service, or a monthly publication called *The Daily Word*. *The Daily Word* is popular across denominational lines; many respondents in this study, including pentecostals and members of psychic awareness groups, were among its regular readers.

Individual Unity members choose the level of commitment that suits them. They believe that within each person, the "individualized expres-sion of Divine Mind," all answers or causes to life's problems are to be found.

Eastern Meditation and Human Potential Groups

This type of group draws from Eastern forms of meditation and exercise disciplines and from popular psychotherapeutic methods, such as sensitivity training and bioenergetics. Examples of this type include Transcendental Meditation, Jain yoga and meditation, Tibetan Buddhist meditation, psychosynthesis, rebirthing, est, and Arica. Some of these approaches are identified by a guru or teacher who promulgates them, such as Muktananda, Meher Baba, or Rajneesh.

These groups were, by contrast to other types, relatively open to forms of healing other than their own, although generally they viewed their own as greatly superior. These groups were widespread throughout the area studied, operating centers and offering classes or programs in adult schools, church basements, and rented temporary facilities. Adherents were generally upper-middle-class and very well educated. Although women were somewhat predominant among members, these groups attracted a larger proportion of men than other types of group. Members were generally younger than in other groups (mainly between twenty-five and forty). In racially mixed communities, nonwhite adherents attended in roughly their proportion of the middle-class population of the community, but no all-black groups were found.

The Yoga and Meditation Center will be used to exemplify this broad type of group. This center encompassed several different healing methods, but the main unifying philosophy was a Jain approach to yoga and meditation. The center was housed in a rented space in a fashionable, older shopping district. It was furnished sparsely to allow space for yoga and other movement activities: Thick carpeting, lush plants, and professional photographs of yogic poses were the main features of the space. Numerous teachers held a full range of classes there, including all levels of yoga, meditation, t'ai chi chuan, vegetarian cooking, massage, and pranayama (breathing) exercises.

Commitment to the center varied considerably. Most persons were —at least initially—merely students taking classes, much as at any other adult school courses. Many students became regular attenders, taking session after session of courses. Full members joined the center for an annual fee. For many members, there was considerable commitment beyond taking classes. They went on center-sponsored retreats and vacations together, enjoyed vegetarian dinners and other center fundraisers, and shared political and social concerns—especially environmental issues. The center also spawned some private healing circles, with yet higher levels of commitment and intensity.

The age range of members was enormous. Classes often included twenty-two-year-olds alongside fifty-five-year-olds. The teachers, likewise, ranged from their twenties to sixties; particularly impressive was one yoga teacher, in her late fifties, whose physical flexibility and strength were an oft-cited inspiration to group members.

A typical Sunday morning session began with warmups, during which members clad in exercise clothes began to stretch their muscles. After working individually for about ten to twenty minutes, the group of fourteen to twenty persons received instruction from one of the teachers on various new poses or refinements of previously learned poses (asanas). Each posture was given spiritual significance. For example, as members held the "tree" pose, they were encouraged to see themselves as a tree, with its roots firmly planted in the earth, receiving energy from the earth, growing straight and tall, making a stand, balanced and poised, one with its environment.

The leader often went around the room, correcting members' poses and offering them personalized advice; she frequently connected their yogic posture with elements of their personal lives and problems, such as needing to "stay in the present" or get in touch with oneself. Despite members' intense work at the poses, the atmosphere was calm and noncompetitive; sometimes, soothing music was playing in the background.

After about one hour of exercise, the leader moved the class into relaxation poses. For meditation, then, several members pulled up pillows to sit on and wrapped themselves in blankets provided. The group sat in a rough circle and began with a lengthy guided meditation:

> In your mind's eye, hold the color green . . . a brilliant, alive color—cool, yet bursting with life, alacrity, and aliveness. . . . Bathe yourself in that green. It envelops your body and the space around you. It lifts you up with new energy and new life. Breathe in the green, breathe in the energy, the new possibilities, the hope. Breathe out the old, the worn out, the truths that are

no longer valid for you. Breathe in the Spring, the new life, resurrection, rebirth. Breathe out Winter. It is past; let it go. With it go the things that hold you back. Experience a new beginning, a new freedom [long pause].

Now let that green move out from you to envelope the whole room, the whole building, all of the space you will go out into this week. See the promise, the freshness, the new life around you. The unfolding of new life from nature, the unfolding of new promise in your relationships. Breathe in the fresh air of those new beginnings. You are alive and experiencing your life more fully. Be with yourself [long pause].

Join your consciousness with the universal consciousness in love and concern [pause]. Share that love and concern with the people of Atlanta. [This was during a period of yet-unsolved murders of several children in Atlanta.] Use that consciousness to protect them from violence. Hold them in that consciousness. Bring the green light of hope and new beginnings to those who are in sorrow.

This was followed by a period of silent, individual meditation. The meditation portion of the session lasted about thirty minutes. To bring it to a close, the leader chanted a Hindu blessing, praying for peace and freedom from violence. She added, in English, a blessing of the new season and those who take up the promise of it.

Then members gathered in a small circle, hand in hand, mentioned the special needs of other members, friends, and loved ones, and meditated for their healing. Often the needs of the world or special social issues were also mentioned. This circle was ended by chants of "Om" and a blessing for peace. Less serious, members gradually began chatting as they moved to put on their shoes before leaving.

Psychic and Occult Groups

This is the most diverse category, and thus the most difficult to describe by generalization. Included are such different groups as Eckankar, Great White Brotherhood, and Spiritual Frontiers Fellowship, as well as numerous individual psychics, spiritualists, and practitioners of astrology, iridology, numerology, crystal healing, divining, and so on.

Like the traditional metaphysical groups, this type of healing tends to emphasize that individuals can gain power and control of their lives.

Typically, however, they viewed the source of this power as being outside the individual. Only persons who were spiritually attuned, psychically developed, or adept in special occult knowledge could tap this great power for themselves or to channel to others.

Several groups included a broad spectrum of ages, although middleaged adherents predominated. Far more women than men were involved overall, but several groups had a substantial proportion of male adherents. This type of healing also includes numerous individual practitioners (such as psychic healers) who had a following but did not usually meet as a group. Many adherents of these practitioners were interviewed, but it is difficult to ascertain how representative they are of each practitioner's following.

A private healing circle is used here to illustrate this type of healing group. Several such healing circles were found. One typical circle met each week in one member's home. This group consisted of eight or nine regular members, ranging in age from mid-thirties to mid-sixties. Because the group met in the daytime, it had only a few members who were employed full-time; its membership was largely female. Newcomers had to be invited, and membership was put to a vote. This group was an offshoot of another healing circle, originally formed by a teacher of psychic healing. Members of the newer group preferred a more democratic style than in the other circle, and they recognized each other as spiritual persons with developed psychic powers.

The group atmosphere was warm and friendly. A specific chair was provided in the circle for each member; if physically absent, members were assumed to be present in spirit, at least. The group expected reverence, concentration, and participation from all. Everyone arrived early, set up the room, and chatted; as the clock chimed ten, all assumed their places. The session began with readings from various spiritual sources (such as the Bible, Unity's *Daily Word*, Swami Muktananda), which members had selected or offered as they felt "led." Setting the mood for their meditation, they chanted three Oms and recited the Lord's Prayer in unison.

A guided meditation by one of the members started the meditation period, after which each person meditated silently until the mantel clock chimed ten-thirty. All stood and moved to the center, holding hands. Lists with the names of persons needing healing were put in the center of the circle, and members around the circle added names. A member would lead a prayerlike meditation for healing; this especially serious part of the session ended with vigorous hugs for each other. Returning to their seats, members shared the content of their individual meditations. They discussed and helped each other interpret these meditations. After announcements and a closing prayer, members enjoyed refreshments and socializing. Although they met once a week as a group, a considerable amount of social interaction took place outside these sessions: shopping and lunches together, attending lectures, and phone calls and visits for further sharing or help.

The group offered much social and emotional support to members undergoing crises, such as cancer or a bad marriage, as well as day-to-day problems. Their interpretations of each others' meditations were similarly supportive. Sharing was open and friendly; it was a gentle learning experience in which fellow members helped interpret which elements of a meditation experience were important and which could be ignored. No interpretation was "wrong" or could be invalidated. Often members deliberately meditated on each other, providing such insights as the need to watch a purse while shopping, reassurance that the member would achieve an advanced spiritual level in this life, or foreseeing that a slightly plump member's weight was only a temporary problem. The group had been together for over six years and provided each other considerable and continuing personal support, friendship, and guidance.

Technique Practitioners

This type is based upon applying a technique, typically in a client-adherent relationship, rather than a group setting. Healing methods of this type include, for example, shiatsu, chiropractic, acupuncture, and reflexology. Related methods, which were sometimes organized as therapeutic groups, include rolfing, Alexander, and Feldenkrais methods. This type of healing is less interesting, because the technique itself—and not the beliefs supporting it—seems to be the key attraction for most adherents. Nevertheless, these methods do represent a nonorthodox approach to healing, are utilized (often in conjunction with some other alternative healing methods) by numerous middle-class persons, and are based upon an alternative understanding of health, illness, and healing. In many cases, experimentation with one of these techniques opened the door for an adherent's subsequent journey into other alternative healing approaches.

Shiatsu exemplifies alternative practitioner techniques. In Japanese, *shiatsu* means literally "finger pressure." Although various techniques are used in shiatsu massage, almost all involve firm pressure to various points on the skin known as "tsubo." Many of these points correspond to those used in acupuncture, so shiatsu is sometimes referred to as "acupuncture without needles," or "acupressure massage." The shiatsu massage stimulates the flow of "chi" or "ki" energy. One practitioner suggested:

> Think of this energy in terms of a series of rivers flowing through the body. If a blockage occurs in the meridian, the cause may be stress and the body falls into imbalance. The water energy becomes stagnant. . . . Acupressure massage keeps the channels open, which in turn maintains the necessary energy current throughout the human system.

While shiatsu may be used to cure, it may also be a tool to discover one's own innate healing powers. Some adherents believe that all people have innate healing powers, as demonstrated by their instinct to place their hand over the part of their body that is in pain. Accordingly, shiatsu therapy amplifies this healing process by using the hands in areas where the body's energy of "ki" is flowing most strongly.

Shiatsu emphasizes preventive treatment, as well as healing. It involves a holistic image of the individual with the need to harmonize the emotional and spiritual dimensions of being with the physical body. Although this emphasis on holism contrasts with orthodox medical treatment, many elements of the shiatsu experience are similar to orthodox medicine, since much shiatsu is given on a practitioner-client model. Appointments are required, sometimes after the intervention of an answering service. In one town, several practitioners formed an association, renting a suite of offices and advertising their services: acupuncture, Alexander technique, chiropractic, Feldenkrais, herbology, shiatsu and other massage forms, meditation training, nutritional counseling, stress management, and various psychotherapies, among others. Most practitioners utilize patient referrals and third-party payments, as do medical doctors.

As with the physician-patient interaction, the shiatsu client has a relatively passive role. The therapist takes a "medical history": Any particular physical problems? Taking any medications? Family history of this problem? She records answers and her observations (such as patient's pallor, iris condition, skin condition) in a small notebook.

In shiatsu, massage is both a diagnostic and a therapeutic method. The massage is quite extensive, lasting forty-five minutes or more. In addition to using her hands, the therapist frequently applies her knees and elbows to various pressure points. At times, she climbs on top of the patient to better utilize her entire body weight to apply pressure. Points that are painful or uncomfortable are given extra attention, because discomfort is seen as an indication of blockage. The feet are also given extra attention, because they are believed to be the part of the body where all the energy meridians meet.

The stomach area, the "hara," contains many of the vital organs, so it is also an area given special attention. The entire body, including the face, is massaged in this manner. Soft music plays in the background. There is little conversation between the therapist and the client. The client has little to do except relax. This therapist also emphasizes the "art of sighing" and encourages clients to breathe deeply, "sending the energy down the spine," then breathing out fully in a loud sigh. To aid in relaxation, the clients might be asked to visualize themselves in a peaceful place: a forest, the seashore, the mountains.

The session ends with a brief gentle massage over the entire body. The client is then instructed to rest a few minutes before dressing. Afterward, the therapist may suggest specific exercises, a change in diet, flower remedies, or other alternative therapies. One therapist also related a vision she had seen of the client while working on her. The therapist rarely urges clients to return for more treatment, but many clients come regularly throughout the year for preventive as well as therapeutic work.

Although she believes that anyone may be able to heal, this shiatsu therapist also feels that she has a special calling to healing for this lifetime. Specifically, the quality of her hands and her use of them in massage were seen as significant of this calling. Other shiatsu therapists held similar views of their special roles as healers.

A Sociological Perspective on Alternative Healing Beliefs and Practices

In subsequent chapters, the beliefs and practices of these and related groups are developed and analyzed in more detail. For each type of healing, several basic aspects of belief and practice are compared and contrasted.

Ideals of Health and Wellness

The idea of health is a socially defined norm. Each group's idea of health embodies its distinctive ideals. It is impossible to understand why a group uses healing as it does without first understanding what it considers to need healing—that is, what falls short of the norm of healthiness. It is difficult, however, to grasp a group's notion of health, because often the ideal is articulated only in formulating responses to illness. A group's overarching meaning system shapes its basic definitions of health. While some aspects of these ideals may be shared by the larger society, many other aspects are peculiar to the group's distinctive belief system. Thus it is necessary to understand each group's ideals of health in terms of its larger belief system.

Notions of Illness and Healing

Adherents' ideas of illness and healing are, likewise, formed according to their overall belief systems. One of the most serious problems with some studies of alternative healing is the assumption that adherents share the dominant medical system's notions of illness and healing. Adherents of alternative healing, however, often have radically different notions of what needs to be healed, what they consider to be a healing, and how healing takes place.

Furthermore, their interpretations of illness embody their attempts to deal with the problems of *meaning* that are linked with illness, pain, suffering, and death. The issue of meaning is generally not addressed by the dominant medical system, but in many alternative healing systems it is central. Why do people suffer? Why do people get sick despite preventive measures? Why do good people have troubles and bad people appear to flourish? Why do some people die "before their time"?[1]

The legitimations with which any group addresses these problems are not mere rationalizing; rather, they are important ways of structuring their world view to handle the potential threat of chaos. Suffering and death create problems of meaning, and they challenge the order of the world view in which the believer operates. Only by creating a satisfactory way of dealing with such threats can any group support and retain its belief system.[2]

Causes of Illness

Underlying all alternative healing systems is an alternative understanding of what causes illness. Part of the healing process in all healing systems is the sick person's and healer's co-construction of an illness etiology. This etiology incorporates an organization of both physical and social events (for example, violation of a moral norm) prior to the occurrence of the illness. These etiologies are typically in the form of narratives with conventional formats. They are analytical, focusing on certain facts and discarding others as irrelevant; they result in a culturally meaningful explanation of the illness that specifies causal relations among selected facts and connects them with the larger, socially prescribed, or "ideal" relations of that group.[3]

The etiology of each person's illness fits a set of culturally understandable explanations; it serves to link the ill person with the larger meaning system of the entire social group. Since these interviews were conducted after the construction of the etiology and therefore are the retrospective reconstruction of events consistent with the etiology, it is impossible to know exactly how these etiologies were developed. Facts remembered are those that were interpreted as causally related or significant for appreciating the value of the healing. It is possible, however, to note the available repertoire of possible etiological factors that are meaningful to each of the groups studied.

One important function of illness etiologies is to link the cause of illness to the necessary treatment. For example, a group might treat an illness differently if it were believed to be caused by Satan than if it were the result of bad diet and self-neglect. Another major function of illness etiologies is to affix responsibility. "Why is this person ill?" is related to the question of "Who—or what—is responsible for the illness?" Virtually every alternative healing system studied had some theory of the degree to which individuals were responsible for their own illnesses.

Diagnostic Approaches

Before any therapeutic approach can be used for an illness, the illness must be identified or categorized in order to know which therapeutic approach is appropriate. Diagnostic methods also link the "causes" with the treatment. All medical diagnoses are transformative. "Signs"—behavioral or biophysical expressions—are transformed into "symptoms"— socially understandable indicators of a specific category of illnesses.[4] In this transformation process, some signs are discarded or recede in importance; others are expanded or elicited. The symptoms are not, therefore, merely products of the illness itself but are, rather, socially constructed, fitting into preexisting socially available categories of meaning.

Diagnostic action typically involves a social interaction (even if mediated by technological devices) between the healer, or healers, and the person presenting a problem. The healer guides or controls the interaction toward constructing the diagnosis.[5] In some of the groups studied, the diagnostic stages sometimes appeared to have been passed over by direct supernatural action (e.g., in a mass healing meeting). Nevertheless, the diagnostic processes are very important functions of alternative healing methods. Indeed, in some cases, determining the identity and causes of illness may be even more important for the individual or group than the actual therapeutic actions that follow.[6]

Source of Healing Power

All healing systems include ideas about where healing power is located and how it is channeled to where it is needed. Etiologies of illness yield information about the group's ideas about disease-causing power, and therapies embody ideas about how that power can be overcome. From this perspective the treatment of illness is essentially the restoration of the balance of power—by weakening the antagonist's (disease-causing) power or by strengthening the victim's power.[7] We can compare groups' images of healing power, its source, and how it is mediated to the ill person.

Healing and Health Practices

How do these alternative healing systems effect health and healing? The specific healing practices must be analyzed and understood within the larger belief system of that group. Often healing is practiced in several different contexts (for example, in group meetings and in private). The social context of healing is, thus, important. Furthermore, most groups have clear ideas about what to do in order to maintain health and prevent illness. These practices, too, are related to their larger belief system and their ideal of health.

Therapeutic Success, Therapeutic Failure, and Death

Consistent with their distinctive ideas of illness and healing, most alternative healing groups employ different notions of what constitutes therapeutic success. What are some of the signs that a healing has taken place? What actions or beliefs are necessary for a healing to occur?

Just as illness and suffering require explanation to restore a sense of order, so too do therapeutic failure and death. Interpretations of therapeutic failure serve to affirm the group's beliefs about health, illness, and healing while explaining the discrepancy as to why a given correctly performed healing seemed to have failed. These legitimations are important to protect the integrity of the belief system itself, affirm the healing power, and assign responsibility for therapeutic failure.

Likewise, the question of responsibility for illness is central to these (and other) healing belief systems. All groups studied addressed such questions as: Who (or what) is responsible for the development of the illness? Who (or what) is responsible for its continuation or for a course of action that would lead to healing? And, if therapy fails, where does the responsibility for that failure lie? These ideas involve important moral evaluations and are not merely neutral descriptions of a situation.

Healing Systems as Ideologies

All healing systems—including "scientific" medicine—have implicit ideological components. For example, legitimations for therapeutic failure serve to justify the actions of those doing the healing and protect their assertions of power. The medical profession, likewise, uses various legitimations for therapeutic failure, generally to deflect responsibility for failure from the physician or medical institution. A study of a hospital's "Mortality and Morbidity" inquiries showed that these sessions served primarily to justify doctors' actions and to certify their nonresponsibility for therapeutic failure, rather than to open the broader issue of why the patient died.[8]

Like alternative healing systems, the dominant medical system in this culture is based upon a number of conceptions of health, illness, and healing—with an implicit belief system regarding the nature of illness and its sources, healing power and its sources, legitimations for failure and so on. In particular, Western biomedicine tends to view disease as a process devoid of social, human value or meaning components. The human body is treated as an object separate from its social, emotional, and other environmental contexts. Disease is often, therefore, reduced to a specific occurrence that simply "happens" to an individualized physical body, either from chance or personal irresponsibility. Thus "scientific" medicine masks its role in moral evaluation and social control.[9]

One especially important point of contrast among these alternative healing systems and between them and "scientific" medicine is the conception of the *self*. Comaroff emphasizes that "healing plays upon the relationship between physical and social being, tapping that primary source of symbolic media, the interface between self and world."[10] In Chapters Nine and Ten, this link between healing and the self is explored. The ideologies implicit in both medical and nonmedical healing systems simultaneously reflect and produce a particular mode of self-in-relation-to-the-world. As we explore these systems of ideas, it is thus important to be aware of these ideological components.

The next four chapters analyze the belief systems of four major types of healing group, using the above categories for comparison and contrast. The fifth type of healing found (techniques utilized in a practitioner-client relationship) was not primarily based upon a comprehensive belief system; thus, it is described only by way of comparison with the other four types. Likewise, responses from the control group are described where relevant for comparison.

3 HEALING IN CHRISTIAN GROUPS

The power of God is central to Christian groups' focus on healing. While most Christian denominations believe generally in God's healing power, the groups in which healing is an important focus are distinguished by their belief in the immediacy of that power. They believe that they have received gifts of power through the Holy Spirit (e.g., the gift of prophecy, the gift of wisdom, and the gift of tongues). One of the foremost of these gifts is healing, which they seek regularly in their individual and collective prayers.[1]

Typically, it is not the need for healing of some preexisting physical ailment that initially brings recruits to the group; rather, through their experience in the prayer group, members come to realize their needs for healing and to believe in dramatic healing power. They usually come to full belief and practice of faith healing gradually, as their general acceptance of the group's whole belief system builds.

Ideals of Health and Wellness

Through interaction with the prayer group, individuals come to share a norm of health centered around the group's spiritual ideals. Accordingly, healthiness is not primarily a physical attribute; health refers to attitudes that are ultimately linked with spiritual sources. One group member described health in terms of several attitudinal qualities: outgoingness, inner vision, tenderness, willingness to listen to people. She added, "I think I could put attitude at the top of every list. I've seen people who are virtually crippled in a wheelchair, and their attitude far surpasses mine. They're fantastic."

Several respondents emphasized that a healthy person copes well with daily life. One stated, "A really healthy person is one that doesn't come apart with every new trial that you go through. It's a growing process with God." Other emotional and attitudinal qualities were specifically linked with spiritual sources. A man emphasized, "A truly healthy person to me would probably have some of the fruits of the Spirit, which would be patience, courage, tenacity, zealousness, faithfulness, kindness."

The ideal of health is, thus, basically a holistic norm. One member commented, "Health, wholeness—all these words to me are Scripture and salvation. It all goes together. A healthy person to me would be one that was whole in spirit, soul, mind, and body." This idea was echoed by another woman, who said:

I feel first they have to be healthy spiritually, to be truly healthy. They have come to know Jesus in a personal way. Come to accept him as their source of salvation. He is their salvation from everything. And give your life to the Lord. . . . And I feel when you're spiritually healthy, everything else will follow. You will become emotionally healthy; hopefully, you'll become physically healthy, because your emotions are healthy; you're spiritually healthy, you're physically healthy. You'll become whole, I feel, in that process.

The key to health, according to this ideal, is a good relationship with God. A minister in one of these groups explained:

Somebody can be the healthiest, first of all, if they know God, because they have the life of God within them. Being born again is more than being recreated, but also the life of God comes within your body . . . and you're permeated with His life. That's why, as Christians learn this, they don't get healed all the time; they stay healthy. They walk in divine health.

Several other members mentioned Jesus as the embodiment of their ideal of health.

Thus, health is defined as holiness (which many members equated with wholeness). Because this ultimate ideal is perfection, many respondents emphasized that it was not possible to achieve in this life. Such extreme norms of health are an important factor in the significance of faith healing. If all believers are so far from the ideal of health, then all require frequent, regular healings, until the final "healing"—death.

For this reason, many respondents described health in terms of a process. For example, one man responded: "A healthy individual really does nothing but focus in on that [holiness], and if he focuses in on that all the time, you can't help but become more and more healthy. *A healthy person is a person who is continuously becoming healthy* [emphasis added]."

According to respondents, relative health (growth toward ultimate health) is all that can be attained in this life. Thus, *healing* (a growth and mending process) produces *health* (progress toward ultimate health—oneness with God).

Notions of Illness and Healing

What kinds of events are described as healings? What kinds of situations are described as needing healing? Members interviewed described experiences of past healings, healings currently being prayed for, and healings they felt they needed to receive. During prayer meetings and informal gatherings, they shared with each other testimonies about healings they or their loved ones had received.

A wide range of situations are submitted for healing. Essentially, any problematic situation that is felt to be "out of order," needing mending and God's power to make it whole, is considered appropriate for healing. Obvious problems, such as physical illnesses, handicaps, chronic conditions, were frequently objects of healing petitions. More often, however, emotional, spiritual, and relationship problems were mentioned by respondents. Fear, depression, anxiety, bitterness, resentment, compulsiveness, grieving, suicidal urges, and tension, were listed by numerous respondents as being healed or needing healing. Similarly, many described social-emotional situations, such as a disintegrating marriage, troubled relationship with a child or sibling, coping with a handicap, adjusting to having an aged parent move into the house, getting along with an obnoxious boss, and so on.

While most prayers for healing for oneself and loved ones were for relatively worrisome personal matters, any disordered situation might be "healed." Respondents described as "healings" such diverse situations as a broken lawn mower suddenly working, a chronically disorganized checkbook becoming balanced, receipt of some unexpected money, or a pet surviving a particularly difficult labor.

Most members sought healing for themselves, their family members, their friends, and fellow members of the prayer group. Although they used similar terms to describe them, healings sought for unknown persons or the larger society were qualitatively different. Typically, these healing prayers implied a judgment concerning the moral character of the object of the prayer. One woman emphasized the need to pray for the spiritual healing of all children exposed to rock-and-roll music. She explained, later, that the music was satanic and influenced listeners without their awareness.

Likewise, one man mentioned, as needing healing, the "bitterness of gangs like these movements like Black Panthers . . . going against authority." He felt the "bitterness" of those on welfare also needed healing. Special prayers of deliverance from Satan were required in order to heal homosexuality, which he described as "demon possession."

Many respondents felt that the whole society needed healing, in the sense that it was not in the right relationship with God. Social problems (as defined by their norms) such as pornography, crime, alcoholism, adultery, and abortion would be resolved only by a spiritual healing of the society. One atypical respondent felt the society needed to be healed of corporate sin that caused unhealthiness through industrial pollution. She stated, "We pray for New Jersey so that God can heal us, so the people can heal these waste matters and things that we're breathing."

As these diverse examples illustrate, these Christian groups used a very broad definition of what needs healing. As one member explained, "I see almost everything in terms of healing . . . healing and deliverance. We constantly need healing. We constantly need forgiveness. I feel that it is always important to be seeking healing; that's seeking the light over the darkness."

This spiritual definition is reiterated by one prayer group leader, who asserted:

Who really loves totally in a powerful way? Who really ever accomplishes the perfection of that answer? It's impossible. We need to be healed back into the image that He had in His mind because the moment we are conceived, we are plagued by original sin. Sin is simply separation from God. There it is Dis-Ease, [meaning] not easy with where I should be. So I see it as anything that separates me from the perfection of God, and God is love. Anything that interferes with the perfection of love in me makes me Ill at Ease . . . and needs healing.

The episodes that respondents described as healings are similarly diverse. To be healed is not necessarily the same as to be cured. It is common to have received a healing and still have symptoms or recurrences of the illness. This is not inconsistent with believers' notions of healing, because a number of legitimations explain why the healing experienced may not be physically manifest. For example, one woman had experienced the healing of her thyroid condition; she added, however, that the thyroid gland is still swollen, and "I get a twinge every once in a while reminding me that if you don't believe that, you know, you take it for granted sometimes when you're healed."

Other episodes described as healings include handicapped or chronically ill persons coping well and using their conditions to the glory of God. Respondents said that they might still pray for the physical healing of these conditions, but they felt the most important healing had already occurred. Indeed, one respondent added that God may have wanted an exemplary person to stay crippled, because that woman's multiple sclerosis called attention to her and made her witness to God more effective.

Other persons described as healings events of improvement or gradual movement toward a full healing. A healer in one group said that often improvement showed only gradually; for example, a person crippled by arthritis might become able to bend down. The small improvement itself is thus defined as a healing, while full healing is still sought.

Members of these Christian groups often included as healing events episodes nonbelievers would attribute to merely natural or human agency. It is not inconsistent with their beliefs to see a healing where, for example, a person under medical care recovered sooner than expected. Even in seemingly ordinary kinds of healing processes, they see instances of divine intervention.

One kind of episode is one in which the healing apparently fails to occur, but there is the discovery that an unexpected healing had occurred in another area or to another person. For example, a woman was disappointed that her vigorous prayers for her daughter's orthopedic condition seemed unanswered, until she discovered that her sister, in another city, had received an unsolicited healing of her chronic bronchitis.

Another kind of episode is one in which one's worst fears are not confirmed. For example, one man was sure his chest pains were signs of an incipient heart attack. He solicited the healing prayers of his prayer group before going to the doctor for tests. His "healing" was that the test results showed his pains were from a minor ailment, rather than the deeply feared heart problem.

It is not necessary to have a medically diagnosable condition in order to experience a healing. In light of these beliefs, the self-confirming potential of Christian healing can be appreciated. More important, however, is that healing "works" first and foremost as a spiritual experience; physical and social-emotional changes are hoped-for, but secondary, aspects.

The key criterion of healing is the process of becoming closer to the Lord. Some described it as becoming able to do the right thing, overcoming sin, growing into a more personal relationship with God. This emphasis on process explains why people must suffer illness; God uses illness and healing to teach people and to bring them closer to Him. Thus, healing is not only the result of faith; it also produces faith.

The following description of one woman's multiple healings (of physical, emotional, and relationship problems) illustrates this spiritual focus in the complex interweaving of aspects of this type of holistic healing:

> It was really inner healing and then through that I got better [physically], because I was sick for eight years. . . . Then I went through inner healing, which didn't happen overnight either. It was a process . . . I mean God usually doesn't zap anyone with a miracle. It's just a natural process. But the more I went through inner healing, I found out what was really bothering me.

> And again, it's a process. Every once in a while, the feelings will come back, but I don't give in to it, because I know I've been healed through all the things that I have done in the prayer group.

> [Describes one healing episode, and the problems that followed it]. I got this feeling—it was like a black feeling. I thought, why do I have this feeling? I am not sick. And they have just finished praying over me too. This feeling, I could literally feel it go. It was like this black going up to the top of the room, up there [pointing up] for a second and was gone. . . . I knew later, after talking to _____ [a leader], I just knew it was a healing, but I didn't have a handle on what the problem was. So, I didn't see any great difference each time, but it was a process.

Like this woman, many respondents distinguished between, on the one hand, the experience of being healed and, on the other hand, feeling healed. It was not necessary to see symptom changes, to feel different, or have otherwise verifiable results. Healing was a spiritual process, known only by faith in that very process.

Since healing is a process, the ultimate goal of which is a perfect relationship with God, it is never fully achieved in this life. A member explained, somewhat humorously, why: "The process is healing. We are in a process of healing from the moment we are born until the moment we die. The Lord decides when we are cooked. We're all half-baked."

Unlike most other types of healing studied, Christian healing groups made a strong distinction between "true" healing and "counterfeit" healing. Both could produce major changes in the healed person, but "true" healing was from God, whereas "counterfeit" healing was from Satan. According to this belief system, both God and Satan are powerful enough to produce healings, which outwardly might appear identical.

Like "true" (Christian) healing, "counterfeit" healing is often mediated by humans, such as psychic healers, occult healers, Christian Scientists, or other groups of which these Christian groups disapproved. One woman explained that the main way to tell the difference was: "Where did you go to receive it? Did you go to a Satan worship or cult and you received it?"

She added another key criterion: "Healing should bring you closer to the Lord in some ways." By contrast, "counterfeit" healing serves to put one in bondage to Satan. Thus it is not merely "false" healing; it is also very dangerous. A person who has been healed by "demonic" means will require "deliverance" (i.e., exorcism) from that influence. A prayer group member asserted: "I believe that there are people who can heal you that are working for the Enemy—they're working for Satan. I believe that he can bring about healings, too. If you get it from him, you might be healed, but the repercussions of getting a healing that way would be bad, would be dangerous."

The experience of illness invites explanation. People want the experience to have a meaning, perhaps even a purpose. They ask: Why do people suffer? Why do people get sick despite preventive measures? Why are there illness and death? For Christian groups, there are additional problems of meaning in reconciling their idea of an all-powerful God with that of a compassionate and personal God. If God is powerful enough to arrange our lives as He wishes, and if He cares about us and loves us so much, why does He allow His faithful to become ill, to suffer, and even die? Some of these groups' responses to these questions are discussed further at the end of this chapter, but some interpretations shed light on the groups' very notions of illness itself.

The meanings given to illness are responses to these problems of theodicy.[2] Suffering, illness, and death create problems of theodicy, not because they are unpleasant, but because they threaten the fundamental assumptions of order underlying the social group itself. Theodicies tell the individual or group that the experience is not meaningless but is, rather, part of a larger system of order.[3]

Virtually all groups studied grappled with the problem of pain: Is pain a necessary—or even beneficial—part of the healing process? Or is it always to be avoided and overcome? On this theme, opinion was divided; Catholic charismatic prayer group members and members of traditional Protestant pentecostal groups generally asserted that pain and suffering were not ever good, that God wanted everyone to be free of illness, pain, suffering, and other problems. One Catholic charismatic adherent represented this point of view: "We were led to believe [as Catholics] that if you had a pain, that was your cross you were carrying. And now the charismatic movement tells us it's really Satan. He wants you down, as that can turn you away from God. But God really wants us to be happy, to be healthy and to be wealthy."

By contrast, Episcopalian respondents (charismatic and noncharismatic alike) tended to see positive aspects in suffering and pain. One leader of an Order of Saint Luke prayer group explained: "His [Christ's] pain was unbearable and yet he took it on. And when we're suffering, we shouldn't deny it, but just recall Christ bore all our pain, and he'll help us through it—not around it or over it, but we have to go through and experience it. . . . Pain and illness aren't the end. You wouldn't know goodness and joy, if you hadn't experienced pain."

Why does a loving, personal God permit suffering and illness, when He has the power to take them away—or to create a world free of them? Most respondents in Christian groups saw experiences of suffering or pain as learning experiences, as opportunities to come closer to God, or as God trying to awaken them to get their attention to speak to them. Accordingly, although God did not wish suffering on His followers, He sometimes permitted it for a reason.

One woman said, "You ask the Lord what you're supposed to learn from this. If He has a reason for this, then please show me what am I supposed to learn from this." Another woman added, "The Lord uses it to chastise us and to get our attention [gives example of person hurt in car accident]. . . . It is good for us if we handle it the way the Lord wants us to. It can make us better and better."

The notion of learning a lesson, combined with chastisement, was more prevalent among traditional Protestant pentecostal and Catholic charismatic groups than among other Christian respondents. Characteristic of this image of chastisement is the statement by one adherent: "God has allowed it [illness], permitted it, let me say, as a chastisement in love to bring you back, so that your soul will be saved."

Dependence upon God should be learned through suffering or illness, according to some Christian healing adherents. One prayer group leader explained, "He may leave us with a thorn in our flesh so that we might know the need for Him." The belief that illness is an opportunity for learning a lesson from God also explains why sometimes healing does not happen quickly. A member stated, "Once we're healed, we have a responsibility to learn the lesson God was teaching us through the suffering. If there is a delay in the healing, we should ask God what He wants to teach us first."

Several respondents emphasized the spiritual secondary gains of the illness experience. Several mentioned that the illness brought the family closer together, reaffirmed the importance of friendships, or gave them more time to read the Bible. Others suggested that the break in routine, along with more need for prayer, helped them reexamine their routine and its priorities. One woman noted: "God means good in everything, and we derive a good experience from everything. Being sick gives you more opportunity to pray." This typical response illustrates how the meanings given to illness serve to resolve the problem of theodicy.

Causes of Illness

As the preceding description suggests, Christian healing groups believe that illness is more than just a physical condition. Accordingly, the causes of illness are not mere physical causes. Respondents in Christian healing groups also attributed illness to social, emotional, environmental, and, especially, spiritual causes.

Respondents asserted that the foremost cause of illness was sin. Some emphasized personal sin on the part of the sick person; others mentioned original sin or the sinful condition of humankind; a small number also mentioned community sin (such as corporate greed).

Characteristic of the interpretation of personal sin was one woman's explanation:

> Sin is probably the root cause; it's probably the only cause. Sin—either your own sin or the sins of others around you or just the sin factor in the world. Not being in tune with the Lord. Not being disciplined enough to hear Him speak and direct your life. . . . Disregarding the laws of God, being not in tune with Him, committing sin. Subtle sins, like hatred of another person that you're not fully aware of. That's sin. Harboring a grudge, letting your temper fly in such a way that you then have guilt. . . . It's because of sin that we derive all the illnesses and evils of the world.

Original sin was also used as an explanation, either distinguished from or in combination with individual sin. Most traditional pentecostal and Catholic charismatic respondents referred to this combination, often giving a version of the biblical story of the expulsion from the Garden of Eden. For example, one Women's Aglow leader explained, "There are germs and things like that in this world, and I belive that they came with the fall of Adam. When God drove Adam out of the Garden of Eden, then he was exposed to the things of the world, the diseases and the illnesses that were already present outside the Garden, because of the fall of Satan."

Another pentecostal adherent emphasized the literal quality of the biblical description:

> When God made Adam and Eve—and I believe that he made an Adam and an Eve, and I believe that they were named Adam and Eve, and that they had a garden that they lived in, and that this particular place that they lived in was perfect—when they decided to do otherwise than what God asked them to do and blew the whole perfectness of the thing, He said right away, "Now sin has come into the world and death by sin and it's passed upon all people." . . . We began to have weaker muscles and I don't know where the colds came from—I guess some flu bug decided to be sinful, too, instead of good. But it all came as a result of that sinfulness.

Further theodical problems arise from this interpretation, however, over the issue of whether a given illness comes from God as punishment for sin. Many respondents were concerned with resolving this problem, because it affected their image of God. Many believed that illness is a punishment/lesson from God. Several said that illness is punishment or the result of general sin, but not necessarily the sin of the person who is ill. In a similar vein, some said that illness comes from Satan, as a result of human sin. One group leader said, "They [illnesses] are not a punishment; they're not from God. Satan is the author of all sickness and disease, but sickness is not a punishment, but it can be the result of sin. Sickness and disease can be the result of sin, of disobedience—but it's not coming from God."

On the other hand, many respondents felt that sickness is a form of punishment for the individual's sin. A prayer group member commented, "The problem with man is sin. And sometimes illness is a punishment, a chastisement for sin." Another person explained, "God chastises His children just like a parent. I don't think He delights in that at all, but He only wants the very best for us. But I think it's tough love."

Several respondents believed that illness is the direct result of sin. While emotional or physical factors may be the proximate causes, the ultimate or root cause is sin. For example, one woman described a young girl who stopped serving Jesus and died of anorexia nervosa. Another person described how her neighbor had been born-again but fell away, and she developed severe recurring bronchitis "as a result." One man articulated an explanation: "People in society have turned away from the way the Lord wants us to live. They're free to do that, but when they do, they subject themselves to whatever it is the Lord is going to send them."

A few respondents, however, struggled with this interpretation and its implications. One young woman had suffered numerous orthopedic problems since birth. She exclaimed, "Illness is definitely not a punishment. I heard somebody say that one time, and it upset me greatly. How can I be punished for a wrongdoing at the age of two—that's when I had my first operation!"

Frequently, Satan was named as the cause of illness. Some respondents used Satan to explain the very presence of illness and suffering in the world; others identified Satan as the immediate cause of individual sickness. Emphasis on Satan as the cause reduced the problem of God's responsibility for illness or other undesirable conditions.

Most of the respondents in this type of healing group had strongly dualistic cosmologies: Nearly everything was interpreted in terms of a struggle between the forces of Good and the forces of Evil.[4] Belief in Satan's general responsibility for undesirable features of the world is illustrated by the statement of one woman, who said, "The causes of suffering, pain, and death and disintegration and corruption and poverty and war: Satan is behind all these things." Another member addressed the theodical issue more directly: "Satan is the author of sickness and disease. God doesn't give sickness, because He's the God who heals us. [Sickness] is Satanic oppression."

Many respondents used the imagery of warfare: doing battle, defending oneself from attack, using prayer and Scripture as weapons, and so on. One woman stated, "I think that sometimes it's an attack, and it's like warfare. And sometimes a good person might be attacked more than someone who has already fallen." Another respondent commented:

> I believe that Satan is in control of the dark side of human nature, unless you don't allow him to be in control. . . . [You must protect yourself through] prayer, fellowship with other Christians, Bible reading, speaking out against Satan. You can carry on a conversation with Satan if you know he's attacking you. You know he's giving you bad thoughts in your mind that would go against God's way of doing something. You can tell him to get lost, especially quoting Scripture.

Thus members attributed illness to Satan, not just in a general sense, but also in explaining particular bouts of illness. Many respondents connected this influence of Satan to individual sin, as well. One woman explained, "A person can experience illnesses because they hold unforgiveness within their heart and it opens the door for Satan to dwell in there. And he comes in the form of disease and illnesses." Another member stated:

> I believe that it's coming from Satan. And he uses it in all sorts of ways to either zap you with something. You know, all of a sudden you feel fine, then tomorrow morning you wake up with something horrible, and you've probably been exposed to it. I mean illness is in the realm of Satan. And however you get it—whether it's through sin or exposure or neglect or whatever—that all is Satan's territory.

Someone else emphasized spiritual bondage to Satan as a major cause of illness: "Some of them [illnesses] are spiritually imposed. I think we all live in certain bondages. I believe there is an Evil One rolling around the earth, and I think he has bondages over certain individuals."

Some illnesses, however, were attributed to a more dangerous form of Satan's influence: possession. Emotional problems and physical diseases with important emotional components are especially likely to result from possession by the Devil. Other conditions defined as illnesses are also likely to be explained as possession, especially when they carry a strong moral connotation (such as homosexuality or alcoholism). Several respondents described cases of possession: an emotional disturbance in a woman who had been to see a fortune-teller, a housewife's depression and subsequent dependence on Valium, extreme fear in a child who had been molested, a college student's sudden change to rebelliousness and sullenness. Possession is very dangerous and requires special prayers for deliverance or exorcism, as described later in this chapter.

Emotional causes of illness were cited frequently, usually concomitant with spiritual causes. For example, anger and bitterness were often mentioned, together with the need for repentance and forgiveness. Other respondents blamed stress and competitiveness, adding that a truly healthy person gave all that over to the Lord and was relieved of the stress and drive to compete for false goals. Some members linked specific illnesses with particular emotional states; arthritis, for example, was tied to bitterness, resentment, and anger. Other emotional factors mentioned included anxiety, holding grudges, lack of trust, fear, perfectionism, envy, sadness, and self-pity.

Respondents typically combined these emotional causes with spiritual—or even specifically moral—interpretations. A person might begin by saying he needed to be cured of a bad case of eczema, but that he had come to realize that the condition was really caused by his nervousness and anxiety. And, although that emotional problem needed healing, the root cause was really his personal sinfulness in not being willing to turn over his whole life to the Lord.

In some groups, certain emotional aspects of illness were described as "memories" that needed healing. These groups attributed the sick person's present emotional difficulties to persistent memories of unpleasant experiences earlier in life—as early as conception or birth. The parallels with psychoanalytic notions of repressed emotional responses are obvious. The spiritual therapy for memories is described elsewhere in this chapter.

According to many respondents, thoughts and words are also powerful influences in bringing about illness. Just as thoughts and words are effective tools in combatting illness, so too can they promote it. A man explained, "The power of life and death is in the tongue. If you say, 'I'm sick,' there's a suggestion you will—a good possibility you will—get sick."

Members of Christian healing groups did not emphasize social and physical environment as the cause of illness as much as did other groups, such as the Eastern-inspired healing groups studied. Typically, they mentioned environmental factors in spiritual terms. One adherent, for example, linked illness with a social environment that promotes materialism, power, self-fulfillment, and idolatry of money.

Only three respondents from these groups mentioned the physical environment as causing illness; they uniformly gave this factor a spiritual significance, as illustrated by the comments of one woman: "When they say New Jersey is known for the cancer cases, it could be because of all the horrible pollution and all the wastes, the gases that are escaping. So that would be the sin of greed from the industry and not cleaning up the water and not keeping the air clean."

Medically induced illness was a surprisingly common causal interpretation among Christian healing groups, given their relatively high opinion of doctors and established medical practice (see Chapter Eight). Most of the problems attributed to medical treatment were children's illnesses and handicaps (such as neurological impairment ascribed to anesthesia in childbirth, or brain damage attributed to high fever following infant inoculation). This nonspiritual interpretation helps to explain why seemingly innocent persons are impaired.

Many of these respondents expressed particular concern that drugs (such as tranquilizers) and other medical treatments for emotional problems were bad. They suggested that such treatments probably do more harm than good. The only other adult problems attributed to medical therapies were negative (perhaps dangerously so) reactions to treatments for diabetes and epilepsy. These critics described the treatment-induced conditions as illnesses separate from the initial disease.

God's will was not cited as a cause of illness, but several respondents answered the theodical problem of God's apparent complicity by emphasizing that there is much humans (in this life) simply do not understand. One prayer group member said, "It's the Lord's will for us to be well. But there are certain things we will never understand, and I don't think we ever will until it's all over."

As the preceding description of causes of illness suggests, one of the key questions believers ask is: Who is responsible? This question is important, not so much to affix blame, but more to determine the appropriate course of therapeutic action. Affixing responsibility for illness is, in many cases, an integral part of the healing process.

Simultaneously, believers are understandably concerned about the problems of theodicy implied by the causal categories. Ideas about responsibility for illness are also linked with explaining therapeutic failure. Most respondents from these Christian healing groups believed that individuals were responsible, to some degree, for their own illnesses. The linkage might be that they had failed to repent of certain sins, forgive people, or turn wholly to the Lord. Or perhaps they did not really want to be well; perhaps being sick was a way of getting attention or playing the role of martyr. People are also responsible for their lifestyle, personal habits, and carefulness. Some respondents pointed out that some people might not be consciously choosing sickness, but subconsciously they select an illness-producing way of life.

At the same time, attributing illness to Satan or to humankind's fallen condition implies a lower degree of individual responsibility for any given illness. The main personal responsibility, according to these interpretations, is to get the Lord's help in becoming healthy again.

Diagnostic Approaches

Knowing which healing approach is appropriate requires "diagnosing" the real ailment and the root cause of it. While the Lord could heal directly without such an interpretation, prayer for healing is more effective if it is guided by an accurate "discernment" of the nature of the real problem. Members believed that, through prayer and Scripture, God gave them knowledge of why a person was ill and how to focus their healing accordingly.

Discernment might guide one's own healing or one's healing prayers for others. One woman explained; "The Lord first reveals what's wrong and then He heals. Yet He can't heal anything that hasn't been revealed.

I mean I guess He could—I'm not saying God can['t] do anything—but I feel this is the way He is working. First He reveals what's there (like that fear in my life). I have to acknowledge it and then He heals it." Another person said:

> Most of the time, if I want a definite healing for a definite thing, I try to ask for the Gift of Wisdom as to what He wants me to do. I find your healings develop faster through prayer and getting a Word of Knowledge, either by radio, tapes, people, music, all kinds of things will give you some inkling as to what you might not be doing that you should be doing and are just made aware of. The Lord lets you know.

While all believers might pray for God's guidance and discernment, some members—typically prayer group leaders—were believed to have received from the Holy Spirit special gifts of Wisdom or Knowledge, enabling them to reliably discern the root causes and prayer needs of others. One healing minister of a prayer group stated, "My gift is getting to the root of the person's problem. I have a—well, it's just a gift from God."

Similarly, a clergyman explained, "I get a Word of Knowledge—God tells me of an ailment that somebody has or a sickness or disease that's in their body." This man practices a special form of discernment, characteristic of many pentecostal healing services: After receiving the Word of Knowledge that someone in the group has a particular disease, he announces this sense aloud to the group. A person in the audience then comes forward for prayer for that particular healing or otherwise claims the healing the minister has proclaimed is going to occur. Interestingly, these publicly proclaimed healings are almost always for physical illnesses or handicaps. In no large-scale healing services observed in any of the Christian movements were spiritual or even complex emotional healings thus discerned.

More so than other types of groups studied, Christian healing groups typically categorized the kinds of healing for which different healing approaches might be appropriate. If an illness were attributed to memories, the person might be led through a series of prayers or meditations tailored to the "healing of memories." For example, through prayer, one group leader discerned that a middle-aged member who had requested healing of her relationship with her parents actually needed a healing of memories of her father, whom she still feared. Thus, before praying for the relationship with her parents, she was told to come in for several sessions of healing of memories.

Similarly, a physical problem might be discerned to be really an emotional one. For example, one woman was healed of migraine head-aches and recurring back pain when the prayer group focused its healing prayers on her anxieties and fears. After several such prayer episodes, she was able to relax more on her job and be less fearful while getting to her workplace on her own. This emphasis on diagnosing the real source of the problem has parallels with the medical conception, except that these believers have quite different ideas of what the "real sources" of illnesses might be.

If evil forces are believed to play a part in an illness, the diagnosis and treatment are even more difficult and serious. Catholic charismatic groups were more interested in "deliverance ministries" than were Protestant charismatics and traditional pentecostals. The Catholic church has long had a ritual for exorcism, but it had been rarely used in recent centuries. With the Catholic charismatic movement's "discovery" of Satan's regular influence, ways of dealing with the Evil One have been refined.[5]

The groups distinguish between satanic "oppression" and "posses-sion." Satanic "oppression" (or "harassment" or "bondage") is a common diagnosis in all Christian groups studied (although they varied widely in the terminology used and the images evoked). This idea refers to how superhuman evil forces can bother, hold down, or control people—even good Christians. Several respondents used the imagery of spiritual warfare, with the notion of Satan "bombarding" people with troubles. Many problems were attributed to oppression by the Devil: depression, overeating, anxiety, fears, compulsions, doubts, rebelliousness, alcohol-ism, chronic back pain, ulcers, heart palpitations, and chronic headaches. Only by discernment, through prayer, could one know whether the problem was due to Satan.

Satanic possession, by contrast, was a very serious, less frequent diagnosis. Possession means the Devil's actual full control of persons, such that they literally are not themselves. The power of the Devil over the afflicted person is so great that only by a more powerful external intervention can the person be freed. Catholic charismatic groups used the ritual of exorcism for this dangerous task. Less ritualistic pentecostal groups also invoked God's power to fight the Devil, but these prayers were only more intense versions of their ordinary healing prayers. Numerous respondents told stories of spectacular exorcisms, but they emphasized that this was a relatively infrequent form of healing.

The ordinary deliverance ministry in all Christian healing groups studied involved a regular, rarely spectacular form of healing prayer. Nevertheless, ideally, anyone seeking healing ought to pray for guidance to determine the type of healing prayer to use. Through this guidance, they would be led to use deliverance or even exorcism, if God showed them it was necessary. One member explained:

> There's different types of healing. There's inner healing; there's spiritual healing; there's physical healing; and then there's healing that we would say deliverance. [Depending on which type of healing is needed], your word will be different. And you have to use the discernment that comes when the person who is praying is a person of prayer themselves. In other words, they should be praying inwardly themselves and before the interview with the person for prayer.

Another situation that requires prayers for discernment is the problem of how to pray for a person who is dying. Respondents believed that God could heal a dying person, but that recovery might not be God's will for that person. Thus discernment was needed to know how to pray for such a person. The same kind of spiritual discernment was needed to know how to pray correctly both for illness and for dying.

Source of Healing Power

Before examining healing and health practices per se, it is important to understand the ideas of healing power used by these Christian groups. Implicit in these believers' ideas about the causation of illness is the notion of a hierarchy of powers—powers to cause illness or to effect healing. Most respondents in this type of group believed that humans have little or no natural power to effect health or healing; one must tap God's superior power to heal and be healed. Accordingly, God's power can be mediated to others, and the Lord often channels His power through human agents. This power can be mediated even through words of power (such as the name of Jesus, a Scripture verse, or a prayer), as well as through medicine or other objects (such as prayer cloths, blessed water, or oil).

Figure 3.1 is a model of power implicit in respondents' healing beliefs. Forces of differing potency are seen as warring with each other; the outcome for the sick person depends upon allying with the right forces. Furthermore, the individual's sin (separation from God) is seen as a barrier between the sick person and the source of help—God. Satan may even amplify the barrier, further hindering healing. Healing is accomplished by strengthening the sick person (through God's power) and/or by counteracting the Evil One's power to cause the illness.

Respondents from all Christian healing groups were unanimous in their belief that all true (as opposed to counterfeit) healing is from God. Traditional Protestant pentecostals were likely to say the healing was from "Jesus Christ," whereas neo-pentecostals (in this case, Episcopalian and Catholic charismatics) were more likely to attribute healing to the "Holy Spirit." Numerous Protestant pentecostals described Jesus as literally the surrogate sufferer, quoting the Bible passage that "By His stripes we are healed." One group leader asserted that Jesus had thirty-nine stripes, one for each of thirty-nine basic kinds of disease in the world. He added, "God doesn't do anything by coincidence."

Members of all Christian healing groups studied were, likewise, adamant that the power of the person doing the healing was actually God's power being channeled through that person. One woman commented, "Right at the beginning [I had a healing ministry], because God empowered me in a powerful way. People were really healed when I touched them, and all I felt was that has to come through them [the gifts of the Spirit]. I'm not involved at all. I'm just the instrument, the leader through which His grace can flow. . . . Really, all I have to do is be willing and God can work."

Healing and Health Practices

As the preceding interpretation shows, healing and health practices in these Christian groups aim, first and foremost, to tap God's power.

FIGURE 3.1   Concepts of Healing Power in Christian Groups

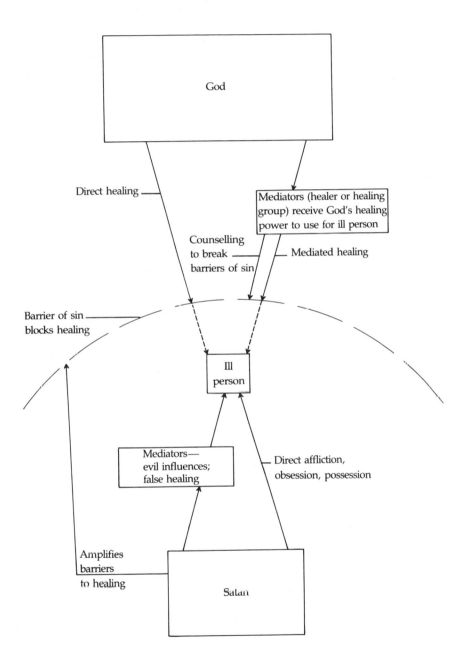

Before looking at the specific healing practices used in these groups, it is useful to examine the various social contexts in which healing was practiced.

When one believes God is active in all spheres of one's life and is listening to one's every utterance, informal and spontaneous prayer becomes a taken-for-granted, frequent healing approach. Virtually all respondents in these Christian groups reported praying frequently throughout the day. Thus many of the healings described were sought in the context of everyday individual activity—in the midst of house-cleaning, on the way to work, while reading the Bible, while tucking children into bed. Typically these prayers for oneself and others were silent—words, thoughts, images; occasionally, they also involved laying on hands or talking to others, or even to oneself. One person described the ordinary quality of these prayers:

> If you wake up in the morning and you have a fever, you can lay your own hands on yourself and say, "Jesus, I'm your servant. I know I have this fever and I have things I need to do today. I ask your healing of this." Then you get out of bed and you start putting your clothes on and get going—acting in the understanding that "I have asked, I believe you want me to be healed, and I know you're healing me." And you just go on your way.

In contrast to the media image of a flashy evangelist doing healing before an auditorium full of emotionally stirred believers, most of the Christian healing described by respondents in this study was quiet, almost matter-of-fact, and relatively private. Only slightly more formal were the organized prayer networks within the prayer groups or churches. For example, Women's Aglow groups had organized "prayer chains" for intercessory prayer.

The "intercessory prayer chairman" of one such group explained that throughout the week people contacted her with prayer requests for themselves or loved ones. Urgent requests were often dealt with immediately by phoning other prayer group members and organizing their prayer efforts. More routine prayer requests were gathered for a general prayer session. She described how they prayed for others:

> Anyone who wants to come and help me pray for all the prayer requests comes in, because we pray for those individually. Last month, only one

woman came to pray with me, and we started at 10:30 and we were still praying at 3:40. Now, yesterday, there were three other ladies who came, so there were four of us and we divided the requests in half and it didn't take quite so long.

Well, the prayer request comes in and it says, "Pray for my Uncle Joe who has just had a heart attack." So we pray for that Uncle Joe; we pray that God will heal him, but we don't know Uncle Joe, so usually we pray, "God, if he doesn't know you as a Savior, we pray to Jesus that you'll just let the Holy Spirit reveal God to him." You know, we pray for his salvation. We pray as though that were the only prayer request we had. We pray for each one that comes in that way, in that manner.

Another kind of prayer network, especially in the Episcopalian and Catholic prayer groups studied, was a more specialized prayer ministry team. This small group met with persons requesting prayer, usually before or after the larger prayer meeting. In this context, they often explored the person's needs more deeply than possible in the anonymous prayer chain. Several prayer ministries used this time to interpret requesters' illnesses to them, and to give advice, counselling, suggestions for reading, and practical suggestions, in addition to the actual prayers for healing. Typically, they laid hands on the person as they prayed. Often they suggested that the person come back for further prayer sessions.

These prayer ministry teams were usually specialized and believed to possess special Gifts of the Spirit that enabled them to be more effective in their prayers than ordinary members. Because these specialized services were highly valued in most prayer groups, prayer ministers frequently had relatively high status in prayer group stratification (although only a few leaders observed seemed to take advantage of their positions).

In some groups the specialized Gifts of the Spirit coincided with other leadership roles. For example, one vigorous and youthful Pentecostal congregation was led by a husband and wife, who together exercised all of the specialized leadership roles in the church. He explained, "Usually I am the one who prays for people. Now there are some times . . . instead of taking time to pray for each one, sometimes I'll have everybody around them lay hands on them—all the congregation—and people will be healed right there. . . . But usually I am the one who lays hands on each one."

Several respondents emphasized how much more effective a healing prayer would be in a group setting. Many quoted the Bible passage about "where two or three are gathered together in my name. . . ." Others noted how good it felt to have others gathered around, showing their concern. One woman added, "If my child is sick, I have fear. I need others to join me in prayer. They are not inhibited, because it is not their child. It frees up the fear, and healing can take place."

While most healing prayer took place in everyday settings and within the prayer group or congregation, mass prayer services and the advent of specialized "healers" were also occasional contexts for Christian healing. Members of every Christian group studied reported attending such services or watching them on television. During participant-observation stages of this research, several such events took place and were observed; group members who believed that they had been healed in these services were also interviewed. These healers were believed to have received extraordinary Gifts of the Spirit and thus to have more potent healing prayers than ordinary prayer group members. Members felt that the healers' gifts worked the same way as their own—as channels for God's healing power—but considered the healers' gifts to be more dramatic. This belief explains their eagerness to put especially difficult cases before the specialized healer and their expectation that miraculous healings would occur.

Some respondents also mentioned a residual situation: when God heals a person directly, without that person or anyone else specifically requesting it. Although this form is not itself a healing practice, some believers mentioned it to show that God need not use any intermediary to effect a healing. And God could, if He wanted, heal whomever and whenever He chose.

Healing Practices

A number of specific healing practices were regularly used in these Christian groups. None of these practices, however, was considered absolutely necessary to effect the healing. While certain practices became almost routine in the prayer groups, some respondents cautioned against assuming that the prayer method itself made the difference. One respondent noted, "God always keeps you off balance. He's not going to let you become an expert in healing. You pray a certain way two or three times and it's successful, and then the pit—the danger—is 'Oh, I've found a formula!'" As noted above, the main focus in healing is asking God to heal the person and effectively channeling His healing power to where it is needed. The following prayer methods are typically used, often in combination, by the groups studied.

All respondents used prayer for healing. Some were quite specific as to how one should pray for healing. Several mentioned it should be a prayer of praise. A woman said, "I think I just bring the problem to the Lord and I pray to the Lord. I try to center my prayer on praising the Lord. So that's what I say the method I do use is—to praise the Lord through the circumstances, or through the problem. . . . I'd say, 'Peter has shingles, Lord, please heal him.' And then 'Praise the Lord.'"

Respondents were divided as to whether one should pray frequently for the same problem. Traditional Protestant pentecostal members were more likely to urge that one pray fervently once and, after that, as a sign of faith, claim the healing as accomplished, even though there are not yet any signs that it happened. Episcopalian and Catholic charismatics were more likely to say repeated prayers. A member explained, "Some people say you pray once for the same thing and that's it. Well, I don't. I guess I do it continuously, because I think that many times there's a gradual healing." This belief is consistent with much of their movement literature, which describes a "soaking prayer" for gradual healing—implying that one applies the prayer repeatedly, allowing the problem to soak in it.

Catholic and Protestant pentecostals alike recommended praying in tongues (glossolalia). One of the Gifts of the Holy Spirit, the ability to pray in tongues, is viewed as a prayer-gift, enabling the believer to pray more deeply and effectively. Accordingly, when praying in tongues, even the words of the prayer itself are in God's control. One healing ministry member stated:

> I pray in tongues all the time in the hospital. People don't know it, because you're praying silently. You wouldn't pray out loud 'cause it would distress them. They wouldn't know what you were doing. But it's beautiful. You say a few English words that were mostly for their benefit. You know, just drop a seed and just put your hand on their head and pray in tongues. And it's just a wonderful feeling. You know that you are just being a co-creator. You're lending your body and then God's perfect will for that person is being prayed.

Respondents recommended other prayers of praise, too. One woman urged singing: "Singing is the most important part of healing. You can be healed of things just while you're singing. [It gives] such a great big opening up, so that you're so receptive to the Lord."

Many respondents also recommended using visualization while praying. Some regularly imagined Jesus doing the healing that was being requested. Others recommended envisioning the affected part becoming well, dwelling on the image of the healed peson while praying prayers of praise.

One special form of visualization was used in guided meditations for "inner" healings or "healing of memories."[6] The following visualization was guided at one mass healing service:

> The healing minister told the members of the large audience to relax and close their eyes; they were then to picture someone who had died with whom they had not been reconciled—someone who needed their forgiveness. The healing minister (a woman in her late forties) led the visualization in a quiet, almost hypnotic tone of voice:
>
> "Visualize Jesus [long pause]. He tells you to walk with Him [pause] and you get to a bridge [pause], but you are afraid to cross that bridge [pause]. Jesus is holding you very securely [long pause]. Now Jesus puts his hand on your shoulder [long pause]. Suddenly something within you melts [pause] and you say [pause] 'I forgive you' [long pause], and the person glows, rushes to you and embraces you [long pause]. Then Jesus steps into the center and embraces you both [long pause]. You have freed another, so you have been freed [pause]. You stand tall and can smile [long silence].
>
> "Lord, only You can hear. Many of us are bruised by problems in life and in our past. We ask You, Jesus, to walk through the dark areas of us and shine your light. Replace the cobwebs with your love" [musical interlude].

Many members believed that the name of Jesus was particularly powerful in effecting a healing. The name itself was a way of channeling God's power, of borrowing Jesus' "authority" over the problem. One woman described a healing of eye spasms: "And I just stopped at the sink and immediately went into prayer, and I took authority in Christ's name over this. And I said, 'I know You've healed me and I will not allow for this to happen in Your name.' And the spasms stopped."

Words from the Bible, too, were believed to be forceful ways of channeling God's power. One group leader stated, "It's a matter of knowing the Word of God, the Scriptures, and when some of these problems come up, you just say 'in the name of Jesus,' repeat the particular Scripture you've been given, and he [Satan] has to back off."

This process is well illustrated in the story of a healing one woman experienced after a severe reaction to what she thought was a spider bite:

[Describing the terrible fear that was building in her] I began to quote that Scripture, "God hath not given us the spirit of fear, but of power and of love and a sound mind." And I recognized where this spirit of fear was coming from. Now if God wasn't giving it to me, it had to be the Evil One.

And then I remembered the Scripture said, "For God hath highly exalted Him and given Him a name above every name, that at the name of Jesus every knee shall bow and every tongue confess that Jesus Christ is Lord for the glory of the Father."

So, I held up my arm before the mirror and I thought, "He's above every name." Jesus' name is above every name. Well, swelling is a name, redness is a name, red line is a name, infection is a name, blood poison is a name, whiteness is a name—every name that I could see as I looked in the mirror that was on my arm, I named. And as I named them, I said, "Bow your knees at the name of Jesus." Every time I would name something— "Swelling, bow your knee; Redness, bow your knee; Red line, bow your knee at the name of Jesus."

Some members described the power of Scripture in other uses. One woman described being healed of arthritic pain through the act of copying Scripture verses. Another woman told of being healed by words of Scripture that flashed through her mind when she was unconscious after an accident.

One of the most dramatic physical practices for Christian healing is the "laying on of hands"—the use of touch to channel God's healing power. Typically, healers or other believers mediated that power by touch to the person needing healing, although some respondents reported laying hands on themselves. The following report illustrates how prayer, Scripture, invoking the name of Jesus, and laying on of hands are combined: "Different kinds of healing Scriptures would come. Like, one time I just had this blinding headache when I was driving home at night and the Scripture came to me: 'If you lay hands on the sick, they will be healed.' So I just touched my forehead, gently and lightly, and just said, In the name of Jesus, I'm healed.'"

Prayer ministry groups that were observed typically prayed for a person by laying on hands. If there were a particular physical part that needed healing, they touched that; otherwise they usually laid hands on the person's head or shoulders. Sometimes, in a prayer meeting, leaders asked everyone to form a chain of touching, such that all persons praying were passing the healing energy through each other to the person for whom they were all praying.

Consistent with the image of transmitting God's healing power, healers reported feeling energy flow through them. One group leader described, "It's like a real mild current of electricity in your hand and you feel it kind of tingly and the heat."

A particular healing practice, usually done through the laying-on-of-hands, involved using prayer to equalize the length of a person's legs in order to relieve some other physical problem, such as back pain. This practice was used widely by visiting healers, some of whom were reputed to have special gifts for healing this way; only a few local healers used it, but some members of all groups studied mentioned it as a valuable healing practice.

One leader described leg-lengthening:

> I've had that same thing happen several times with people who had very bad back problems and when you get them to sit down and check to see whether there appears to be a difference in length of legs or not, there is. And you ask for a healing and the one leg—it either goes shorter or longer—I've never been able to figure out which. . . . But it makes sense, doesn't it, that the back—if you have one leg shorter than the other, you're going to correct, to make a straight walk and so as you bend that back, you're going to get a pinched nerve or muscle out of place or something.

Many Christian groups teach that the Holy Spirit sometimes manifests its power by overcoming the person. Traditional pentecostals typically call this experience "slaying in the Spirit"—highlighting the dramatic way the affected person falls down, as if struck by that power. Neo-pentecostals (such as Catholic or Episcopalian charismatics) often call this same phenomenon "resting in the Spirit" to emphasize the quiet, spiritually salutory state in which affected persons stay for a brief while after falling down.

A Pentecostal minister explained, "Many times when I pray for people, they feel the power of God coming into them, and—nine out of ten—it just knocked them right on the floor. I didn't do it. I just laid my hand barely on them. It was God's healing power going through me into them, effecting a healing and cure and undoing the works that Satan had done in their body."

The process is sufficiently common and ritualized in some prayer groups that persons who request healing stand in line and, as they are touched, fall into the waiting arms of an usher, who lays them on the floor gently while another usher covers their legs for modesty. In such a context, the "slaying in the Spirit" is expected; not to fall is deviant and disturbing to the rest of the group.

Many respondents described fasting, combined with prayer, to promote healing. Fasting was believed to enhance the power of the prayer by demonstrating the person's seriousness and by making the person more receptive to God's communication. Some persons felt they were asked by God to fast on certain occasions in order to receive a healing. One member described a prophecy she received during the "Daniel fast" (a particular form, patterned after a biblical account).

Catholic and Episcopalian neo-pentecostals were more likely than traditional Protestant pentecostals to use blessed substances ritually to promote healing. They kept blessed oil, salt, and water to apply or ingest whenever needed. They also emphasized the blessing of medications before taking them. The use of blessed substances for healing is actually a continuation of traditional Catholic and Episcopalian ritual practices that are now being revived, especially by the charismatic movements in these churches.

All Christian healing groups studied used some form of prayer to protect and deliver members from the influence of Satan. Traditional Protestant pentecostals regularly rebuked the Devil and countermanded him by the authority of Jesus. Catholic charismatic prayer groups typically had a more complex approach to exorcism. They distinguished ordinary exorcism from the official exorcism of the Church, for which specially appointed priests are required. Official exorcism—reserved for cases of Satanic possession—is practiced and encouraged by the movement, and several instances of this more spectacular and dangerous "official" type were reported.[7]

Ordinary exorcism occurs often in prayer meetings and everyday life situations. One woman explained:

I haven't had experience with [the deliverance ministry], but it is very much a part of healing. Sometimes you realize that there is an area under the control of evil spirits. We [our prayer group] don't have a deliverance ministry, but we do pray a simple prayer of deliverance which anyone is capable of.

Sometimes you do get a sense—like one time a person had such unnatural fear—that possibly it was a harassment by evil spirits—not a possession. They [evil spirits] get into a natural weakness and use it against us. I explained this to the person and took authority over the evil spirits, because they do have a way of stifling, harassing. It is simple to just take authority, because Jesus has given us this authority, but deliverance is a special ministry. . . . If the person needed deliverance—if the body [prayer team] discerned this—we could, on the spot, take authority over any and all evil spirits and then we would take this up with the pastoral team and we would speak the truth with the person and put them in touch with someone who could help them—such as Father _____. He has a real deliverance ministry.

Regardless of the form these encounters took, however, all groups studied had some healing practices specifically for counteracting the power of Satan.

Health Practices

Reflecting the emphatically spiritual definitions of health held by these groups, their health and preventive practices also had large spiritual components. Several respondents urged "spiritual nourishment" or strengthening one's relationship with the Lord as the best preventive measures.

Their emphasis on prayer as a preventive practice is consistent with this notion. One group even had a set of "preventive healing" services, illustrating their belief that healing prayer affects health, even in the absence of illness. One respondent urged that before even getting an illness one should always "rebuke it in the name of Jesus." Another woman described her daily prayer as her "spiritual fitness exercises." Like many other respondents, she explained even physical preventive measures, such as eating wisely and getting enough rest, in spiritual terms ("Your body is the temple of God").

Fasting is also a preventive measure, because—like prayer—it gets one better in touch with the Lord. One advocate of fasting explained:

You see, fasting doesn't change God. . . . [A] lot of people fast to try to change God. . . . But he always has good things intended for you anyway. . . . What it does is it changes you—the person that fasts. The main thing is you become more spiritually attuned or aware of God. It's a lot easier to hear him. . . . And your body is quieted down when you don't have all this food from eating. Also, you're showing God . . . you want to hear from Him— more than you want food.

Members of these Christian healing groups favored various lifestyle practices to promote health, but even these practices were done for spiritual reasons. The foremost spiritual reason cited was that one should not rely on anything (substance or habit) except God. A member described giving up the vitamins she was using, because "I realized I was trusting vitamins and not the Lord." Similarly, several respondents thought that drinking in moderation was acceptable, so long as one did not come to rely on alcohol, rather than on the Lord. Another woman said Christians should not make a fetish of their health practices, because even good practices could get in the way of relying on the Lord. She stated, "I don't think junk food is really good for you, but if you come to the point where you can't even buy a quick hamburger or something, then you're in bondage to that."

Another spiritual reason for certain health practices is to avoid conditions that are an opportunity for Satan's influence. Several respondents were against using tranquilizers, because they dull one's ability to hear God. Worse yet would be the use of hallucinogens and strong drink; these weaknesses leave an opening for Satan to enter. A related preventive practice involves controlling exposure to negative influences. One woman commented, "I think it's essential that we watch what we read and what we listen to and what we see."

Several members described following certain ordinary health practices (such as giving up smoking or getting more rest) because the Lord instructed them to do so. One woman was on a particular diet "because the Lord wants me to eat that way. He wants me to lose the weight. He wants me to follow the prescribed formal program for me at this point. So that's why I'm doing it."

A final health practice was mentioned by only a few respondents. They urged close interpersonal relationships, especially with fellow believers. One member said, "You can protect your body . . . by being in contact with people and having loving relationships with people, and not just living closed in by yourself—but reaching out to others and sharing and giving."

Therapeutic Success, Therapeutic Failure, and Death

Since these Christian groups believed that God did the healing, all conditions necessary for effecting a healing pertain to the supplicants' relationships to God. Sometimes healing appears not to have occurred. Since healing is such an important part of the Christian groups' faith and practice, therapeutic failure and death are potentially very threatening. Typically therapeutic failure was attributed to the absence or insufficiency of one of the factors needed for a healing to occur. Further theodicies were employed to provide meaning for real therapeutic failures and to explain why some failures were only apparent.

Although approximately one-third of the respondents mentioned physical criteria for healing, these indicators were usually in the form of broad symptom relief—such as reduction or cessation of pain. More typical were respondents who used spiritual or emotional criteria for therapeutic success.

The Christian healing groups studied distinguished between the healing itself and the *experience* of healing. Sometimes, accordingly, a healing has already occurred but the person cannot experience it because he or she has not "claimed" the healing. Some other event or learning may be necessary first before the healing can "manifest." For example, one woman told a lengthy story of her healing: She had gone to a healing service at church and the minister and healing prayer group had prayed for her hearing and a blockage in her ear. "I felt heat in there, but it wasn't manifested." The blockage was still there throughout the day. That evening at a Bible study session, another member asked this respondent to pray for her healing. After praying for the other woman, she realized her own ear blockage had disappeared. She concluded, "God had me immediately impart the healing to someone else, and then my blockage was healed."

Asked how one would know desired healing had occurred, a member exclaimed, "You'd be full of joy. You'd know! You'd have a good feeling. You'd be excited about the Lord." Others replied that recipients would know because they would be closer to the Lord, the Lord would touch them in a special way, the Lord would give them a Scripture verse as a confirmation of the healing, or their faith would grow. Many respondents noted that healing almost always went hand in hand with forgiveness; if you had experienced a healing, you would also be aware of letting go anger or resentment toward others.

Sometimes these spiritual and/or emotional changes were accompanied by a cathartic experience. Numerous respondents described crying, trembling, or laughing. One person described her healing at a service: "[After we sang the song 'I am the Bread of Life'] I started to cry. And it was uncontrollable, and I'd just stand there, and I would sob, and I couldn't stop it, and it was the most beautiful [experience] that I ever had. . . . So I felt the ulcer that I know I had was healed."

Other members, however, were sometimes disappointed that they did not have a special experience or feel different after a healing was supposed to have occurred. One woman had undergone a special deliverance session and had been told by the prayer ministry team that she was healed. Although she, too, subsequently considered the event a healing, at the time she was very disappointed: "I expected to come out feeling great. I came out feeling so empty and so horrible. And I came home and [the group leader] called me. You see, I always have great expectations. And she said, 'Well, that's how you feel; that is how you feel, because you're emptied of everything. . . .' But I expected to feel wonderful, and I felt crummy."

Another source of knowledge that healing had occurred was the sensation of the healing energy. Most persons reporting this experience were those who regularly engaged in healing ministries as clergy or laypersons. One woman exemplified this sensation: "And sometimes when in prayer and in a group, I would feel the healing power of the Lord was very present and then I would feel it in my hands. Then I would wonder who was to be healed. And the Lord would say who, and then I would go to that person, and then that person would be healed." In this and similar examples, the certainty of healing preceded both the healing itself and even the knowledge of the identity of the recipient.

Similar sensations—typically unrelated to the nature of the illness itself—were described by recipients. One man knew his healing had occurred because he felt a warmth and a glow come over his body. A woman described feeling "a weaving" sensation in her entire frame, especially her spine. These sensations were taken as evidence of the flow of the Lord's power into the body.

Most respondents believed that faith was necessary for a healing to occur. Usually, they expected the person seeking healing to have strong faith; they did, however, allow that healing could be channeled even to an unbeliever through intercessory prayer. Thus a healer or prayer group could use their strong faith as sufficient basis to ask the Lord to heal someone of weak or no faith. In general, adherents believed that the stronger the faith of those praying, the better the results.

The faith of the person being prayed for is important, not only to increase the whole atmosphere of faith but also to increase receptiveness to the healing. One man stated, "I would not go so far as to say that someone who doesn't believe in God couldn't be healed by God or through Christians who believe in God. But I would tend to think that in most cases starting with repentance, being open to God, believing in God would be primary for healing."

Members urged that one should have positive faith—faith without doubts or conditions—that God has healed the person. A group leader stated, "It's a matter of positive faith. I ask and I believe He's doing it, so I'm not going to mess around finding out, 'Did He?' It's like planting something and then pulling it up to see if it's growing. We're tempted to do that at times rather than Praise the Lord." Another member affirmed, "You have to believe in the Lord Jesus Christ. You have to be firm in your belief. You have to ask unconditionally and open yourself to whatever it is that the Lord wants to give you. You can't lay a condition on your request."

Such faith is often critical in the gap between the healing and the experience of healing. One man explained, "I believed I was healed before I looked like or felt like I was healed. My faith was what brought the healing up. I had to believe in order to make the healing come."

Many respondents indicated that, just as strong positive faith is necessary for healing to occur, so too a failure in healing is often due to lack of faith. A group leader explained, "Jesus expects your faith. . . . You see, the reason many people don't get healed is because they're in unbelief." Another respondent stated, "The Lord won't heal someone who is a doubter. You have faith in Jesus and in His power. . . . You have to have strong faith. The Lord will not heal someone who is wishy-washy."

Respondents recommended that the person seeking healing (and others praying for that person) should purify themselves and remove impediments to the flow of healing power. The foremost blockage mentioned was sin; the person seeking healing should repent of past sins. Unforgiveness, anger, false beliefs, and bad attitudes must be shed in order for God's healing power to flow fully to where it is needed.

Thus many healing groups began their healing requests with a search for anything that might be a blockage to subsequent healing. They sometimes began by "counselling" the person about his or her blockages, or by asking God to reveal what those blockages were. One person described this: "First of all, the person comes to you if he wants healing, but most times you have to pray that the person is open. Sometimes they have to be forgiving, and you almost have to go through and find out what it is. And as you talk to a person, you find out that maybe they're harboring resentments or unforgiveness toward someone or something." Another member said, "Very often your healing is dependent upon scrutinizing your own life and deciding if there might be something blocking your prayers, like sin in your life, that has to be dealt with." She described a time when her son's healing would not come until she repented of her own sins that were directed toward the child.

As shown in Figure 3.1, the image of healing power used means that blockages hinder the flow of this power. Respondents urged that the recipient must be "open" to God's healing power; people must want the healing and remove blockages of sin, unforgiveness, and unbelief. This emphasis was summarized by one member: "I feel that health and healing is there for the taker. That Jesus wants to give it to all of us and we just have to open ourselves up and let Him in and let Him do it. . . . The more open we are to His power and to His healing love, the more healing that we get."

According to these interpretations, some blockages are due to the sick person holding on to the sick role for its secondary gains. A member who had been healed of migraine headaches said:

At that time in my life, if Jesus came along and said, "Do you want to be healed?" . . . if I'd really be honest, I'd have to say "No, I don't want to be healed; I'm enjoying this pain, because it's my whole identity." It's not that I enjoyed the pain so much, as it was that that's who I am: I am hurt; I am crippled emotionally; I am bitter; I am angry; I am all these things. And to get rid of it is to get rid of a part of you.

A group leader explained, "Some people like being sick. It gives them a lot of benefit. They get a lot of attention. They're the center of someone's life, the life of a given home; the disability is the focus."

Some respondents believed that Satan, too, sometimes obstructed healings. In those cases, prayers of deliverance and protection were necessary before the healing could take place. More typically, however, human failings were blamed as blockages. Often members interpreted therapeutic failure as God trying to teach them a lesson. One woman felt that her healing had not come, because she needed to "become more worthy of a healing." Another person explained, "Perhaps because the Lord's got things in store for you, or perhaps because He wants you to believe in Him a little more strongly and He's trying to pull this belief out of you by not healing you right away. He's saying, 'Come on, believe in me a little more, come on.' And He's just taking you on to believe in Him more."

Another factor promoting successful healing is the ability to pray correctly. First, it is important to pray for the kind of healing appropriate to the kind of illness (e.g., a spiritual healing for a spiritual illness). According to prayer ministry leaders, this linkage often takes much discernment, because persons seeking healing may not know what is really wrong with them. Nevertheless, the more accurate the group/ healer is in praying for the right need, the more effective the healing prayer.

Also, it is important to create an atmosphere of faith. Several respondents mentioned the helpfulness of having more than one person praying. One explained, "It's stronger if two or three pray together what's called the 'prayer of agreement.'" Furthermore, it is better not to have detractors present. Obvious unbelievers can raise doubts and reduce the atmosphere of faith.

Respondents mentioned several factors that focus the healing energy. They recommended that one be specific in requests (unless the person's needs are unknown). One should specify the name of the person needing healing (e.g., not just "my uncle" but rather "Joseph Smith"). Ideally, persons laying on hands should directly touch the person. One woman noted, "There is something about the channel of healing between God and you and this person. It flows. And if God is going to put healing power in you, His power for this person, a lot of times it will flow best if you touch them."

Several respondents mentioned that it is preferable to lay hands on the person at the affected part of the body. One man stated, "When someone says 'heal my headache,' it seems to me, this is where you should pray. . . . It would be better to go to the spot. Of course, it could be embarrassing—if it's a female, or male—but that's God's problem [laughter]."

In order to focus the healing energy, many believe it is preferable for the person who is the object of the prayer to be present. One interesting device to approximate channeling healing to an absent person is to have another person, typically a relative, serve as proxy. Several respondents indicated that God's healing power flows more effectively if the person is physically present and can be touched. One prayer group leader said:

> It helps for the person often to be present, because there are things that happen in the interaction, the prayer interaction, that enables the person to really be healed. . . . If there's a person out there who just doesn't even know they're being prayed for or might be in opposition to this happening or discounting it, there's probably less of a chance anything is going to happen. But if a person comes seeking and can allow themselves to be touched, it seems to me they're drawn. And then there's more of an opportunity for something to happen.

Another way of focusing the healing energy is for those praying to visualize the person or the affected part. One adherent said that it helps to "visualize this person and actually see them [while praying]." It is not enough to "pray words. But I think it's to focus in on them and the place where they are hurting."

Although these ways of "praying right" are not viewed as fixed rules, therapeutic failure is often attributed to the failure to pray correctly. Respondents used this interpretation mainly when they felt that they had not correctly discerned the person's real need or the Lord's will for the person.

Problems of discernment are especially difficult when the ill person is near death. One should pray differently for someone who is dying, if it is discerned that death is God's will for that person. Otherwise, prayers that the person stay alive may actually hinder the person's peaceful death. Several respondents described how they, in their selfish wish to keep loved ones alive, had prolonged the persons' passing. On the other hand, it might have been God's will to miraculously cure even a desperately ill person, so discernment is needed.

One woman described how she received the discernment that God wanted to "take" a dying person: "A peace came over me, not to pray for healing. Her time had come and she was going home to the Lord. No more was I led to pray for healing. My prayer was that Jesus would be glorified through her death, and he was glorified 'cause she was the most beautiful. . . . It was just nothing morbid; it was the glory of . . . going back to heaven. I just know in my heart she did."

Many respondents were emphatic that one must always pray in accordance with God's will. Before specifying a healing request, one should ask God first what He willed for that person. One member stated, "I hate to limit God, because I don't want to come saying, 'Lord, I need to be healed in this area,' when He may be saying, 'But you need this area much more than this other area.'" Similarly the Lord's time is a factor; it may not be the right time to ask for a particular healing. Another woman said, "If the Lord is ready, He will heal. If not, healing won't take place."

All these factors, while believed to contribute significantly to successful healing, are themselves subject to God's will—which is above human standards and rules. Having stated firmly that faith is necessary for healing, one person added that the Bible tells of Jesus healing a person who did not believe (although the person's friends did have faith). She concluded, "So I don't think we could limit God. I think He could heal . . . whatever way He wants to." This idea was echoed by another woman who observed, "So it seems as though there are requirements in some cases, but yet . . . if these requirements are not met, God still in His love and mercy will do it sovereignly."

Several respondents commented that, ultimately, God's will is a mystery that humans should not expect to understand. One member concluded, "God answers every healing prayer. Is it worth praying for healing? Yes, it is. Do I have to see the answers? No, I don't. God doesn't owe me. He very graciously lets us see, as I said, but He doesn't have to reveal His plans to us."

Many instances in which the healing appeared to have failed were interpreted as successful healings. The apparent-versus-real distinction mitigates against disappointment and affirms the Lord's healing power. This legitimation should not be viewed as a mere rationalization, however; it is completely consistent with these Christian groups' understanding of how healing works and with their emphasis upon spiritual aspects of true healing.

One such interpretation is the idea that the healing has already occurred but is not yet observable or "manifested." Therapeutic failure is only apparent, not real. After describing several healings where this interpretation applied, one group leader recommended, "Don't be moved by your circumstances. . . . Just keep thanking God for His healing. . . . Healing manifests different ways. . . . The main thing is: Just stay in faith and you won't be concerned about whether you felt it or not."

Another situation where healing is believed really to have occurred is when the healing is "undone." Just as one must claim one's healing, so too must one stay close to the Lord to keep the healing. One member stated, "If you start going the wrong way, away from the Lord, then I say yes, the symptoms can completely come back." Another woman commented, "Some people don't know how to accept the healing. They go all out and do completely wrong things. People, most of the time, make their own mistakes by not thanking the Lord every day." Such recurrence of symptoms, however, does not mean that the original healing was not effective; rather, it is interpreted as a failure of the person to stay close to the Lord.

The most commonly cited examples of apparent failures that were really successes is when the healing is believed to have occurred in an area other than the one requested. One person stated:

> Sometimes people will go for a physical healing and they'll come back and say, "Gee, nothing happened." Every time that you pray for healings, some healing takes place. It may not be exactly in the way that you have prayed for it, but your prayers are answered in some way. . . . It could be healing psychologically. It could be a healing that's applied to the people around the person who is sick.

One particular form of the real-versus-apparent distinction is in how these groups interpret death. Death is not usually therapeutic failure; rather, it is the ultimate healing, the perfect healing. This interpretation is not merely a rationalization; it is consistent with the groups' image of healing. If the primary goal of healing is to bring people closer to God, then death—the threshhold to eternal union with God—is a perfect healing.

A leader described his consternation when he had prayed for a man and a woman, both with advanced cancer:

> I prayed for [them] in exactly the same way. The man got better rapidly. Boy, it was just startling. The next day they said he had a remission, which is what they like to call these things. As far as I know, he's still alive today. . . . The woman got worse and worse and two days later she died.
>
> I went and sat down and said, "Lord, what did I do wrong? One was healed and one wasn't." And He said, "Oh!" I said, "What do you mean 'oh'?" He said, "I healed one of them perfectly. The other one is still around and he has to battle with colds and sore muscles and those sorts of things."
>
> I said, "Oh, yeah. When you take us to heaven, you heal us perfectly. There's no more sorrow, no more tears, no more illnesses, no more financial problems, no more of this, no more of that. We've made it. We got it made. There is no problem any more." And so I said, "Thank you, Lord. You tell me to pray for them, and then you decide which way they should be healed—perfectly, by going to heaven, or their disease taken away or stopped or whatever it may be."

Explanations of therapeutic failure exist partly to show how, according to the belief system, therapy could have proceeded better. They confirm an ideal of the therapeutic process. Alternative healing systems differ from the dominant medical system in how that ideal process is defined, but legitimations of therapeutic failure in both healing systems serve this same function.

Similarly, both the dominant medical system and alternative healing systems favor legitimations that adequately protect the power of the healing agent and satisfactorily give meaning to the event of failure. These legitimations may be categorized by the degree to which they deflect responsibility for the apparent failure from the primary agent of healing, thus protecting and affirming that agent's power. The two main legitimations used by these Christian healing groups are that the failure is not really a failure but merely apparent and that God was not responsible for the failure.

Legitimations that acknowledge that people have not been healed typically assert that responsibility lies with the individual, prayer ministers, or the larger social group, but not with God. The primary beliefs—that God is all-powerful and that He cares for individuals enough to want them healed—are thus protected.

Less common is the situation in some groups in which individual gifts of healing are the basis of status. In these, prayer ministers were less likely to assume responsibility for therapeutic failure than were ordinary prayer group members who also prayed for others. Even more dramatic a disclaimer was that of a travelling healer who proclaimed many people healed in a mass healing service. He then left the region, taking credit for these therapeutic "successes"—no comfort to those who had been proclaimed healed but who subsequently had relapses. There were serious problems of responsibility for therapeutic failure for some of these people, because of the anonymous setting, the high levels of expectation from their families and friends, and the subsequent "success" of the healer and their own "failure."

One young woman, struggling with the responsibility issue after her proclaimed healing, said, "Initially, I had an experience where for a moment I felt like I was healed, but it didn't last. I could feel a change, a difference." A few hours after the healing service, it was obvious that her physical condition was not substantially healed. "I didn't know why I didn't have enough faith to say it would last. After it was over, it took me a couple of days to get over it." Then she and her mother redefined the healing as more of a psychological healing. She described the healing as more like "a pep rally." Regarding the severe physical problems for which the healing had been proclaimed, she concluded, "Obviously it's not my time to be rid of this problem."

Despite her successful legitimation of the failure, she was still caught in the responsibility problem. She said:

A lot of time people wonder why I haven't been healed yet. [They think] that I lack faith or that I'm doing something terrible. I don't think that's what it is. If the Lord wanted to, He could heal all the people in this world that were sick. I don't think it's that He doesn't want to, but it's not part of His plan. Sometimes I think that He's trying to use me to do something, and I really don't know what it is. There's always a purpose for something, and I don't believe that a person who's looking for a healing is not going to lack that much faith. Because if they have faith enough to think that they're going to be healed, . . . you have to have faith to think that the Lord is going to heal you.

According to these explanations for therapeutic failure, a considerable portion of the responsibility lies with the recipient of the healing. Insufficient faith, failure to forgive, the presence of blockages of sin, and lack of openness are all attributable to the individual recipient. Sometimes the prayer group or prayer ministers might share the responsibility: failure to create a whole atmosphere of faith or not praying right. In contexts in which healing is a basis for stratification, however, leaders are less likely to accept the shared responsibility.

Explanations that Satan had intervened serve to deflect responsibility all around. These explanations were not often used, however, partly because the groups shared a general emphasis on individual responsibility before God. Even respondents who believed that Satan caused illness were unlikely to interpret therapeutic failure as Satan's responsibility, perhaps because such explanations attributed to Satan more power. Since adherents linked healing with growth in faith and positive changes in one's life, they were less attracted to legitimations that blamed failed healing on outside forces.

These beliefs about healing power shaped Christian adherents' ideas about the role of the healer, their help-seeking practices, and their healing rituals, as subsequent chapters illustrate. In many respects, Christian healing groups closely resembled other types of healing group. At the same time, they generally differed from other types in their dualistic emphasis on God and Satan and their more authoritarian notions of a singular path to true healing.

4

TRADITIONAL

METAPHYSICAL

MOVEMENTS

Like Christian healing groups, traditional metaphysical healing groups believe that health and healing come from tapping a powerful life force. Unlike Christian healing, however, this type of healing is based upon a wholly immanent power, fully within the reach of each believer. Ideas of health and illness, imputed causes of illness, and appropriate diagnostic and therapeutic responses are, accordingly, quite different from those in Christian healing groups.

Healing was a major emphasis of the turn-of-the-century metaphysical movement. As used by these groups, the term *metaphysics* refers to "the deeper realities of the universe, the things that are external, standing above and beyond the outer phenomenal realm."[1] Drawing eclectically from several strands of thought, including Eastern religions, mesmerism, and transcendentalism, the metaphysical movement first emerged in the middle of the nineteenth century. The teachings of Phineas P. Quimby served to articulate the movement's philosophy and give it its distinctive emphasis upon healing.[2]

The main strand of this movement was loosely organized into an association called "New Thought," which spawned such groups as the Church of Divine Science, the Church of Religious Science, and the Unity School of Christianity. Quimby and later spokespersons for New Thought were adamantly against establishing a fixed, orthodox creed. As a result, New Thought groups have remained relatively nonauthoritarian and loosely affiliated—essentially cults or denominations, rather than sects.[3]

The most familiar offshoot of the metaphysical movement, however, is Christian Science, which was based upon a more extreme interpretation of metaphysical healing than that of the New Thought groups. The founder of Christian Science, Mary Baker Eddy, had been healed by Quimby and relied on many of his teachings in developing the principles of Christian Science. Christian Science underwent considerable scrutiny, harassment, and control by medical and legal authorities, because its healing beliefs and practices were so central to its existence and were in direct opposition to much established medical practice.[4] Christian Science is unlike New Thought and other metaphysical movements of that era in that Mary Baker Eddy successfully arrogated to herself all teaching authority, centralized decision-making and organizational power, and developed the movement's sectarian character.[5]

Christian Science has greatly routinized its practices in subsequent years. Its worship services are uncontroversial and denominationlike, and its current system of Christian Science practitioners and nurses is less of a threat to the medical establishment.[6] By redefining its healing as teaching, counselling, and caretaking, Christian Science has avoided most of the kind of head-on confrontations with the medical system that characterized earlier periods.

Unity, or Unity School of Christianity, also emphasized healing from its inception; however, Unity was never so extreme as Christian Science in its recommended beliefs and practices. Furthermore, as Unity developed, it increasingly emphasized teaching and meditation rather than healing as key functions of its centers. Healing became an important by-product of these other aspects.[7] Also, unlike Christian Science, Unity's members often belong to other churches simultaneously.

In this study, Unity was of particular interest because its local centers appeared to be attracting growing numbers of new participants, many of whom were young, relatively affluent, well educated, and not from New Thought religious backgrounds. This vitality was in marked contrast to the aging and apparently declining congregations of Christian Science churches in the area. Unity was also interesting in that it was achieving some of the universalist interracial ideals of New Thought. In racially integrated communities, Unity was one of the few groups studied that achieved a racial mix comparable to that of the larger community. Another New Thought movement with adherents in the catchment area was Religious Science. Some respondents in this study had attended a Religious Science center in a nearby city; this center was not studied directly, but interview data suggest strong parallels of its form of healing with that of Unity.

Recruits to traditional metaphysical healing groups, like adherents of Christian healing groups, rarely come to the group primarily out of the need for healing of some preexisting ailment. Rather, Christian Science adherents typically were raised in that tradition. Some Unity adherents had grown up in Unity or Christian Science, but many were attracted initially by Unity's meditation services. Through their learning and experiences in these groups, then, members came to believe in their distinctive healing approaches. Full belief and practice occurred gradually.

Ideals of Health and Wellness

Like Christian healing groups, metaphysical groups also emphasize a holistic image of health. By contrast, however, they believe that the key to the desired wholeness is mental more than purely spiritual. Unity members define health as wholeness—oneness with the "Christ Mind" (i.e., the part of the Divine Mind that is within the human individual). One woman stated, "Well, I think a person is a mind, body, and soul. So, first, you have to have a healthy mind. Of course, a healthy mind will help you to have a healthy body, and eventually the soul is the result of your mind and your body. So, it's a three-way thing to keep yourself healthy."

These adherents believed that health—indeed, perfection in all aspects of life—is the *normal* condition of all persons. A Unity member explained, "We're made perfect; it's what we do—it's our wrong thinking that brings about the imperfections." Similarly, a Christian Scientist described a "truly healthy person" as loving, kind, thoughtful, caring, intelligent, honest, cheerful, courageous, and moral. She added, "We have those qualities because we're a likeness of God. They're not personal possessions that we're apt to lose. That's man's innate nature, but he chooses not to accept that nature [bringing on unhealthiness]."

Notions of Illness and Healing

Illness, according to Unity, is "an inharmonious condition in mind and body." It is, by definition, an error. Illness does not exist in Truth. Illness comes to have existence and power only when people allow it to reign in their consciousness. Thus, while pain and other "symptoms" of illness are real enough in the individual's experience, they are not necessary parts of human existence. One who walks in Truth need not experience any such negative conditions; pain and other "inharmonious" experiences serve only to remind people that they need to "work" to affirm the Truth and deny Error in their lives.[8]

This "work" is essentially mentalistic, because, as one woman emphasized, "all healing takes place in the mind; all healing begins in the mind." "Work" in metaphysical groups refers to using reason, knowledge of Truth (as revealed by movement literature and leaders), and examination of one's thoughts and practices in order to discover the source of error-thinking and to overcome its destructive habits in one's life. Mental "work" is the principal healing activity, since healing involves the correction of thought. One necessary aspect of metaphysical "work" involves the effort to reject the notion of illness itself. A Unity minister urged, "We have to fight that [acceptance of disease and illness] all the time. We have to constantly remind ourselves that the natural state of the human being is to be well."

Unity members typically had very general notions of what needed healing. While they emphasized that individuals' ways of thinking and speaking must be redirected, they applied this approach to all areas of human need, not merely to physical problems. Since virtually every imperfection is ultimately reduced to an issue of consciousness or mind, Unity adherents recommended the same healing process for every need from physical problems to relationship problems and economic troubles. As an example of something needing healing, one woman suggested:

> A man or woman who can't pay their rent—that's a tremendous problem, and there again, that's related to consciousness. What they're saying when they can't do these things, is that they don't believe in a world that is full of abundance or a world that has been divinely created for good. They don't know it, but they don't believe it. Because if they believed it, there would be abundance and there would be a means and a way to overcome these problems.

Members of metaphysical groups mentioned many social, political, and economic problems that they felt were appropriate focuses for healing efforts: greed, dishonesty, hatred, unkindness, pornography,

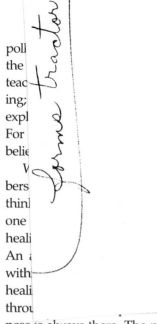

poll
the
teac
ing;
expl
For
belie
V
bers
thinl
one
heali
An
with
heali
throu

oblems, wars, and societal treatment of
ed, and other needy persons. Unity
dual mental processes that need chang-
ciousness needs healing. As one man
cumulation of the beliefs of mankind."
healing for "our mass thinking, our
nd all that will give us peace."
at they had experienced, Unity mem-
very of the element of error in their
ar changes in their condition. Indeed,
r bouts of discomfort, but the actual
of Truth and the rooting out of error.
ss: "This healing process is going on
pend on somebody to actually do the
whole—even though I might be going
rtain time—but to tell me that whole-

ness is always there. The perfect life is always there, because I'm a part of
the whole." Thus the healing experience was primarily that of discovering the error thinking that needed correcting; whatever physical, emotional, or spiritual effects that flowed from correcting that error were
secondary.

Indeed, since too much attention to one's illness might inadvertently
affirm the illness and prevent or delay healing, members avoided focusing on their nonmental conditions. Some even told, with some delight,
stories of not realizing that physical healings had occurred until some
time later; they had, appropriately, been too preoccupied with mental
work to notice the physical changes.

Simultaneously, respondents were adamant that, without correcting
the error-thinking, any improvements (such as pain relief) were purely
temporary. *Real* healing required a new way of thinking. Unity adherents
used medical doctors, but they believed that any true healing required
more than medical attention. Christian Scientists, however, explained
their avoidance of medical doctors by this real-versus-apparent dichotomy. One woman explained, "The medical, they don't heal anyone.
They just don't heal, because our sense of it is if someone is ill, it's a
product of his thinking. And [doctors] don't correct thinking."

The ultimate goal of this lifelong developmental process is perfection:
the restoration of persons to their natural state. One's true self is a

perfect being, but healing requires the gradual gaining of control of one's thoughts and words so that perfection can be realized. As one man stated, "If the thinking changes—really changes—and you can accept the new ideas or the new-formed positive, good thoughts you are using, then the body, the physical body, will follow along with the thinking."

The mental process, then, is central. Particular unpleasant setbacks that may occur during the process are minimized, because they are only external "appearances"—part of the fundamentally unreal material realm. One Unity adherent noted, "Once you come into that awareness that the healing process is going on, you will believe you are healed, and whatever appears is just an appearance, and it's changing, because under that appearance is the healing process." This emphasis upon healing as a gradual process reduces the problem of therapeutic failure, as it does for many of the other types of groups studied. Failure is only "apparent," not real, because the real healing is the larger process.

Unlike some other types of groups studied, however, metaphysical healing groups saw no benefit in pain or suffering. One Unity member emphasized, "There is no merit in suffering. If it hurts, you're doing [something] wrong." Accordingly, illness is viewed as a sign of error and the need for "work." One woman gave an example: "If I got an ulcer, that would be telling me that I should be healing something, maybe my worrying thought . . . I should get my anxieties and my worries taken care of." Similarly, a Christian Science adherent explained, "Maybe the pain would be a help to you, if it awakens you. If you connect difficulty with thought, then you would naturally think there's something. If you have pain, then there's something you'd better do about your thinking."

Some illness, thus, is the inevitable result of people failing to discover the root error and change their ways of thinking. As one Unity member explained, "People really cause a lot of their own problems. They keep on the same treadmill. . . . You keep on perpetuating the same mistake over and over, instead of stopping and saying, 'What am I learning from this experience?' They are their own enemies."

Causes of Illness

According to Unity adherents, illness itself is error, and the primary cause of illness is error-thought. The corollary of this concept is the belief that error-thoughts can be eliminated by denying their reality and power and by affirming the Truth of Being. This mentalistic concept of illness is illustrated by the comments of one woman: "When the mind has an idea about something, and you identify with the mind, you say 'I am [that quality or thing],' then whatever negativity is in there, you become the negativity. That's the beginning of illness."

Likewise, another Unity member emphasized, "The cause is always within the person. Illness is a misuse of your own creative power. . . . For example, if there is a pain and I know that the pain started first in my thinking somewhere, I [tell] my upstairs to clear up my act."

The mentalistic concept of illness is taken quite literally: Most members believe in the power of words to effect a person's well-being. For example, one woman told of an experience in which she was in such pain that she could not get out of bed one morning. She began to meditate to discover what error-thinking could have been the source, and she realized that she had developed the bad habit of saying, especially at work, "I will not stand for that." She interpreted her inability to stand up as the literal manifestation of that negative thought.

Illness and other human maladies thus proceed from misuse of mental processes. One Unity member explained:

I think this has a lot to do with creating it [illness]. Because what we think and what we know is energy and that energy gets translated into, manifested in, our bodies. . . . People say, "I just don't believe [in healing]," but . . . they believe in other things. They believe in germs; they believe in colds. I think we create these paradigms of beliefs and I think this has a lot to do with creating illness.

Some Unity members acknowledged the influence of "evil forces" in the development of human illness, but they defined these evil forces quite differently from the Christian healing groups. One woman explained this approach:

Evil forces, like good forces, stem from our own thinking. In other words, the wars, hurricanes, the tornados and things like that are caused by mankind and their own thinking. So, it goes right back to that. I heard recently a woman who kept saying "That burns me up!" Two times. This was a common expression of hers. You know, eventually she got a burning sensation all over her body. Of course, she had to go to all kinds of medical doctors to find out why, until this friend of mine said to her one time, "Do you realize that you keep saying 'that burns me up' two times?" "Yeah," she said. Well, she stopped thinking about it, and well eventually the burning sensation cleared up. That's how powerful thought is!

While most respondents from metaphysical groups emphasized individual error-thinking as the cause of illness, they also used a broader concept of "race consciousness." As in the above quotation, this concept often refers to the thinking of humankind, in general. The idea has obvious parallels with the distinction made by some Christian healing groups between individual sin and general or "original" sin as causes of illness.

The concept of "[human] race consciousness" is also used to explain how erroneous thoughts are inadvertently learned in socialization, because the whole social group shares error-thinking. For example, one woman said, "It starts with young children. They hear, 'Oh, you're going to catch a cold, because you're getting your feet wet.' " Thus, while these groups emphasize a highly individualistic notion of the causes of illness, they also recognized the influences of the larger social group.

Diagnostic Approaches

Unlike Christian healing groups, metaphysical groups observed gave little attention to diagnosis. For the purposes of their alternative healing practices, there was no need to distinguish different types of illness; all healing proceeded by the same approach. The main "diagnostic" effort was for the individual to examine his or her thoughts and words to find a negative pattern that might be connected with the particular malady experienced. Regardless of what the individual discovered in this process, the main healing practice involved the "affirmation of Truth" in thoughts and words.

Adherents who had sought diagnoses from their medical doctors referred to their illnesses in terms learned from the doctors; many respondents, however, recommended avoiding thinking or talking too much about the illness, lest they affirm the reality of the illness. Many of these respondents used medical diagnoses to determine whether treatment by a doctor were necessary, but they believed their full healing would be accomplished best by refusing to dwell on the idea of the illness (see Chapter Eight on patterns of use of medical treatment).

Source of Healing Power

Consistent with this notion of the causes of illness, members of traditional metaphysical groups held essentially mentalistic and individualistic ideas of healing power. One man said, "The healing power comes from the individual—the individual with the change in their concept, a change in their attitude, with a change in what they are accepting, can just about heal themselves." He added, later:

> I use [the word] "process." I use "healing activity," the healing "energy." I believe it is an energy that is everywhere present in all forms of life. I believe that we can allow that energy to do its work. . . . Some people sometimes call it "God," sometimes "spirit." I think of it mainly as a creative energy that is in the universe and its purpose is to keep the universe and everything in it perfect and free. . . . I can heal myself. I can be healthy and wealthy and live a harmonious, beautiful life. It's still the same; it depends on me—no one else or nothing else outside of myself.

Like him, many respondents avoided talking about "God" but attempted parallel concepts: force, creative energy, life-giving spirit, universal consciousness. The ultimate source of healing, thus, resides in some highly abstract spiritual power, which, at the same time, each individual can tap through concrete mental processes. The individual must get in touch with his or her own powers—the Divine Mind within, becoming attuned through affirmations and meditation. Through knowledge and use of the laws or principles of Divine Mind, the individual gains *control* of life and fate. Figure 4.1 depicts this emphasis on mind as the immanent source of healing power.

The individual's mind regulates the body's well-being through words or thoughts; incorrect use of words or thoughts, conversely, produces illness. The body's "natural" state is health, so healing is essentially a matter of undoing illness-producing mental processes, thereby self-healing the body.

FIGURE 4.1

Concept of Healing Power in Traditional Metaphysical Groups

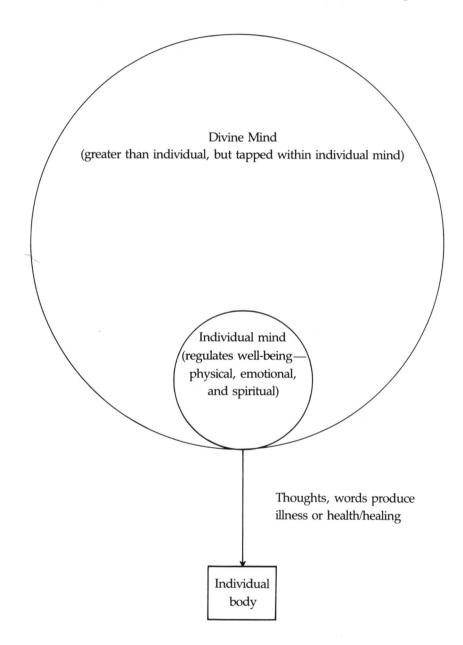

Divine Mind
(greater than individual, but tapped within individual mind)

Individual mind
(regulates well-being—
physical, emotional,
and spiritual)

Thoughts, words produce
illness or health/healing

Individual
body

Since the greater power of the Divine Mind is reached from within each individual, there is no conception of transmission of healing power. This notion explains the relatively minor role of the group or leader in the healing process. At most, the group or leader teaches members about Truth, while providing an atmosphere conducive to affirmation rather than negation. The group, thus, helps individual members learn and maintain positive thinking, but the healing process itself is essentially individual.

Healing and Health Practices

Like members of Christian healing groups, adherents of traditional metaphysical groups were not attracted primarily out of a need for healing. Rather, they became interested in and convinced about healing after learning the groups' approaches to it. Unity's emphasis on affirming Truth and denying Error is the all-purpose response to any adversity: ill-health, poor interpersonal relations, unsatisfactory job, lack of prosperity, inclement weather, social and political concerns, emotional problems, marital and family problems, and so on.

Accordingly, healing is the process of restoring the afflicted person to the perfection that exists within. The healing process is not medical. Although all Unity respondents used medical services, they were quick to add that real healing had to take place within. The doctor may be necessary to help relieve pain, set bones, or treat the symptoms, but medicine deals only with proximate causes, whereas *real* healing must deal with the ultimate causes—mental patterns.

Healing is, therefore, primarily, a "mind process" (not an intellectual process, however, since intellectualizing can lead to error). It is a process of growth involving much "work." This "work" consists of examining one's thinking habits and then eliminating all negative thought and substituting positive thought.

The typical formula for these positive thoughts is an affirmation, a statement of the desired, positive condition. Members viewed affirmations as the equivalent to prayer, except that they are not supplications; they are declarations of what has always been there but has been unrealized. One man described his treatment of his arthritic ankle: "I may be sitting in a car waiting for a traffic light and I may feel the ankle twinge and I direct my attention to the ankle and I begin to know in myself that there is a perfect prototype of that ankle right there, seeking toward its perfect self."

Unity meditations are filled with such affirmations; the local recorded Dial-a-Prayer service and *Daily Word* magazine offer different affirmations for each day. Attached to the monthly contribution envelope of the Unity centers studied was a set of recommended affirmations, for example, including, for healing, "The consistent flow of God-life within me heals, restores, and strengthens my mind and body," and, for prosperity, "The steadfastness of God's care assures me of unending supply and abundant prosperity."[9]

Even more specific affirmations should be used for specific conditions. One dated but still widely used Unity book interprets numerous illnesses in terms of the group's beliefs and recommends specific affirmations for each. For example, it states:

> To be delivered from the error called bronchitis, one needs a greater sense of vitality and a freeing and harmonizing of the life forces. When these two changes are brought about, the congested thought which is centered in the bronchial tubes will be released. Hold [the affirmation]: *The purifying, vitalizing, healing Christ life is now doing its perfect work in me and through me.*[10]

This mental "work" is essentially individual. Even when a minister or other member works with someone for a healing, the process consists of showing the affected person how to change error-thinking. The group does offer some moral support to individual members, although support in the metaphysical groups studied tended to be more impersonal than in Christian, Eastern, and psychic healing groups. For example, Unity offers a national telephone prayer service, called "Silent Unity," which responds to letters, telegrams, and telephone requests for help through prayer.[11] One respondent described developing a painful bladder infection at 4 A.M.: "I called Silent Unity . . . and the lady there spoke nicely, gave me some affirmations and said they would be praying with me. And I was sitting in a chair in my bedroom, and . . . as soon as I hung up, I felt like an explosion in the bladder area; it was completely healed. I never had any more problems."

Unity ministers and teachers also often lead relaxation meditations as part of accomplishing a healing. This emphasis on relaxation considerably predates the current notions of stress-reduction; rather, relaxation is viewed as a form of mental denial of error and a preparation of the mind for affirmation. Such meditations were the central part of every Unity service observed.

Meditations and guided visualizations observed at Unity services were highly effective; several recruits to the centers described these as the feature that initially attracted them to Unity. Guided visualizations are meditations that are led verbally, invoking images for the meditators to use individually.

A typical Unity meditation began with relaxation exercises. The leader instructed the congregation not to concentrate on her words as ideas, but to let them invoke individual personal meanings. She described relaxation as a wave, flowing over them; she commanded each part of the body to relax: jaws, neck, shoulders, solar plexus, and so on. The leader's voice was quiet, calm, monotonous but emphatic. A long silence followed while individual members deepened their relaxation and began meditating.

The leader used the pronoun "I" ("so I don't interfere with each meditator's space"): "I am creating a new world [pause]. I am continually creating it anew [long pause]. God gives me wisdom [pause]. Wisdom to grow [long pause]. And peace [pause]. Mine is a creation of peace [long pause]."

The main phrases of the meditation had been prepared in advance. The leader read a passage, then was silent. Not all the phrases were separate ideas; some were rephrasings of a previous statement or further images or adjectives to add vividness to the visualization. Repetition of statements with slight variations, together with the pattern of speaking-and-silence, resulted in a sense of continuity without direct linear development of an idea. Meditators described this kind of guided visualization as images floating by.

The leader often used nature imagery: wind, waves, ripples on a wheat field; many of these images evoked sound, motion, or other sensations. Typically, the meditations included "I am" affirmations: "I am making my new world with confidence"; "I am at peace"; "I am one with the universal light energy." Prayers requested for others were not in the form of supplications. Sometimes prayers for others were affirmations: "My loved ones are being brought into that energy and light; they are becoming whole and well." Other times, the leader suggested expanding one's consciousness to engulf others in need; she urged, "Whisper their names." Silence followed, while participants meditated on their separate prayer requests. At the end of the meditation session, the audience was "brought back" gradually; the leader directed them to move first one and then another part of the body. Deep exhalations and stretching were also recommended.

Many Unity members also used meditation individually to make their affirmations more effective. The individualism of Unity's approach to healing helps to explain the low levels of reliance on the group and the low levels of commitment to the local center. Unlike Christian and psychic groups, in Unity the group is not a channel or source of greater energy for the individual. The center is a source of teaching and creates an atmosphere for individuals to do their own "work."

Mental "work" through affirmations, visualizations, and eliminating sources of error-thinking is the primary healing and health practice of Unity and related traditional metaphysical healing groups. Many members, however, freely borrowed elements of healing and health practices from other healing groups. For example, some members believed strongly in the effectiveness of laying-on-of-hands, although they did not share Christian or psychic groups' explanation for its effectiveness. Consistent with the pragmatic approach of traditional metaphysical movements, their emphasis was simply on its effectiveness; little attention was paid to "why" the practice worked or the fact that the practice was not orthodox in their own belief system.

Similarly, individual Unity members reported borrowing some other practices, such as fasting, vegetarianism,[12] chiropractic, herbal remedies and special diets, exercises such as yoga, and other stress-reduction notions. There was no consistency, however, in the kinds of practices or their interpretation by Unity members who used them. Often, the explanation was that a friend suggested a practice and the respondent had tried it and liked it. This approach reflects the pragmatic and nonsectarian attitude of Unity and related New Thought groups.

Whereas Eastern and some psychic and occult groups typically had complex interpretations for their exercises, diets, and meditations, members of traditional metaphysical groups were generally satisfied with a, simple reduction of "why" to a mentalistic interpretation. They did, however, share other groups' metaphorical use of some practices and rituals. For example, one woman emphasized that she fasted, abstaining not only from food and wine but also: "from hating. I fast from being impatient. I fast, fast, fast. Fast isn't doing without a certain kind of food; it's doing without all that awful thinking that people are taking up with. That's the way we see fasting."

Therapeutic Success, Failure, and Death

Therapeutic success, according to these groups, is essentially only the process of realizing the perfection that already exists. Thus, while successful healing is an important confirmation of their beliefs, members generally emphasized the larger mental process rather than specific instances of healing. One woman noted, "A healing makes it easier for the next healing; each one builds upon the remembrances—even in the subconsciousness—and makes you more receptive." Christian Science congregations held regular meetings for testifying to healings; Unity centers studied rarely gave public mention to successful healings.

Consistent with their mentalistic emphasis, several Unity members suggested that individuals would always know if they had experienced real therapeutic success, since it is the individual who accomplishes the progress. At the same time, believers might not notice the physical manifestation of that progress, because they are appropriately focused on the mind and not the material (physical) realm.

Therapeutic failure was generally attributed to a lack of positive attitude or a lack of full faith. One man explained, "They have to eventually believe that they can be healed, . . . because it will be done only if they believe." He expanded this emphasis upon belief to include medical treatment, too: "You have to believe in what you're working with—medicine, doctors, physical processes, prayer—you have to believe in all that."

Traditional metaphysical groups hold the individual responsible for developing (or failing to develop) the consciousness necessary for full health. One woman emphasized that, while it is unkind to make people feel guilty or blameworthy for their illnesses, ultimately they need to take responsibility for their conditions. She added, "I do feel that we are responsible for a lot of it. I mean, sometimes I'm sick and I know that I chose it. I can see exactly what I did and how I wanted to rest."

Similarly, therapeutic failure can be explained by the individual's failure to recognize and change negative thought patterns underlying the illness. A Unity member explained, "I think that when a healing doesn't occur, it's because there's a reluctance on the part of the person to part with some of that personality. . . . People are reluctant to give up part of themselves that they've held onto for many years—their beliefs, their attitudes, and their approaches to life. [If these parts are not changed] that interferes with healing."

Therapeutic failure is, thus, less of a threat to the larger belief system in these groups than it is in Christian healing groups. Therapeutic failure, in many Christian healing groups, potentially results in questions about God's goodness and healing power. In traditional metaphysical groups, by contrast, responsibility and power reside within the individual. Failure is merely individual shortcoming and error, not at all inconsistent with the groups' beliefs about God or Truth.

These groups' beliefs about death are somewhat more ambiguous, however. Metaphysical groups do not share traditional Christian notions of heaven and hell; historically, some held general notions of reincarnation, probably borrowed from Eastern religions. In eighteen months of field observation, there was no mention of death or dying in any of the traditional metaphysical groups studied. Was this due to decreased emphasis upon these groups' traditional teachings about death? Was it perhaps a reflection of their emphasis on positive thinking (together with an acceptance of the cultural notion of death as a negative)? In contrast to adherents of Christian healing, members of these groups articulated no clear connection between the process of healing and the problem of death.

Historically, most metaphysical movements had clear-cut, distinctive theories of death. They generally viewed the mortal body as an illusion; thus, the finality of death was an illusion, since what was real (i.e., mind) was eternal. Fillmore even went so far as to teach that death was not necessary. Accordingly, one with a fully developed consciousness would never die. Fillmore asserted, "The mind can be so filled with thoughts of life that there will be no room for a thought of death. Death can never take possession of the body of one whose mind is thoroughly charged with ideas of life."[13] Indeed, Fillmore believed that he would enjoy such eternal life. None of the Unity members interviewed expressed comparably extreme beliefs, but they did share the movement's traditional mentalistic notions of health, illness, and healing.

5 EASTERN MEDITATION AND HUMAN POTENTIAL GROUPS

The central thrust of groups in this category was predominantly some adaptation of Eastern spirituality. A secondary source, interwoven with these spiritual notions, was some form of psychologism, emphasizing self-awareness, self-realization, self-fulfillment, or self-development. This latter set of beliefs and practices is quasi-religious but lacks emphasis upon any transcendent religious reality or power, leading some observers to refer to such beliefs and practices as "self-religions"[1] or the "cult of man."[2] In this latter approach, the individual self is the end, and the health of the individual is an ultimate good.

The overlap in membership, the syncretic amalgams of beliefs and practices, and the fuzzy combination of terms from both traditions make it virtually impossible to create neat distinctions between the Eastern and the human potential aspects of these groups. Furthermore, given a methodological focus upon individual adherents rather than movement spokespersons and official literature, this study encountered very few persons who practiced "pure" forms of any of these approaches. Very few respondents identified themselves primarily with the nonspiritual, psychologistic methods, even though a sizable proportion had taken courses or workshops about these approaches. Typically, our respondents wove together complex, eclectic, and continually changing strands from several approaches for their personal beliefs and practices.[3]

Although the press and the public became interested in these religious and quasi-religious movements in the late 1960s and early 1970s, they are hardly new to the American scene. Several forms of Eastern spirituality were transported to American audiences before the turn of the century, and there are links between these movements and other spiritual movements of that time in the transcendental, occult, and psychic traditions. The 1950s saw another increase of enthusiasm for Eastern meditation. Thus, the "new" Eastern religious forms of the 1960s and 1970s could be seen as a reemergence of earlier themes.[4]

Similarly, the human potential movement did not appear from nowhere. It had its roots in previous forms of psychotherapies, although the proliferation of various forms of human potential or growth therapeutic methods is a relatively recent development.[5]

Many of the earlier studies of the current Eastern movements assumed their development to be a youth culture phenomenon. More recent research, however, has shown that, like the groups studied here, many Eastern spiritual forms attract middle-aged, educated, and established persons more than they do the stereotypical countercultural youth.

In the communities studied, the dominant form of these groups was an Americanized variant of some Eastern spiritual belief system, such as Zen or Tibetan Buddhism, Jain, or some other form of yoga and meditation. Less spiritual but still-related Eastern variants include Transcendental Meditation and 3HO (Happy, Healthy, Holy).[6] Frequently group members also participated in various human potential groups or workshops (such as Neurolinguistic Programming, Progoff Process, Cornucopia, or rebirthing). They typically viewed them as incomplete but valuable learning experiences. Conversely, recruits were often set on the path to "self-realization" in human potential groups but turned to the discipline of Eastern spirituality for long-term development. They were often disparaging of persons who expected human potential groups to give them an instant self-discovery "fix."[7]

Adherents were particularly critical of two well-known human potential programs, Scientology and est. Despite their generally eclectic and tolerant approach to methods other than their own, a large proportion of adherents in Eastern meditation groups expressed criticism or skepticism about Scientology and est (which are, interestingly, two especially authoritarian human potential approaches). Only two respondents had tried or would try Scientology. Of those who had taken some est training, most felt that it was far too narrow, authoritarian, and short-term an approach. Those few who felt they had gained something valuable from est training generally accepted only a small portion of est "information" and eclectically amalgamated it into a personal framework.

The following material, then, is a composite, focusing primarily upon the more stable and committed Eastern meditation groups. With the exception of these groups' emphasis upon self-discipline and their use of Asian cosmological notions, such as karma and reincarnation, virtually all Eastern and human potential groups studied were remarkably similar in their notions of health, illness, and healing.

Ideals of Health and Wellness

The foremost concepts mentioned by respondents in describing their ideals of health were energy, balance and flexibility, holism, self-awareness, and responsibility. For example, one woman described a "truly healthy person" as one with "high level energy, positive thoughts, the ability to accept responsibility for one's mental and physical state of being. And I think mainly it's this high quality of energy, which is fed by and conversely into one's power of thought."

The holism of their definitions is exemplified by another adherent: "I think of health at every level: a healthy mind, a healthy spirit, as well as a healthy body. So that person would have to have energy, alertness, enthusiasm, a love of life, a love of people, a love of themselves."

Most respondents considered self-awareness to be a necessary precondition to true healthiness. One should really "know" one's body, emotional reactions, spiritual situation, true social and psychological needs. Self-awareness was necessary in order to evaluate one's problems and potential solutions. Only through self-awareness could one achieve self-fulfillment. As one person explained, "A first prerequisite, I think, is being insightful, and being insightful means, to me, being aware of yourself, knowing what your needs and your wants and your desires are, and then getting it."

Several respondents were emphatic that true healthiness must come from inside oneself—an inner strength, an inner peace. One woman characterized the necessary inner qualities as "knowing you're doing your best . . . flexibility in life, an openness to life, open to change." Another stated that the inner strength comes when one's entire energy field is raised and balanced.

In contrast to psychic or traditional metaphysical groups, however, these groups used concepts of "energy," "balance," and "flexibility" literally as well as metaphorically. They believed that the literal condition of the body both reflects and produces larger spiritual, emotional, and social conditions. For example, if one is able to be physically balanced, one is more likely to become balanced in one's emotional, social, and spiritual states, as well. This literal/metaphorical connection explains a number of the healing practices described below.

Another contrast was that meditation groups tended to emphasize physical well-being and physical lifestyle qualities more than other groups studied. This emphasis is consistent with their focus on balance; the ideal lifestyle is one of balance, moderation, and flexibility, in all aspects of life.

Notions of Illness and Healing

When identifying areas they felt needed healing, members of these groups frequently mentioned physical conditions—as did many members of other groups. They sought healing especially for chronic conditions such as "bad backs," allergies, asthma, migraine headaches, elevated blood pressure, arthritis, and sciatica. More than members of other groups, these respondents emphasized lifestyle issues, such as weight problems, stress responses, smoking and other cravings, and other physical-emotional conditions related to lifestyle. Whereas other groups viewed lifestyle problems as secondary symptoms of deeper problems, such as not relying enough on the Lord, these respondents considered lifestyle a central issue in well-being.

Another point of contrast was the emphasis placed by meditation and human potential groups upon social factors needing healing: family life, interpersonal relationships, job troubles, and so on. In contrast to Christian and metaphysical groups, however, these groups saw such problems as a way of making decisions. Whereas many other groups interpreted interpersonal problems as a need to adapt to a bad situation (or "submit," in the case of poor marriages or relationships with authorities), meditation and human potential groups considered healing to involve choosing—including the choice of getting out of the situation.

Furthermore, groups in this category were unique in this study in their strong emphasis on larger social, environmental, or politico-eco-nomic issues. Only in these groups were political concerns publicly discussed regularly. Whereas Christian healing groups tended to empha-size mainly issues of private morality and personal choice, such as pornography, abortion, divorce, drug abuse, and alcoholism, these groups focused on public morality issues of environmental pollution, world peace, injustices, prejudices, nuclear destruction, poverty, malnu-trition or famine, political oppression, and unemployment.[8]

Despite their virtually unanimous definition of social issues as needing healing, respondents were nearly evenly divided between activist and quietist approaches to social problems. Some groups encouraged letter-writing campaigns, marches, and political action; others saw meditation and private behavior as the primary approach to healing for social problems. For example, one member stated, "I think we're on a merry-go-round that leads to destruction. Of course, that's one reason why I've been working for the freeze, because I feel as though we must stop this business of throwing money down a rathole that leads only to holocaust, that is going to use these weapons on each other, either intentionally or by accident." By contrast, another explained:

> I think society does need to be healed. I think countries need to be healed. But I think that's a real macrocosmic view, and that [healing] can't take place until we begin with the microcosm, until we begin with the individual. And I think that's really symbolic of—once we begin to heal ourselves as individuals, then we can work on a much more global space. . . . The people who are working with healing global problems—people working on ecology, people working with world peace—are people who are aware of their own healing powers and are working on healing themselves individually, so they have taken on responsibility for that [larger healing].

Alternative healing, according to these groups, is not extraordinary. They believe that normally the body heals itself; medical and nonmedical intervention alike merely aid the natural processes to effect a faster, better, or longer-lasting result. One woman explained, "I feel pretty strongly that we have a natural healer within. . . . I work with people and myself . . . to move the energy more freely in the body, opening the channels of the body would have natural healing effects."

Like other groups, these adherents distinguished between healing and mere symptom relief. While they respected the need for symptom relief, they emphasized that long-term healing of the underlying problem required something deeper. For example, one member of a yoga/meditation group criticized overreliance on chiropractors (whom she also used): "I don't consider [chiropractic] healing. It's temporary relief. I think a healing has to come from someplace else." Real healing comes from an inner awareness, openness to the flow of energy, and inner freedom. One woman, who described numerous extensive healings in her life, said:

> It feels like a total surrender, a total letting go, a total opening, a heightened degree of awareness of every cell of your body, and a connectedness between your body and your mind and your spirituality, an incredible, incredible connectedness there. Just wonderful! [You know a healing has occurred, because] there's a freeing in your body and your mind. There's more space. There's more energy. And your mind has let go of whatever it was you were tenaciously clinging to. That's the only way I can describe that. I mean, I just know.

Thus Eastern/meditation groups shared other alternative healing groups' notion that real healing must address the real causes, not merely the symptoms. Unlike some Christian healing adherents, however, these respondents had no category for "counterfeit" healings, because their worldview is essentially monistic, rather than dualistic. All healing energy (including the power of medicine) is one.

Similarly, these groups shared with other groups the notion that healing is a process rather than a discrete event. Since real healing occurs through gradual increased awareness and lifestyle changes, the whole healing process takes place over time—often a lifetime. One man described his healing of a chronic painful sinus infection:

> It can be a very gradual process where there's no one specific event that you can pick out. But, the body, like in a case like me, being healed of my sinus condition, it was a very gradual process. There was no one particular time that I can pick out. It's just that the metabolic process started in the body and the healing, you know, just continued over a period of years. It would get less and less and less.

The meaning of pain and illness was a more complex issue to Eastern healing adherents than to some other persons using alternative healing.

Although pain and suffering were not particularly problems of theodicy, respondents did distinguish different meanings of pain. Some persons contrasted "good" versus "bad" pain. For example, one woman with a painful chronic illness explained that good pain is a temporary clue to some change that is needed, whereas bad pain is meaningless and fruitless suffering.

Similarly, some distinguished between "normal" pain or discomfort and pain that is a sign of trouble. These adherents believed that the key to distinguishing the two lies in being fully aware of one's own body. For example, a woman who had years of problems with arthritis told of being able to distinguish when her discomfort during yoga poses was acceptable—perhaps even a good sign that the stretches were doing what they should for her—in contrast to when the discomfort was a clue to avoid a pose. She said her gradual healing was due partly to becoming willing to engage in exercise; previously, fear of each experience of pain crippled her physically and increasingly had limited her range of motion. Thus some pain is seen as a valuable clue to the lesson to be learned in order to bring about growth and real healing. One person commented, "I think that illness sometimes is a very creative way of growing, of learning. I think that's why we're here, to kind of progress, to be more loving, to learn certain lessons. And illness sometimes can be a way of stopping ourselves and bringing ourselves up short to look at our priorities to see what's really central. I don't see it as a bad thing."

Another woman said, "I knew there was a destiny for this confinement. . . . It really did give me time to develop my insight as to what was wrong with my lifestyle." And another yoga adherent explained:

> Pain is your body's way of saying, "Hey, something's wrong, do something about it, don't block it out, and notice you're tense all the time" instead of taking a tranquilizer or something like that . . . I think it might be a signal to look at: Maybe I'm in the wrong job, maybe something in my family life needs to work out, maybe I'm not getting along with people I'm living with. So, in that way, it can be a way of turning your life around.

She added that illness was not only a lesson for this life, but also for future lives—part of an ongoing process of growth and development.

Several members emphasized that pain and illness can teach other qualities, as well. One can learn endurance and patience. One can learn to be more compassionate toward others who are suffering. For example, a nurse said it was not until she was immobilized in great pain following a cesarean section that she learned how to give compassion to her own patients. Numerous respondents added that without pain, growth is impossible. Although such attitudes are not unique to these groups, they gain particular emphasis in this type of group because of the focus on personal awareness and development.

Other members of these groups articulated a very different interpretation of pain and illness: that pain and illness are the natural by-products of the body's attempt to rid itself of pollution. Accordingly, illness is a purification process. One woman explained that the "illness crisis is when all of the toxins seem to accumulate at once, and your body is pushing all these toxins out." The discomfort or pain is experienced as evidence that the purging or purification is taking place.

Like respondents from other groups, these adherents shared the notion that pain and suffering were often retained because of secondary gains to the sufferer. They were more likely, though, to attribute the illness to avoidance of some decision or awareness in their lives. For example, one woman explained a series of events leading to her breaking an ankle: "I thoroughly believe that I didn't want to make the decision for myself, and so I let it be made for me." Another yoga adherent interpreted her prolonged partial paralysis: "I wanted to paralyze myself, because I felt there were a lot of things I did not want to face. And so I used the paralysis of my leg (which is a typical Freudian interpretation) to keep me from going where I knew I needed to go and was afraid to go."

Causes of Illness

Adherents of these groups held beliefs about the causes of illness that, in some ways, paralleled the beliefs of other groups reported here. In their interpretations, however, member of Eastern/meditation groups typically emphasized specifically spiritual causes somewhat less and focused more on lifestyle and environmental factors. Another interesting point of comparison is that only in these groups and Christian healing groups was doctor-caused illness mentioned, although it was not a common response for either type of group.

Pollution

The foremost cause of illness mentioned was pollution. This cause had, simultaneously, physical, social, and emotional aspects. The concept was also used both literally and metaphorically. Members of these groups typically emphasized both pollution brought on by others and pollution resulting from individual lifestyle choices. There was a sense of constant threat, perhaps all the more acute because of the community's proximity to numerous nuclear power plants, petrochemical and other environment-threatening industries, toxic waste dumps, polluted rivers, urban noise and congestion, and so on.

One woman observed, "I believe the causes are the contaminants in the atmosphere, in the water, in the food. It's all around us; it's difficult not to become contaminated." Another woman, in addition to mentioning the ill effects of being around crowds of people, attributed illness to "polluted" food and drink: "I think it's a lot of the stuff we ingest. I believe we pollute our own bodies, and that brings on illness." One man illustrated the connection of environmental and personal choice issues:

A person could be exposed to an environmental poison without them knowing about it, and get sick from it. . . . A lot of people get sick from environmental pollutions, workplace conditions. . . . Even if we are exposed to environmental poisons, which we all are to a certain degree—smog, pollution in the air, the water is polluted—we can minimize the effects by a good nutritional program.

Pollution is pervasive. It emanates from large-scale and small-scale "problems." For example, one man listed a string of causes of illness: "Three Mile Island, asbestos and uranium processing, eating white bread, chemicals in meat, impurities in the water." Similarly, many respondents in these groups saw a threat not only in the pollution of the physical environment but also in the larger social-political atmosphere. The prevalence of war mentality was associated with pollution as a threat to health. One man exclaimed, "Environment especially—the chemical assault on our bodies. Acid rain, pollution. The planet is in big trouble. It's got a cancer. Anybody who believes the unbelievable brainwashing we get that we need more defense weapons . . . they can destroy the whole planet."

Many respondents mentioned specific lifestyle factors as illness-producing, because they pollute the body. Obvious pollutants include cigarette smoking, taking drugs and tranquilizers, and eating unhealthful foods (of which refined sugars, red meats, and white bread were almost universal symbols). Many members of these groups emphasized that noise, confusion, social pressures, and stressful conditions were also polluting. The time-clock, assembly-line pace, urban noise, frustrating traffic conditions, and similar pressures were all named as causes of illness.

These groups' concept of pollution also had a spiritual tinge; self-pollution often comes from attachment. One woman emphasized, "[Illness comes from] bad living, definitely. Bad, bad living. Self-abuse. Attachment—that's where ego comes in—attachment. Attachment to alcohol, attachment to cigarettes, to coffee, to love—possessive type of love; attachment to wealth, money. Food, sweets. Those things make people sick." In many Eastern religions, the goal of eliminating all attachments (as illusory sources of happiness) is a spiritual purification. For most adherents interviewed, however, purification meant merely avoiding excessive or unhealthful attachments—that is, imbalance and immoderation.

Imbalance

As a frequently mentioned cause of illness, imbalance was often connected to pollution and lifestyle. It was also a sign of not being in touch with oneself. Lifestyles of excess—too much work, too much food or drink, too much alcohol or drugs, too much activity—represented harmful imbalances. Even essentially pleasurable and helpful activities, such as sleep, exercise, and sex, could be harmful, if they were allowed to "take over" one's life.

Injuries and accidents, in particular, were attributed to imbalance. For example, one woman, who had fallen down a flight of stairs, attributed her injuries to the fact that her social and emotional life were out of kilter. Another woman, who had painfully injured her back and leg, explained, "I think a lot of illnesses that people have are either they just are so busy and not being in touch with themselves, but being in touch with everything else, that they plow through and injure themselves, on a big level or a little level."

Emotions and Stress

Another major category of causes of illness included various emotions. Many members mentioned anger, resentment, bitterness, self-hatred, and residual anger from childhood or other earlier experiences. Like physical pollutants, these negative emotions were viewed as toxins to the body, introducing illness or making the body vulnerable to external sources of illness.

Linked with emotions, but more importantly with pollution and lifestyle, was the factor of *stress*. Members linked stress with numerous emotional and physical maladies, including cancer, heart disease, migraine headaches, chronic back pain, asthma, allergies, and colds and viruses. One woman described these causes:

> Anxiety and stress. A lot of my stuff comes from my own ego's need to collect my being, my energy and make an impact in the world, and in doing that I end up leading myself and defiling myself. So that it has to do with some kind of thing that's very much a part of our Western culture— accomplishment-oriented, striving, being seen, having a big voice. That certainly drives me and . . . a lot in this community that there's such a need for making that impact. Making it, striving, getting ahead, that kind of thing. Really makes us crazy and makes us sick.

Another member emphasized that stress could be productive and linked with creativity but that, given societal values, it was often illness-producing, because people push themselves too hard for the wrong reasons:

> I think stress is a tremendous cause, and the expectations that we have of ourselves to be all things, to prove ourselves in some way (probably the old ego)—it's a very powerful disease-maker. How do I mean that? Well, in the desire I might have to prove myself, to accomplish, to drive, to compete with other people, to be better than another person—that can be constructive, but I think it can also be destructive.

Far more than in other types of group studied, respondents in Eastern meditation and human potential groups emphasized social causes of stress and other emotional strains. Members cited job pressures, discrimination, pressures of family life and marriage, isolation and loneliness, and pressures of unsatisfactory role-expectations, such as gender or family roles. So, while they emphasized the need for individuals to choose healthful lifestyles and personal stances toward life, they also recognized the assaults on health posed by the larger society.

Like metaphysical groups, these groups held that mental processes— thoughts and words—are important causal factors. Accordingly, thoughts are connected to one's energies. One may use thoughts to mobilize energy for health and well-being, or one's thoughts may produce negative energy, bringing on illness. One woman said, "I like to believe that if thought creates form, then the way we're thinking does influence people around us, that it goes out in ripples and it can have some small effect, at least on the lower consciousness." By contrast, negative thought produces illness, as illustrated in another woman's explanation: "I would relate illness to the way the person thinks. There's no question that some people are down all the time. And they think of their ills all of the time, and not think of their wells."

Spiritual Causes

Groups emphasizing Eastern-inspired spirituality were especially likely to mention spiritual causes of illness. One leader of a Jain yoga and meditation circle said, "It's all ego-involved, and us through ego hanging onto things we no longer need, our inability to surrender, our inability to let the natural process of the universe and the body take place." Thus, ego-involvement and its concomitant attachment to illusory sources of happiness misdirect the individual's energies and produce illness. These ideas are closely connected in one person's explanation of the causes of illness:

> Not thinking of the higher qualities but of the lower needs. A lot of physical things. And it's not the most important things. People's wants and needs. Wants—I would say, people's wanting things. Anything having to deal too much with the physical world. I keep in my mind a lot of affirmations that

help me to live in this world, but don't be of it, because it's only a transient experience. We're here to accomplish certain things and certain purposes on this earth. And when it's our time to leave, it's time to go someplace else. But people shouldn't get too caught up in the physical things of living, the mundane things like greed, with money.

There was no parallel concept in these groups to the Christian or psychic notions of evil forces as a cause of illness. The Eastern-inspired belief system held no dualistic notions of good-versus-evil. All energy— positive and negative alike—is essentially one.

A more common spiritual explanation was karma. According to this interpretation, the individual's fortune or misfortune is attributed to positive or negative actions of the past, including past incarnations. One man explained, "According to the Law of Karma, everything that we do in our individual sphere and our social sphere has certain repercussions. So, if we do things that are negative, negative results are going to come back to us, eventually. So I think, in that sense, [we] were punished for actions that we do that are not in harmony with the greater good."

Because the concept of karma includes reaping effects of previous lives' behavior, it is a useful theodicy for the suffering, illness, or death of a good person. Many respondents believed that suffering resulting from karma was a "natural" effect. For example, one young woman stated:

Well, karma comes into this now. I believe in reincarnation. I would say it's a payoff. There was another life in which maybe that person wished evil upon somebody else, and now in this life they are getting it back in this form, whether they know it or not. It's something that they have to go through. That's how I feel.

That's the only way I can make any sense out of it, because of cancer and everything today, even with senseless murders—like with John Lennon and that guy that killed him. People say "How horrible," and it was. It's horrible to us to think that somebody has to die like that. But you look at it from another perspective and say there was some kind of a debt there. There was some kind of a debt and it had to be repaid. It's nature. It's nature's way of working, and it's not always the most fair thing, but it's nature.

Like Christian believers, adherents of Eastern healing approaches distinguished between individual and general sin—or karma. One's illness or other misfortune could be the result of one's personal wrongdoing or could be the more general negative effects of world karma. This latter concept is somewhat similar to the notion of original sin, in that the wrong adheres to a whole social group and its ill effects fall upon all heirs, no matter how personally righteous or good.

Unlike sin, however, karma was not considered an affront to a personal god; it was more like a violation of nature. It was not a punishment, but a simple matter of reaping what one sowed. Furthermore, the idea of karma implied more remote responsibility than the notion of sin, because it allowed that the offense may have taken place in a previous incarnation. Unlike psychic or occult adherents, Eastern/meditation groups showed very little interest in discovering their identities or basis of karma from previous incarnations. The emphasis was on being "in the present." Thus, karma did not serve as a basis for guilt; the primary appropriate response was to become as pure and self-aware and good in this life as possible.

Responsibility for illness is, however, implicit in these adherents' belief system, just as it is in other types of group studied. There is strong emphasis on personal responsibility for health or illness, especially the responsibility for one's self-awareness and lifestyle. At the same time, there is the sense that some problems are larger than individual (e.g., environmental pollution); there is also a sense of political responsibility—more so than in most other groups studied. For example, some groups took part in a campaign to prevent the regional aerial spraying for gypsy moth infestations.

Most concern with pollution, however, took individual forms, such as the installation of elaborate water purification arrangements in the home, rather than campaigning for clean water supplies. Likewise, although these groups gave greater recognition to social sources of stress, their responses were largely individual; one was responsible for simplifying one's lifestyle and learning to tune out the clamor and pressures. No external evil forces, devils, or temptations could be blamed for one's plight. Ultimately, too, one was responsible for one's own karma and working it out.

Diagnostic Approaches

There appear to be no diagnostic approaches peculiar to this type of group, yet these groups—far more so than any other type—are concerned with discovering both the physical and symbolic meanings of persons' illnesses. Respondents from these groups typically used medical doctors' diagnoses in combination with their own self-"understanding." One yoga adherent said, "We need understanding [of] our own body. Feeling. Being aware of when we're out of sync with ourselves, because the body gives every indication."

These groups emphasized self-awareness, including bodily awareness, more than other groups studied. Accordingly, persons who are really in touch with their own bodies are best able to evaluate their own health needs. For example, one woman described changing doctors in complete frustration, because her first doctor did not take her symptoms seriously. She had gone to him twice with what he diagnosed as "flu," and at the second visit he had implied her problem was mainly emotional. In the interview, she exclaimed, "But I know my body and I know what flu does to it, and I knew that this thing I had was far worse, affecting me in ways that flu never had. I knew I had something serious, but I didn't know what." A new doctor did diagnose something serious, aided partly by additional symptoms that had subsequently developed. This kind of experience with doctors is probably not unique to adherents of alternative healing. Attention to such experiences is heightened, however, because many adherents of alternative healing are more aware than most patients of their own bodies' normal functioning, more attentive to changes or problems with their bodies, and more committed to optimum physical well-being.

Furthermore, these groups focused on teaching members to experience themselves differently. They believed that one of their healing functions was to show people how to get in touch with both their real needs and their sources of energy or strength. One woman explained:

> And I think there's so much healing that comes from a person if they just know how to really source into it, that they can be trained . . . or shown how to go to your different levels of strength. I believe in medicine; I'm a nurse, and of course, medicine definitely has its place. But I think so many times . . . if you can step back from your situation when you're not feeling well, whether it's aches and pains kinds of thing, if you can assess your whole emotional, psychological, nutritional—the whole thing—and work at that, you can then encourage your own healing.

Many respondents from Eastern and human potential groups were especially attentive to pain, viewing it as an indicator, not necessarily a bad thing in itself. They often resisted medicating the pain if they felt that the pain was needed to diagnose the *real* problem. One respondent explained, "In America people rely too much on drugs, don't allow pain, don't allow for pain. Sometimes you have to listen to pain—if it's a good pain or a bad pain, because pain is the only way you can diagnose anything. But we never do; we run to a drug as soon as we have pain."

For these reasons, members of these types of groups generally avoided taking painkillers, over-the-counter medications of all kinds, and especially tranquilizers, sleeping pills, or other psychotropic drugs. They believed that fully experiencing one's condition was a necessary prerequisite for accurately diagnosing what one needs—physically, emotionally, and spiritually.

These respondents had strong interest in determining the symbolic meaning of their illness. Thus diagnosis meant not only identifying the physical/emotional condition responsible for one's problems but also discerning the "ultimate" meaning of that condition. (Some adherents of psychic and traditional metaphysical healing also evinced interest in the symbolism of their illnesses, but not to the same degree as these respondents.) For example, the diagnosis of varicose veins was linked with the blockage of energy in the lower part of the body; dizziness and falling were interpreted as middle ear problems and as a sign of imbalance in one's personal/emotional life; the diagnosis of arthritis was linked with the need for greater flexibility in interpersonal relationships and in facing changes in one's life; and so on.

So, while a doctor would typically be consulted to identify an unknown physical problem, the adherent would simultaneously meditate and examine self and personal life for the "higher" identification of the "real" problem. One young woman, who had described healings of ovarian cysts, as well as emotional and relationship healings, said:

> Sometimes "illness" is even a bad word to put on something that's going wrong. And another way of looking at it is blocking energy or whatever. I know for myself and my own energy that some of my stuff in the reproductive system has to do with my own sexuality and connecting with that, and [problems I had in] connecting with the real pleasure I get out of getting turned on all over the place by life.

The primary reason for this emphasis on identifying the symbolic meaning of illness is these adherents' notion that the body-mind-spirit connection works both literally and metaphorically. The metaphorical implications of any given illness are, thus, not merely thoughts to ponder; rather, they may show the way to effecting changes in the physical aspects of the illness. For example, in order to correct a condition of physical imbalance, one may need to work simultaneously upon improving emotional and interpersonal balance, diet, posture, and inner, spiritual energies. Before appropriate healing practices are chosen, however, it is important that the ill person identify the significant deeper issues to be addressed. The symbolic or metaphorical meanings of illnesses give clues for this level of "diagnosis."

In addition to these distinctive approaches to diagnosis, some members of this type of group also share some methods used in psychic groups. Many respondents had considerable faith in well-developed intuition. Many also used Therapeutic Touch for diagnosis. Sharing the psychics' general notion of the illness-producing effects of energy blockages, these persons "felt" for the sensation of energy "congestion." One member of a yoga and meditation healing circle explained, "For me, where there is a lot of static or pressure is an area that needs to be worked on. And where there is an area that's low, I work there too."

Typically, Therapeutic Touch was employed to diagnose developing problems as yet too minor to take to a doctor, or something a doctor would not consider medically significant or treatable. Therapeutic Touch (despite its tactile emphasis) does not involve actually touching the ill person, but some members used physical touch for diagnosis. Like Therapeutic Touch, shiatsu and other massage-diagnostic methods involve theories about the proper flow of energy in the body. Respondents who used these methods believed that a skilled massage practitioner could feel the areas where blockages had occurred and gradually help open the blockage through manipulation. These methods were typically practiced on a client-practitioner model, but adherents of meditation groups were often among the practitioners' adherents as well, because the underlying concepts of illness and healing overlapped.

Source of Healing Power

Drawing from Eastern religious notions, most respondents in this type of group believed that the source of healing power was a universal force in which humans and other living things participate. One woman said, "The source is essence, or 'prana,' which is the yoga way of thinking which is spirit, all the same thing—life's force. It's got a lot of different names, but it's something that is around us, in us and of us." For another member, the connection with healing power was even more intimate. The interviewer had said, "This natural healing power which you are describing, is it within the individual?" To this, the respondent replied, "We *are* it."

Like psychic healing adherents, these respondents emphasized the natural quality of this force or energy. One woman said:

> It comes from within. . . . Sometimes internal things might have to happen to do it; medical procedures, in some cases, are certainly necessary. I think you should depend a lot on your own body. I think [the healing source] is built in. I think it's a natural thing. In general, I think your body's really meant to be healthy, and is suited to be, and does a good job of [healing itself] if you take care of it.

At the same time, however, their image of healing energy was more spiritual and less mechanistic than most psychic healing adherents. One man explained:

> Call it God, or the Divine Consciousness, the One Mind, whatever. I feel there's one infinite source to this universe and that all healing and all spiritual awareness and all life comes from that source. In yoga we call the life force "prana," and in Chinese philosophy, they call it "ki," but it's the same; it means the good dynamic life energy that's present in our bodies, that flows from one infinite source.
> And even in modern physics now, they realize that everything is energy. And they break down all components to their essential nature. And they're energy, and that is the same energy that is within our bodies. That energy is consciousness and intelligence. And that energy is the source of healing.

Several respondents were uncomfortable with equating this notion of energy or force with the Christian notion of God, but they saw similarities. One adherent stated, "Well, of course, I do not believe in a personal God, so I suppose that I would say [the source is] the power of love." Another person emphasized, "I just think it's pure love. Love is vibration; love is energy. And we can direct that. And that's it [the source of healing]." This linkage of love, vibration, and energy was common in the explanations of these respondents. A meditation teacher, too, said, "The source is love. And love translated into concrete physical terms is energy, is vibration."

Another concept linked with love and energy was "harmony," which is also critical to these respondents' definition of well-being. One woman commented:

> The source of healing power is probably the whole universe. I'm just thinking in terms of spirituality. There's an energy level that's not to be measured in machines and I think there's a harmony. . . . I think definitely the source is to be in touch with or in harmony with a much bigger force—what some people call God. And in a generic sense, maybe it is a kind of God. It's spiritual . . . and it's something that's a lot bigger than anyone. A combination of every-thing—maybe a combination of all the energies.

Like other adherents of alternative healing, these groups taught that healing energies could be channeled or communicated from one individual to another or from the source of healing power to the affected part of the person needing healing. Like psychic adherents, these respondents had images of the flow of energy or vibrations, but their conceptions were generally less mechanistic. Similarly, like adherents of Christian healing, their conception of the source of healing power implies the communication of spiritual qualities, such as love, peace, and harmony.

The following quotation is given at length to illustrate the images used literally and metaphorically to describe healing power and its communication in the healing process:

> It [healing power] is coming from somewhere outside of yourself. So I really think that there's a very strong spiritual-like atmosphere that's there, and I think if you plug into that or if you let that sort of roll over you, that's when all these good things can happen. That's the only way I can locate it. Everywhere.
>
> Oh, and one more thing. I think the sun. The sun, by the way—on all levels—spiritual and physical—represents also a very good source of healing and of well-being. There's something I think very maternal and very positive about the sun and how it functions.

[Interviewer: How is the healing power released or channeled to where it is needed?]

It can be with direct communication. For a lot of people, this type of thing where you put your hand on someone—like E.T. touched a finger, okay?—there's the contact probably helps most people directly. It's probably like conducting electricity. But it's not necessary. . . . Energy is just all around. I think it just went wherever people were receptive. And wherever the weaknesses were, it just seemed to like flow in. Like a sandcastle when the tide comes in, it just goes in all the little holes.

I think it comes basically through energy, and energy does not have to be confined to one touching point, but it probably helps. Maybe it just helps the person who's about to be healed, because they can feel the love more directly.

Touching and breathing were two frequently mentioned ways by which one could tap or channel the necessary energy. Special breathing exercises were taught in several groups; these practices were to balance energies, purify the system—literally and metaphorically—and open the individual to the flow of healing energy.

Figure 5.1 illustrates meditation groups' complex images of how healing power works. The monistic unity of universal energy or life force is difficult to depict, because it is considered to be simultaneously *there* ("everywhere") and yet *within* ("we are it").

This conception is also more adamantly holistic than most other belief systems studied. In these meditation groups, body, mind, and spirit are equally important in together tapping or enhancing healing power. By contrast, other types generally emphasized mind or spirit, even while holding that all three are linked. For this reason, healing power is multidirectional in this diagram. Work on the body (e.g., exercise) also affects the spirit, mind, and emotions; work on the mind (e.g., meditation) also affects the spirit and body; work on the spirit (e.g., purification or experiences of oneness) also affects mind and body.

Beliefs about the source of healing energy have implications for the role of healer. Some images of healing energy imply a reservoir of energy to be tapped by anyone who wills and knows how; concomitantly, the energy might be available more readily or powerfully to certain individuals, who channel it to where it is needed. One woman explained, "I am a vehicle—I am not a 'healer'—but I am a channel who pulls the energy from the universe and focuses it." Another said, "I'm merely an instru-

FIGURE 5.1   Concepts of Healing Power in Eastern Meditation Groups

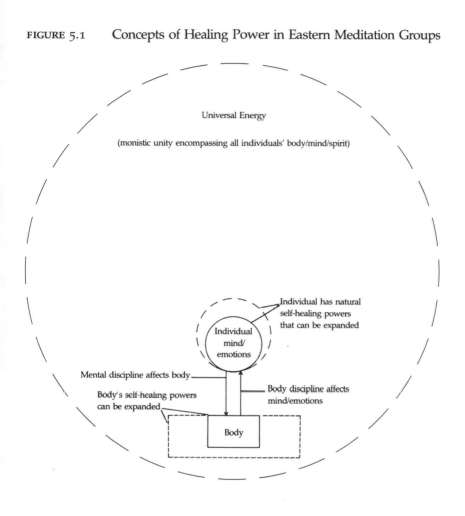

ment of universal energy. There is energy all around us, and all I am doing is directing it."

Another notion was that the teacher or healer was a helper who enables the individual to heal him or herself. Several respondents saw this role as no different from that of the medical doctor. One man commented, "Ultimately, you heal yourself. Or your deeper essence, divinity, or whatever life wants to continue, to heal itself; our cells want to be healthy. . . . I think we heal ourselves. But with the teacher or medical practitioner, the meditation teacher, yoga teacher is a stimulus, a catalyst."

Whether healing was done through another or individually, the ability to focus the healing energy was important. Most respondents in these groups believed that some way of focusing and directing the healing energy was the key: imaging, centering, focusing, using meditation to balance and direct the energies of one's own body and the larger world around one. One nurse, who used alternative healing professionally as well as personally, stated, "I think any holistic modality has, at its base, the ability to center, the ability to go into that quiet place."

Healing and Health Practices

In Eastern meditation groups, the foremost healing practices consisted of purification and adjusting energies. Related groups that were not based so directly upon Eastern thought often used similar practices, but with less-spiritual explanations for them. All of the groups studied were, nevertheless, quite eclectic. Members tried, simultaneously or serially, numerous different healing techniques—some suggested by their central group, others borrowed from elsewhere. For example, the central practices of one not atypical woman were based on Zen meditation, but she also occasionally tried (and was generally pleased with) rebirthing, crystal healing, colonics, meditation journals, shiatsu, and dance therapy. These respondents were generally more likely than members of other types of group to use herbal and folk remedies (such as aloe for burns, warm milk and honey for insomnia, yogurt for vaginal infection). They emphasized trying milder ("safer") remedies before resorting to pharmaceuticals. In their eclectic borrowing, these adherents frequently reinterpreted the diverse practices, thereby integrating them into their central approach. There is little distinction between health practices and healing techniques. The same processes that prevent illness can be used to bring about healing.

Meditation, a major spiritual practice in all of the Eastern-inspired groups studied, can be done as a neutral technique, divested of its symbolism and spiritual values. Some of the more commercial approaches, such as TM, have partially eliminated the spiritual significances—at least, for beginning meditators. Various pain- or stress-reduction programs also teach meditation techniques that are relatively value-neutral. These latter approaches were not specifically studied in this research, since practitioners believe only in the effectiveness of the technique for very limited purposes and do not relate the technique to any larger significance of health, illness, or healing.[9]

Healing, in Eastern meditation groups, is essentially an individual activity; one works on oneself, one's own self-awareness and energies. Group activities are, then, typically a context for learning techniques (such as yoga postures, breathing, or meditation techniques). There is some sense of experiencing greater power or energy in a group, and there is some mutual support in most groups observed, but these functions of the group and leaders are much less significant than in Christian healing groups.

Group-oriented healing settings include a ritual healing circle toward the end of many group meditations. After meditating individually for nearly half an hour, members sat close together in a circle, held hands (the postures of hand-holding were precise and important), and figuratively "placed in the circle" the names of persons in need of healing energies. The group then concentrated on sending its collective energies as needed. Similarly, several of these groups held special collective functions, such as silent retreats, feasts, and other celebrations, which also created and focused group energies. At the same time, however, the dominant focus was essentially individual.

Purification

For these groups, the logical healing practice is purification, because they generally consider pollution a major cause of illness. Pollution is taken both literally and metaphorically; so, too, are purification practices viewed as producing both symbolic and physical results. Furthermore, the desired results are holistic. Just as illness cannot be neatly separated body-from-mind-from-spirit, so too the salutary effects of purification are simultaneously physical, emotional, and spiritual.

Physical aspects of purification include fasting, special diets, exercises, and certain ways of breathing. Rarely are these purification techniques used alone; ritual, spiritual and emotional purification belong alongside them. For example, the individual who is fasting may also be meditating on purifying imagery, emotionally shedding "toxins" of anxiety or anger, and opening "chakras" (i.e., certain energy centers in the body).

Adherents in this type of group—far more than in any other type studied—emphasized purification and avoidance of pollution in their health and healing practices. More than a quarter of these respondents fasted regularly; some used lengthy and severe fasts. One woman who fasted frequently described it: "It's a cleansing process. You actually feel the cleansing process going on. You feel a light-headedness. You feel a cleansing effect going on. I don't know of another instance when you feel the way you do under a fast." One man commented, "I also find that when I fast, the energy flowing through me gets greater, and therefore fasting is conducive to high-energy states of meditation."

About 30 percent of these respondents practiced vegetarianism, although the degree of strictness of definition of "vegetarian" varied. Eating meat is polluting; it is tied to the karma of the killed animal, as well as to purely physical pollution by chemicals (e.g., antibiotics) put into the meat, environmental pollution that made its way into the animals' organs, or by diseases animals had when slaughtered. One member said, "The reason why I can't eat any meat or fish or any formerly living creatures is because I don't believe they should be killed. And I believe that if I contribute to their death, then to some extent I'm taking on that karma which is going to bring something negative back to me."

Several members maintained organic gardens, and nearly all respondents attempted to reduce their consumption of processed foods and food additives. Several persons had elaborate water purification systems in their homes; many more bought spring water rather than use tap water; a handful used only distilled water. These respondents tended to be somewhat more politically active on environmental issues, such as air pollution. At the individual level, they addressed the problem of air pollution by installing air purifying machines in their homes, and by adamantly forbidding smoking in their homes and workplaces. Virtually all respondents in this type of group were strongly against active and passive smoking. By contrast, in other types of groups members may have felt that smoking was not a good health practice, but did not treat it as a moral issue. For persons in Eastern-style groups, however, pollution is a moral issue, as well as a physical concern.

Special methods of breathing exemplify these groups' literal and metaphorical approach to healing. For example, in much yoga practice there is an emphasis on "prana" (loosely translated, referring both to energy all around one and to air); "pranayama yoga" is, thus, the discipline of breathing by which the individual takes in and uses, physically and spiritually, that energy. Several yoga instructors taught breathing techniques to be practiced throughout the yoga poses. Meditation instruction also emphasized breathing. Rhythmic breathing was used to focus meditations; for example, one might breathe in very slowly while meditating on the first syllable of the mantra "Vi-rum," and then breathe out to the same rhythm while meditating on the second syllable.

One breathing exercise specifically used for purification and balancing energies is "alternate nostril breathing." In this exercise, the meditator gently pinches to close first one and then the other nostril, while breathing rhythmically and very slowly in and out of each nostril in turn. This exercise is believed to be a strong corrective to imbalances created when the individual unknowingly has come to breathe disproportionately through one side of the nose.

During the practice of yoga poses ("asanas"), care to breathe properly helps to center the attention, eliminate distractions, and deal with discomfort. Some yoga teachers emphasize "ujjay" breathing during exercise; this method involves considerable control of breathing, increased use of the diaphragm and lower lungs, and eventually lung capacity and control in which the person sustains extremely long, rhythmic inhalations and exhalations. The following excerpts[10] of instructions during an hour of yoga exercise illustrates the many metaphorical uses of breathing in these groups:

> Breathe energy into the part of the posture that needs work. If there's pain from stretching, send your breath to that part. Use your breath to focus, to center, in order to hold the posture and balance. . . .

Breathing enables you to experience yourself, to be present to yourself. It is this presence, then, that you take with you as you go about daily life, in relationships with others. This presence within yourself is a protection against the needless stresses of life. . . .

Breathe in new life, breathe out old. Old truths are no longer valid. Breathe in new possibilities, a freshness of life and living. . . .

Always relax thoroughly between postures, mentally checking out each part of your body for any tension or stress. Release it. Let go. Full relaxation needs its counterpart—full outpouring of energy during the posture. Even while relaxing, hold your breathing. Don't lose the breathing. It gives you the necessary focus to relax fully too. . . .

Breathe out negativity, frustration, and fear. . . .

Picture yourself in the pose. . . . The mind offers other images. Reposition it. Bring it back with your breathing. Use your breath to bring awareness to your body. Focus. Hear your own breath.

Similarly, guided meditations often involved the use of breathing as a metaphor for directing energy. A commonly evoked visualization, often used for cleansing at the beginning of a meditation session, involved imagining one's breath going in through the nostrils, passing through and cleansing the lower chakras, and going out through the base of one's spine, expelling negative emotions, worn-out attitudes, and all other impurities. One woman described, "As I breathe, I breathe in light. As I breathe out, I breathe out the tension or . . . the toxins that are in the body."

Balancing Energies

Another focus of healing and health practices involved balancing energies. Since, according to these groups, imbalances and blockages of energy cause illness, various healing techniques are used to restore equilibrium and harmony or to open blocked flows of energy. Again, members typically used the ideas of creating balance or opening blockages both literally and metaphorically.

Exercise in yoga poses, for example, led to physical, emotional, and spiritual balance, simultaneously. An experienced member explained, "As we work within the context of the poses and the postures, an internal massage is effected, not only on the muscular system but also on the entire endocrine system, therefore eliciting the proper amount of hormones needed to create a balance in the body . . . reducing stress. We're much better able to cope."

One instructor reminded students, as they struggled with the "tree pose," a posture involving extended balancing on one leg, "Standing postures are for balance and stability. Feel the earth; it is your grounding. Lift up from the ground to higher consciousness. Avoid the temptation to collapse to the ground. . . . Focus on a spot on the wall; focus your attention; breathe into your foot." Members used both exercises and meditations to "open" the flow of energy in the body and eliminate illness-causing blockages. Similarly, massage and other manipulation of the body was believed to open the flow of energy. More so than other types of groups, these groups held that things done *to* the body effected changes in emotions, relationships, attitudes, and spiritual qualities of the person, as well. They believed both that healing spirit or emotions could produce healing effects on the body and that healing efforts on the body could affect problems of the spirit or emotions.

Many respondents in these groups emphasized creativity, use of color, sound, dance, fantasy, imagery, and "getting in touch with" nature as healing or healthful practices. In their belief system, such activities were tied to the enhancement of the individual's energies. One person stated, "I really believe in the healing process of the arts. For me, it's poetry. It's saved my life more than once, and I mean that quite literally. . . . I found my way intuitively to the pencil and paper and the poetry. And it was the poetry that got me out of there. The pursuit of the creative is the most constructive healing process we have."

A therapist who used yoga and meditation personally and with her patients said, "What I will do is imagine a stream of light coming into the area, using a lot of creative fantasy imagery—you can call it anything you choose, but I call it creative imagery. . . . I imagine light coming into my head." She added, "Giving yourself time to dream, and getting up and writing down the dream—that's also a way of healing yourself." She recommended creating desired endings to one's dreams, like myths and fairy tales, except that the creative energy focused around fantasy has impact; it is not a "mere" story.

Guided meditations frequently utilized colors that symbolized healing. The following excerpt[11] illustrates the use of such imagery:

> In your mind's eye, hold the color green—a brilliant, alive color—cool yet bursting with life, alacrity, and aliveness. Bathe yourself in that green. It envelopes your body and the space around you. It lifts you up with new energy and new life. Breathe in the green, breathe in the energy, the new possibilities, the hope. Breathe out the old, the worn out, the truths that are no longer valid. Breathe in the Spring, the new life, resurrection, rebirth. Breathe out Winter; it is past. Let it go. With it go the things that hold you back. Experience a new beginning, a new freedom.
>
> Now let that green move out from you to envelop the whole room, the whole building, all of the space you will go out into this week. See the promise, the freshness, the new life around you. The unfolding of new life in nature, the unfolding of new promise in your relationships. Breathe in the fresh air of those new beginnings. You are alive and experiencing your life more fully. Be with yourself [long silence].
>
> Join your consciousness with the universal consciousness in love and concern. Share that love and concern with the people of Atlanta. Use that consciousness to protect them from violence. Hold them in that consciousness. Bring the green light of hope and new beginnings to those who are in sorrow.

Another way of enhancing energy is through proper relaxation. Relaxation is crucial to the healing process, not merely as the reduction of stress, but as the best way to control energies in preparation for and conclusion of exercise, meditation, and healing. A member described:

> [Healing comes] by relaxation, by calmness, and once you calm yourself down. It's like the classic example would be the reflection of the sun on the lake, knowing the lake is all moving from the wind or from your emotions, you can't possibly reflect the sun. When you calm that down, and there is no wind, then the lake automatically reflects the sun. . . . It's that relaxation that lets the energy in.

Order and balance are also emphasized for health and healing. Ways of maintaining order and equilibrium in one's life include moderation in food, drink, exercise, temperatures, commitments, and so on. Several members emphasized the need to avoid excesses—even of good things. Staying "centered" is especially important to maintaining one's equilibrium. One woman commented, "I know that during the day a lot of times at work, I will have to go and kind of recenter. I have quick little ways of doing that: I'll drink some water, and take a couple of deep breaths, and do visualizations. So then I'm not as sensitive to this very disordered environment."

Related goals include maximum stability and flexibility. Seemingly opposite, these two concepts refer to the desired equilibrium in everyday life. On one hand, one should be strong, well-rooted, grounded, firm in one's sense of self; at the same time, one should be open to change, willing to bend when necessary, and able to move freely. These goals, again, are meant literally and metaphorically. The believer uses meditation to center the self (producing stability) and to release the "old truths" (enhancing flexibility). At the same time, yoga postures emphasize bodily balance, stability, and flexibility—metaphorically producing those qualities in the mind, spirit, and emotions as well.

Restoring equilibrium and harmony are, accordingly, healing factors. One adherent explained, "The person is healing himself. We're [the healing group] just boosting that ability of his own, getting him in touch again with that own innate sense of order within him that will produce healing." Another person emphasized the connection between harmony, "grounding," change, and energy:

> We are involved in the whole rhythm of the universe. We are just an extension of the changing seasons, changing times, and we are in flow with the universe. So, by tuning in and just listening to the peaceful sound of the rain or the summer breeze—to me bringing myself more to the connection, rhythm and harmony. . . . That's why I use the earth images [in visualizations].
>
> Often in meditation you think of a grounding, and one of the meditations that I teach in yoga is that you stand very still and imagine yourself with roots that go down as deep as you are tall, and these roots are drawing up energy the same way the roots of the tree draw up energy. And you are able to bring this energy to the center of the earth. And there is an energy field—the gravitational force—that you are able to bring that into your body . . . [producing] harmony and stability.

Dealing with disorder is, for members of this type of group, more a matter of active decision-making than it is for traditional metaphysical or

Christian healing groups. Persons who experience their lives as disordered, frustrating, or upsetting should make decisions and take actions to remove sources of stress. Whereas metaphysical and Christian healing groups generally emphasized ways of coping with daily problems, Eastern and human potential groups were more likely to pose the possibility of change: leaving an unpleasant work situation, getting a divorce, moving from an apartment or community, dropping excessive commitments. One member attributed her healing to "just deciding that some things were more important than other things and that feelings I had about what I should be doing or shouldn't be doing that I had to decide. Not maintain this eternal conflict about—I wish I were doing this, but I'm not, and if I were doing that, I wish I were doing this. . . ."

Therapeutic Success, Failure, and Death

Members of these groups were generally more pragmatic about evaluating therapeutic success than were members of traditional metaphysical and Christian healing groups. Their attitude seemed to be: Try something, and if it works for you, continue to use it; if not, drop the practice. No particular meditative practice, remedy, or technique was considered essential in itself. Indeed, insights, practices, beliefs, and ways of managing one's life that were previously useful may be "worn out" or "no longer valid" in an individual's life. In contrast to the traditional metaphysical and Christian healing groups' value of tenacity and unswerving faith in immutable beliefs and practices, the general philosophy of most of these adherents is: All things change.

Although they emphasized that healing was a growth process, often gradual, they were typically more likely than psychic or metaphysical groups to identify discrete healing experiences. Several respondents described, in detail, what a healing experience was like. One woman said:

> [It was] very overwhelming and very happy, very much like a release where you're bursting out, almost like a source of energy. All of a sudden, something is lifted, so it's a total feeling of being liberated from something that you didn't even realize how bad it was—that thing that was there—until it was

lifted from you. It feels almost like you shed your body. It feels almost like you become a spirit for a moment. You get so light from the lack of the thing that's been holding you down.

Like many Christian respondents, some adherents of Eastern groups suggested that the disappearance of physical or emotional problems is not, itself, the key to whether the healing had occurred:

> You're walking in the same place and everything is the same, but you're different. You're just walking lighter, and you're walking in such a clear way into a situation, whether the physical pain or the emotional pain is gone, it doesn't matter. It's just so much calmer. . . . It's just a very nice calm—sort of control without being in need of being in control.

What is necessary for a healing to occur? For respondents in these groups, the foremost factor was self-awareness. One woman explained, "Healing does not come from keeping busy and keeping yourself away from what is inside of you. But to learn to take time out to get inside of you. Yes, I do think that healing deals basically with taking the time and doing that." Although most of these respondents did believe that it was possible to send healing energy across a distance and help, to some extent, even a person who was not working on self-healing, they greatly emphasized self-awareness and self-healing as the path to the real, long-term process of healing.

Several respondents connected this self awareness with the necessary openness, which eliminates some blockages to healing energy. Another woman stated:

> There's a time period that leads us to that recognition. Sure. Then you recognize that [e.g., why you have the problem in the first place], and that's when the healing begins to take place. I think it has to be recognized and, I think, first of all is the recognition and acknowledgement. And the second step for the healing to take place is for the person to open themselves up to the healing process, to let go of any resistance. Because if there's resistance there, it's just not going to happen.

Such "openness" is tied to spiritual and emotional qualities—almost a life-stance. Openness to change and new ways of thinking and experiences is important. One woman felt that some people were not healed because "they were clinging to their belief system a little too much, and not being open." One adherent described the requisite openness as "just openness to God. It's like a relief of obstacles. The greatest obstacle is the ego. The ego is the sense of oneself as being separate. The sense of one's needs as being incompatible with the needs of others and others' needs as being incompatible with ours." Another person explained:

> I think, ideally, the healing power is flowing all the time, and that the natural state of the body is to heal. I think there are blocks that get in the way— having to do with emotions, improper diet. And so when there are blocks, if you can recognize them, . . . you can work on whatever you think might be blocking. . . . The healing energy is always trying to move through. It's trying to circulate, and you have to remove the blocks.

Often, respondents felt that the requisite self-awareness and openness were impeded by the individual's other needs and attitudes. Secondary gains from illness make it unlikely that the person would confront the real issues needed for self-awareness.

Like other adherents of alternative healing, members of these groups considered faith an important requirement for healing. By contrast, however, they did not consider any particular faith to be critical—just a generalized faith or expectancy in whatever approach one is using. Indeed, it was often necessary to use an approach that fit the beliefs of the person needing healing. If, for example, the person were very religious in a Judeo-Christian sense, then healing should proceed from that approach; other people might be more receptive to an Eastern or Native American or nonreligious approach. No single approach was "right," but one approach might inspire more faith in an individual than another, so it would be "right" for that person at that time. One respondent asserted, "If you believe something will work, you'll have more of a chance of it actually working. If you have confidence in your doctor. If you think he doesn't know what he's doing, you're gonna be all tense, you're gonna be nervous and not relaxed. Even if he does do something that could work, you're going to be resisting it. If you think it'll work, you're more open to it."

Several respondents emphasized that "faith" did not necessarily mean religious faith. One woman explained, "You have to believe that healing can occur, and you have to believe in the source that you're using. I think it's a matter of faith—and I'm not religious. I'm saying that from a nonreligious point of view. I think it's a matter of true faith—to truly believe and to have confidence that it's going to happen."

Without some faith in the healing process, the person would lack the necessary motivation to engage in the whole healing process, but faith alone was rarely viewed by these adherents as sufficient. Faith, without awareness and personal change, would not have much effect. One woman stated, "I think first they have to believe that they can be well. And then, I think they have to explore the things in their lives that have caused them to break down—whether it's diet, stress, emotional, psychological, or against spiritual qualities."

In contrast to respondents from other types of group, these respondents gave greater emphasis to action on the part of the individual—action to change lifestyle, to correct bodily imbalances or breathing, to change the larger society into a more healthful environment. While most such adherents focused on personal, lifestyle actions, about one-fifth of the members of these groups also mentioned social actions. One man said:

Not just we pray for [healing]; that's still not enough. We all have to work toward it. I mean we have to become—everyone on this planet has to become—aware of the way we contribute to the well-being of the earth that we live on, which is our maintainer of life. I mean we can't defile the environment that we live in and expect to be healthy and well. We have to clean the oceans. We have to clean the air. We have to have the technology that is not destructive. I feel that we have to be aware that we're stewards of the earth, and we have a certain responsibility toward the well-being of the environment.

I also feel before a total healing takes place on the earth, people have to be aware of their inner relationships. And, in a larger sense, things like poverty and conditions where people live—like in parts of the world, where they have just the bare minimum amounts to sustain themselves—that has to be changed. They [should] have adequate medical treatment, adequate clean water, adequate food and housing. That should be a priority all nations should work toward—like remedying the conditions of poverty and subhuman conditions that exist in the world.

I feel these [conditions] are a direct result of all the emphasis going on the military budgets of the superpowers. The nuclear arms race, I think has to be changed before planetary healing can take place. We have to stop the madness of just continuously putting trillions of dollars into military machines. Instead, put that money into healing of the earth and the environment.

The corollary of these prerequisites is that the presence of doubt, confusion, distraction, and emotional blockages can prevent the flow of healing energy and explain why healing does not occur. While respondents from this type of group attributed many therapeutic failures to individual responsibility, they also generally believe that the individual cannot control everything. There was a sense of being a part of a "larger flow" with which one could move but not control. Indeed, they downplayed the need to "be in control." Healing practices were primarily paths to self-awareness and understanding; any control they gave one over one's situation or life-course was a pleasant—but secondary— by-product.

Like respondents from other types of group, these adherents believed that therapeutic failure was sometimes only apparent, not real. One woman said, "It may not happen the way that we want it to happen. It may be happening in another way that we may not see happen with our eyes, but maybe in another plane it is happening in a spiritual sense or in a way that we can't see. We can't always see everything. Things are always happening around us that we are not able to see, but they happen." Similarly, these respondents often viewed the seeming failure of healing as evidence that the process was gradual and would take a long time. One member explained, "I think sometimes, if something doesn't work, then maybe there is something that is meant to be learned yet. . . . I think there can be learning from pain and from illness. Maybe it's going to take a long time. There's a lesson that it's just going to take a very long time to learn." Some adherents of Eastern healing approaches also shared the notion that healing occurs when the "right" time comes. One respondent said, "I think there's a critical time. And I think there's a time that it's too late."

For members of this type of group, however, death was neither a healing in itself nor the end of growth. The belief in reincarnation, held by many respondents in these groups, was a buffer against the apparent failure of healing when death occurred. In the face of death, the appropriate healing approach consisted of such help as "bathing them in light," supporting them in their "acceptance of death," in addition to ordinary love and attention.

One woman described a healing that "didn't work," of a man with a heart attack: "Probably . . . it was time for him to move on and make room for someone else, because he was not responding whatsoever. And, as long as he and his wife both agree that they did not want any outer interference, it was their decision to make." Another woman described the death of a loved one: "And as she was dying, we did a lot of healing. What it was was mental and spiritual healing to allow her to surrender to the dying process. And I would surround her in light, cradle her in my arms, and chant. . . . It was right; I know it. And I think that those experiences with her really helped her to surrender and let go."

Thus, peaceful death is also a goal of the healing process. Since many respondents believe in reincarnation and karma, healing that occurs in the dying process is believed to be carried forward in the next life.

Responsibility for therapeutic failure, according to these groups, is largely the individual's: Therapeutic success depends upon developing self-awareness, adopting a healthy lifestyle, opening blockages to one's energy and learning to channel that energy effectively, purifying oneself and avoiding a polluting physical, emotional, and spiritual environment. The individual alone cannot accomplish all of this; larger social change is needed. And, even with dramatic efforts toward health, some things are out of the individual's control.

Therapeutic failure and death are, however, less of an issue for these groups, because such events are not a threatening: Neither the individual healer's power nor God's power or goodness is undermined by therapeutic failure. Despite their otherwise activist stance, many respondents in these groups held a quiet fatalism about "the flow"—one could not fully understand it, control it, or be responsible for it.

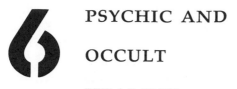

PSYCHIC AND
OCCULT
HEALING

Psychic and occult healing is the most diverse category of healing groups studied; it is thus the most difficult to describe by generalization. The variation in beliefs and practices between and within these groups is enormous and fascinating. Respondents' healing beliefs and practices were extremely eclectic, individualistic, and continually changing.

Like Christian healing, psychic and occult healing is based upon a notion of a transcendent healing power—something outside and greater than the individual. Thus, healers in the psychic tradition, as in Christian healing, view themselves as mediators of that healing power to others who need it. Unlike Christian healing, however, psychic and occult healing groups emphasize that healing power may be readily tapped by any knowledgeable or spiritually developed person. This essentially gnostic approach also distinguishes psychic healing from Eastern and traditional metaphysical groups, in which technique and personal spiritual power are less important.

Psychic healing has been associated historically with the nineteenth-century Spiritualist movement and the contemporaneous interest in mesmerism. Other historical strands contributing to these current groups' beliefs and practices include: occult and esoteric knowledge brought forward from medieval times (e.g., astrology, cabalism), enthusiastic Christian sects (e.g., Shakers), American transcendentalism, New Thought, the "I AM" movement, Theosophy, and Eastern thought imported much earlier in the twentieth century (e.g., Vedanta).[1] There is also a pronounced interest in trying the beliefs and practices of Native (North) American, Polynesian, Latin American, and Caribbean peoples.[2] Recently, psychic healing has gained somewhat greater respectability and some scientific attention through parapsychology and related research.[3]

Some observers treat psychic and occult healing in all its forms as part of the broader "metaphysical" movement.[4] Others suggest a distinction between "manipulationist" movements (e.g., New Thought, Theosophy, occult groups) and thaumaturgical groups (e.g., Spiritualism). Manipulationist groups, by this definition, include all those that cultivate special knowledge or spiritual power that adherents can tap for their own use; thaumaturgical groups are characterized mainly by their emphasis upon communication with the dead. Spiritualistic groups, generally, lack the coherent belief systems characteristic of manipulationist groups; their concerns are typically very particularistic: individual guidance via mediums and spirits; spirit direction in place of universal ethical concerns; personal reassurance and security.[5]

Historically, all of these groups borrowed extensively from each other, and their beliefs and practices are interwoven in complex ways. For the purposes of this study, however, it is important to distinguish between groups that relate to an external, transcendent healing force and groups that have an image of an immanent, internal healing force. This distinction accounts for marked differences in the healing approaches of the two types. For example, if the healing power is internal, mentalistic methods of healing are appropriate (as in Unity and Christian Science). If healing forces are external, they must be reached, tapped, and channeled to where they are needed (as in what we are calling psychic and occult healing).

Since the groups studied tended to be highly eclectic, they often used images and phrases from other belief systems but applied their own meanings to these concepts. For example, most adherents of psychic and occult healing believed in reincarnation, like most Eastern meditation groups. They typically used this concept, however, to refer to specific external forces in the individual's life that could be understood, tapped, and used. By contrast, for most members of Eastern-inspired groups, reincarnation was simply a "fact" of existence, having some explanatory usefulness but not particularly amenable to direct human manipulation. Thus, unlike Eastern meditation adherents, psychic and occult adherents often used their psychic energies to discover their identities and experiences in prior incarnations in order to use those forces in this life.

Using groups' ideas about the source of healing power as a criterion, some forms of Spiritualism could be considered "psychic and occult healing" if they emphasized proper technique and embraced a larger ideology, beyond the particularistic concerns of communicating with the dead. Likewise, much "Christian Spiritualism" is more appropriately viewed as a form of Christian healing—albeit one in which the mediators of God's healing power are both the living and the dead (analogous to some traditional Catholic healing cults that draw upon saints to mediate God's healing power).

Classical Spiritualism was not a significant part of any psychic or occult healing encountered in this research. Spiritualism has been historically identified with psychic healing, and it should be considered as one strand of the alternative healing phenomenon. For this reason, we are presenting a brief description of Spiritualist healing, but it was a very minor—almost negligible—element in any of the psychic, occult, or Christian healing actually found in the catchment area of this study.

The two definitive characteristics of traditional Spiritualist belief are the continuity of life after physical death and the possibility of communication with those who have "passed over into spirit." The movement began in the middle of the nineteenth century in New York State, but it has been far more successful in England than in the United States. Loosely organized Spiritualist "churches" developed, usually around a particular medium whose ability to communicate with those spirits enabled her (or him) to tap the knowledge, powers, presence, and affections of the dead for the benefit of the individual members of the congregation.[6]

The role of healing in Spiritualism has varied over the years. Most commonly, adherents sought contact with spirits of their own loved ones for guidance and reassurance; at the same time, though, mediums often claimed contacts with other, powerful spirits who might aid in healing Spiritualist adherents. Spirits of "Red Indians," Chinese sages, or wise doctors were believed to aid the healing process and give diagnostic or therapeutic advice. In Britain, where Spiritualist healing enjoys greater freedom from legislative controls than in the United States and Canada, it has a wider following and even a limited acceptance for its healing practices in hospitals and other medical settings. In the United States, however, Spiritualists appear either not to emphasize healing so much or to avoid direct references, especially to physical healing.[7]

None of the groups studied were affiliated with any national Spiritualist societies, but a small number borrowed some Spiritualist concepts. Spirit mediumship, the major element of traditional Spiritualism, was relatively unimportant in the groups studied. A few groups believed in the existence of spirit guides; the "appearance" of such guides was considered worth attention, but seldom were spirits consulted to advise about or intervene in life situations. Spirit communication was treated with little reverence. Mediumship was not the role of a few leaders; it could be exercised by all believers. One healing circle had a spirit guide (a deceased member) who frequently attended their meditations. His presence was welcomed, but his absence did not diminish the meeting. In groups that believed in them, spirits were considered useful sources of information and advice, but individual members were so empowered through their own heightened psychic awareness that spirit intervention was seldom sought.

The foremost unifying feature of these diverse and eclectic groups was belief in the mental and/or physical transfer of external energy as a basic healing tool. More so than in any other type of group, these respondents emphasized the necessity of technique in successful use of that energy. No one perspective was shared by all members. This chapter presents the most commonly cited views, but in no way could this descriptive generalization be attributed to all psychic healers.[8]

Psychic adherents get their information from various workshops, books, magazines, audio and video cassettes, adult school classes, and psychic fairs, in addition to private healing circles. Some adherents in this category also had participated on an occasional basis in workshops, retreats, or other experiences in national organizations, such as ARE (Association for Research and Enlightenment) or SFF (Spiritual Frontiers Fellowship), but there were no ongoing local study groups (branches) of these movements, and few respondents considered themselves "members" of these groups. One national occult movement, the Great White Brotherhood of Elizabeth Claire Prophet, did have several local groups; it did not much overlap in membership with other psychic or occult groups, because of its atypical sectarian closedness.[9]

The psychics discussed here belonged to both large, loosely structured organizations and small private healing circles. Representative of the larger organizations was one group that held public meetings in a local library. Announcements of forthcoming meetings and topics were posted in local papers and flyers. A typical pamphlet described the smorgasbord of future topics:

"Some of My Experiences with Baba-Ji"
"Peace and Self-Healing"

"Hopes, Dreams, and Aspirations"

"Life and Transition"

"Do-It-Yourself Shiatsu"

"UFO's and the Hollow Earth"

"Dowsing"

"The Human Aura, Meditation, and Therapeutic Touch"

"Numerology"

"Astrology for Fun"

"Self-Healing and Gestalt Therapy"

These topics were generally covered in a lecture format. Some of the course descriptions even resembled academic classes, such as Astrology I and II.

Members attended only those lectures that interested them, discarding unimpressive ideas and integrating attractive new information into their prior assortment of beliefs. These meetings were well attended, with over one hundred people packed into the library conference room. Members dressed up for the occasion. Many in attendance knew each other from other "classes," but it was possible to attend these meetings and remain anonymous. Numerous participants brought tape recorders to the meeting; others took notes studiously. When interviewed, many adherents proudly pointed out their extensive collections of lecture tapes. Organizing sessions as lectures, locating them in libraries or classrooms, encouraging other aspects of classroom behavior (e.g., note-taking, recommended readings, raised hands for the question-answer period), all promote the larger definition of the situation: This is not religious ritual, but rather the learning of important knowledge. The classroom environment is considered "safe"—not weird; and acquiring knowledge is valued in this culture.

Although the lecture topics varied widely, most speakers used scientific or quasi-scientific terminology to support their positions.[10] For example, one lecturer described holograms as a model of consciousness, informed the group that gravity was the physical force most amenable to conscious manipulation, and cited the Big Bang Theory and the idea of black holes to support the Eastern circular concept of time. Statistics were also frequently cited to support points.

Smaller healing circles demanded more commitment and gave more personal mutual support. Members telephoned each other if unable to attend a meeting, and a physical place would be reserved for the absent in awareness that the member would be present in spirit. The healing circles were relatively small (between six and thirty persons) and usually met in a member's home. The atmosphere was relaxed and chatty; dress was casual (see Chapter Two for some descriptive details). Family, work, and everyday problems were broached to a concerned and caring audience. It was a safe and supportive atmosphere in which to experiment with a variety of new beliefs and practices. Much of the meaning of illness and the therapeutic response was negotiated in the small-group setting, rather than in a one-to-one relationship with a healer.

Most psychic adherents interviewed were involved in both the large, loosely structured organizations and the smaller, more tightly knit circles. The two forms of association served complementary but different functions. The larger organizations satisfied the membership's endless quest for new information and techniques, while the intimate circles provided ongoing social support on a personal basis. In both networks, members were selective, weighing new information in terms of their previously held beliefs. They evaluated speakers' effectiveness in guiding meditations. Members considered themselves well informed and quite capable of evaluating the speakers' information. One member observed, "People are finally realizing that we must live our own lives—we've trusted the experts: They gave us sugar in our babies' food, Valium, the Vietnam War. We're through being manipulated." Adherents considered each individual to be capable of making evaluative decisions; indeed, choice and taking responsibility are mandatory. This theme of individual responsibility resounds throughout the psychic and occult belief systems.

Ideals of Health and Wellness

Psychic adherents emphasized control, spontaneity, and flexibility as the foremost characteristics of true health. These qualities include the ability to be in control of one's daily life and to handle crisis situations. One member of a psychic healing circle illustrated a number of these groups' key themes:

I think that they [truly healthy persons] are very spontaneous and flexible, and I think they have more options that they experience. I think they have a sense of aliveness and a feeling of being in the flow. . . . They are feeling connected to a larger purpose and connected with other people. They are in touch with their rhythm, whether it's to be withdrawn and hang out by themselves for a while, or whether it's to be in a crowd. And to sense where their needs are at. Sensitivity is an important part of being healthy. I would also say that being in power, feeling powerful in your life, feeling responsible for your life is a very important part of it.

The idea of "being in the flow," or recognizing one's connectedness with the larger cosmos or universe, was another frequently mentioned characteristic of healthiness. One should realize one's place in the universe and accept this position as "where one is destined to be now." The goal is not to change the present situation, but to discover the larger meaning of it.

A healthy person, according to psychic adherents, is energetic, vibrant, alive. This aliveness refers to psychic energy and vibration, not merely physical energy. Accordingly, a healthy person is characterized by a healthy energy field, or "aura." One member explained, "There shouldn't be any holes in the aura. The aura should be colorful and vibrant and have a bright and full color to it—whatever the colors are, it doesn't matter. The person should be vital, like in energy. You should have physical energy, desire to do things, healthy mind."

Psychic adherents considered love a necessary quality for healthiness. One respondent emphasized, "[You need] love for all beings on the planet, and the planet. And I would say not only all beings but for the universe and the cosmos. . . . That would be the nature of a healthy person." Another person explained:

Your whole life is centered more around love. It's expressed more through love. You're just perceiving higher vibrational feelings, rather than lower ones. . . . And as it filters down into the physical, then you receive the benefits of endurance and rosy cheeks, and clearer eyes and nice coloration and healthy aura, powerful energy body, so that you can come into the presence of another person and just influence them, because your energy field is of a strong vibrational nature that you just elevate the other person.

By "love" these adherents do not mean being swept off one's feet, help-lessly infatuated, or feeling an uncontrollably overwhelming emotion. Rather, love means an emotional state of power and control.

Healthiness was typically associated with a state of mind, more than a physical condition. A man explained, ". . . health is not the absence of disease. That's not health. . . . Health is an experience of vitality, energy, aliveness, goodness, feeling warm inside." Accordingly, high level healthiness is not incompatible with serious physical problems.

For most psychic adherents, however, health and wellness meant wholeness of body in conjunction with mind, emotion, and spirit. One could not be truly healthy if illness disturbed any of these areas. Healthi-ness is not merely the absence of disease in body-mind-spirit, but real health requires balance among the three. There should be a sense of harmony in all areas of life, and an inner state of calmness and peace. An adherent said, "I think a healthy person has to be healthy inside and out. In other words, total health. If you build a beautiful body and you don't have a beautiful mind to go with it, it can't last. So the beauty has to be more than in the body. The beauty has to be in the soul."

Physical characteristics are important—mainly as indicators of health or illness. One psychic healer explained, "Well, you can usually see it in the skin tone. . . . If you see a redness, a healthiness, a glowing almost in the skin tone. The eyes can certainly tell you. I can look at a person and tell if they're experiencing health problems by their mouth . . . because you know the mucus membranes are the first to show if something is wrong."

Physical qualities themselves are less important, however, than mental characteristics. A "good" mental outlook precedes health. One respon-dent stated, "I think [one needs] a mental outlook that's very positive, basically optimistic, and seeing the glass of water half full instead of half empty—that kind of mentality. The healthy people that I meet are usually very positive about their health; they expect to be healthy for whatever reason."

Psychic healing adherents considered health the natural condition; only when "disorder" enters one's life does illness occur. Healthiness is not something that one must strive to achieve. It requires only returning to the normal state. One respondent noted, "At the alpha state, health occurs naturally. You don't have to work for it. You don't have to do anything for it. . . . You were designed to be healthy. You were not designed to be at dis-ease."

Notions of Illness and Healing

Psychic healing adherents had very broad notions of what conditions required healing. Their perspective was truly holistic: Healing is physical, social, emotional, and spiritual.

Physical conditions treated by the psychic believers in this study ranged from commonplace bouts (e.g., colds, flu, headaches) to acute conditions (such as broken bones, hepatitis, and ear infections) to chronic conditions (like arthritis or paralysis). While removal or alleviation of physical symptoms was the goal of healing for most participants, they believed that healing sometimes occurred even though physical symptoms persisted.

Pain is more than just an obstacle to overcome or eliminate. Many respondents felt that pain was a prerequisite to growth, as the following excerpt suggests: "The miracles of my life have always been preceded by pain for some reason. I am a resister. Whenever you resist, there will be pain, when it is necessary for something to change in [your] life. Through the pain and only through the pain will you really grow and understand."

Pain was seen also as a warning: "God's method of 'waking up' the person," an indicator that one is "on the wrong track." Pain may serve the positive function of signaling that something is not right. One woman, for example, interpreted her partial loss of hearing, after being struck on the ear, as a sign that she had been avoiding events in her life. She believed it was her inner self's way of saying: "Wake up! I've got your attention. Now listen."

Several respondents stated that pain and pleasure are not dichotomous. One woman described this awareness in her self-healing:

Pain and pleasure come from the same place. It's a pressure. It's a tension. . . . The mind interprets that tension as pleasure or painful, but it's the same stress. It's how we view it. . . . So it became very apparent to me that I had to refocus my attention on something healthy. And so I began to experience this pain and equate it with the healing process. In other words, every time I experienced pain, in my own mind, I saw it as a battle between the healing forces in my body and the ill forces in my body—the tension of the battle, but that this was an indication that I wasn't giving in to it. In other words, that I was fighting it and that every pain was making me better and better.

Thus, pain is a necessary part of the healing process, rather than something to be feared or avoided. The individual needs to learn from the experience of pain. This belief gives the ill individual a sense of meaning and control over the illness experience. Pain, viewed this way, has a purpose.

Another interpretation was that pain could be a mechanism for transmuting karma for deeds in a previous lifetime. Accordingly, pain is a necessary process for spiritual growth, even though the physical body temporarily suffers. A psychic healer explained:

> There are many times when I go in and try to make direct contact with the soul first, and then the soul will often say to me, "Look it, I know the body is suffering, but this is what we have to go through and this is part of the plan for us, and thanks a lot, but no thanks." And it's very difficult to say to someone who's suffering and thinks that they want to be well, that it's not in the plan for this time.

Many psychic and occult practitioners also believed that certain individuals may have transmuted all of their personal karma but were reincarnated voluntarily to assist with planetary karma. This explanation gives psychic adherents a further sense of order and control; it enables them to experience illness as having meaning and purpose. It is a useful explanation for the seemingly senseless suffering of good people.

Many psychic healing adherents also believed that illness is a necessary cleansing or purification process. One woman explained, "All disease is caused by too much toxic waste in the body." This respondent saw the symptoms themselves as part of the healing process. A fever, for example, "burns the disease-causing elements." One woman said, "The cold is the cure—the releasing of the body's metabolic wastes and acids." Accordingly, healing consists not of the relief of physical symptoms but of the search for why the illness occurred in the first place.

Some psychic adherents, however, believed that physical symptoms are *not* real. A group leader added, "Members find that hard to accept when they ache so much." Another adherent observed, "I don't believe in colds, I don't believe in sore throats. . . . I believe that you can bring those about yourself. . . . Nobody can find a cure for the common cold. That's because, medically, I don't believe that it exists."

While several psychic healing adherents professed this notion, they acknowledged that often it was necessary to treat the symptoms while the believer built up strength and searched for insights into this illness event. Although relief of physical symptoms was not the primary goal, it could be used as a therapeutic tool to tackle the "real" cause of the problem. Nevertheless, remediation of physical symptoms was received enthusiastically when it did occur, even though theoretically it was of low priority.

A real healing occurred when the believer gained insight into the illness, accepted responsibility, and began the process of changing his or her life. The transfer of energy from a healer or healing group often began this process. The healing itself did not necessarily entail immediate changes in symptoms. Pain or other physical or emotional symptoms might continue, but the *process* was defined as the true healing. One respondent noted, "Once you've made up your mind that you're going to get well, even though the symptoms or the pain are there, the knowledge of being well should be there with it. What you're dealing with here is really an echo of a past creation."

Social issues were also recognized as requiring healing, although they were mentioned less frequently by adherents in this type of group than in others. Problems cited as needing healing included, for example: decrease in morality, traditions "going down the drain," family and other primary relationships diminished, stresses due to the "money situation," the congestion and confusion of modern life. The appropriate response to social needs was wholly individualistic. One man commented, "The best way to heal the world is to heal ourselves."

Economic concerns were frequently mentioned as needing healing: the national debt, inflation, unemployment, high interest rates, the difficulty in affording a home. More so than in Eastern meditation and some Christian healing groups, these adherents sought "healing" for personal goals: winning a tennis tournament, their children's success on college entrance examinations, or finding the right summer camp for a child's special needs. Like adherents of traditional metaphysical groups, these respondents used healing techniques as all-purpose methods of achieving many kinds of needs and wishes.

Many physical ailments were considered manifestations of emotional tensions. According to this belief, different emotions caused illnesses in specific parts of the body. Psychic healers thought emotional problems were often more difficult to treat than physical ailments. Emotional healings described tended to be general, such as dealing with grief over death of a loved one, or learning to handle life's problems in a calm, organized, responsible manner. Other healings cited included the treatment of professionally diagnosed problems, such as depressions and phobias.

Less important to psychic adherents was the spiritual category of illness. Ultimately, every healing required a spiritual dimension, but this underlying theme was so vague and pervasive that adherents rarely made it explicit. Spiritual healing meant growth and development of spiritual powers, such that one could cope with life's difficult situations and take responsibility for one's situation in this lifetime.

Causes of Illness

Like adherents of other types of healing, persons who used psychic and occult healing sought meaning for the illness experience. While they accepted medical explanations for the causes of illness, they also believed that larger forces were at work. Psychic healing adherents believed that *nothing* occurs by chance; thus, their search for meaning was especially important. Psychics' explanations of illness emphasized factors over which the individual has control: mental habits, attitudes and values, patterns of response to stress, and lifestyle.

Their belief that individuals are responsible for their condition implies that there is no need for sympathy. Accordingly, one reaps what one sows (i.e., karmic illnesses), or one might "choose" an illness for a variety of reasons, such as to learn a needed lesson or to get attention. While these groups offered empathic support and comfort to sick persons, they believed that the sick must accept responsibility for getting well.

Karmic reasons for illness were often given. Psychic believers stressed that karma is not punishment. Rather, illness is merely the fulfillment of the "natural" law that one reaps what one has sown. One person stated, "If you kill somebody, which is contrary to the rules of life, then there's going to come a time that you're gonna suffer for that. And it's not because some God up in heaven is lashing out at you or angry with you. . . . You've upset the balance of things and so you're going to be upset by it. What you put out comes back."

According to this belief, then, people may voluntarily take on serious ailments to permit them to work out large amounts of karma quite quickly. Hence, one should not judge an individual by the illness. The severity of symptoms is not directly proportionate to the amount of karma for past misdeeds; rather, it may represent an individual's courage in taking on a large amount of karma to be transcended in this lifetime. There is also the possibility that this illness may be doing a service for humankind. The sick person may be a surrogate sufferer or taking on world (rather than personal) karma.

Handicaps and retardation were interpreted in this light. A handicapped child may be born into a family that needs to work out karma through the extra care the child requires. Respondents gave numerous examples of families that had learned the true meaning of love, caring, and giving by having a child handicapped in some way. Likewise, adherents explained epidemics as the result of group karma. The frequency of heart disease in this society, for example, was interpreted as the result of a large amount of planetary karma on the heart chakra (i.e., the body energy center influencing capacity for love).

With an illness that seems to have no underlying genesis in this lifetime, it may be necessary to search other lifetimes for the origins— often with the aid of meditation or hypnosis. For example, a man with an inexplicably sore shoulder learned, through hypnosis, that in a previous lifetime he had been pierced with a sword in that exact region. Underlying such beliefs is an assumption that, once the cause is understood, it is possible to transcend the symptoms—on an emotional and spiritual if not always physical level.

Responsibility for illness was even greater for problems created in this life. "Bad habits" like smoking, eating "junk food," or other self-harming practices were viewed as the result of people's choices or needs. Why are they choosing to abuse their bodies now? What is happening in their life situations that causes them to behave in this "unnatural" way? In order to heal the illness brought on by abuses of the body, it is necessary first to address the causes—the reasons for that choice.

The concept that one chooses an illness is closely connected with the idea that one is responsible for bringing on the disease, even if unconsciously. Many respondents mentioned that sick persons chose their illnesses to gain attention, affection, or reduction of responsibilities and pressures. The idea that illness is choice was applied even to very serious problems, including cancer and heart disease. This quote from a healer working with a paralyzed young person represents such a view: "It's hard to convince N_____ that she chose her karma. Who would want to choose being paralyzed in a wheelchair? But this has been a learning experience which means her next reincarnation will be that much better for what she's doing now."

One explanation of why an individual would "choose" a serious illness is that illness is a growth experience. One woman said, "Each person takes on the kind of illness they need for their own growth and development and the lessons they have to learn in this life. So I feel that each individual tailors his own illness to fit his emotional needs." Whether a conscious choice or not, illness is something for which one is totally responsible. Another respondent stated, "Many people then blame all their problems on something out there—other people, different forces in their lives, that they feel helpless. That's one of the biggest causes of illness, is helplessness, and hopelessness, as far as feeling that you don't have control over your life."

This explanation is not a denial that biological factors play a role in causing illness. Several respondents pointed out that, while germs and viruses are always present, not everyone exposed to them succumbs. Rather, one is much more likely to develop the symptoms if one has a specific undesirable mental, spiritual, or physical condition.

Likewise, harmful "accidents" may be chosen. One man asserted, "The choices that we make between life and death, and illness and health, are very much within our capabilities. That when we choose to die; whatever route we choose, we choose—no matter how devious or deceptive it is, to ourselves. . . . We'll be faced with presumed accidents; we've invoked that." Thus even tragic accidents, such as being murdered, can be interpreted as choice. The "victim" may not want to be murdered, but may bring on personal harm as karmic payment for misdeeds committed in previous incarnations. The "victim" sends out mental signals that attract the murderer.

Thoughts also create accident situations, for which the "victim" is indirectly responsible. Constant fear of being harmed or robbed can itself create the situation. One respondent illustrated this point: "If you think that you are going to trip, chances are increased that you are going to trip." Thoughts and emotional states, therefore, may create physical events.

This line of reasoning was also used to explain illnesses like cancer. Some psychic adherents interpreted diseases that "run in families" as the result of the family's fear. For example, if one member of the family develops cancer, everyone in the family begins to fear cancer, and these negative thoughts and fears actually create the illness or cause other members to be prone to it. People attract illness by their thinking; it is like a self-fulfilling prophecy. The individual is fully responsible for bringing on illness through thoughts. An adherent stated, "It's what's programmed in when they're young. People that believe that when [you] get old, you get senile, get senile. People that believe [that] with age comes wisdom, get wiser." Another respondent noted, "People say 'my father died of a heart attack, so I'm going to watch my heart.' Well, you're creating a condition by putting your energy into that particular problem."

Like adherents of traditional metaphysical groups, these respondents emphasized the role of negative mental thoughts in causing illness. One respondent said:

> A sense of lack that the person interprets within themselves creates a dis-ease within one's body. And it shows up in different aspects, whether it's your mental thoughts that are poor and then that will create illness, or if it's emotional upset which does manifest on their physical level, or a person just seems to abuse their physical body.

Explaining how thoughts effect illness, a man explained:

> Like, your lungs only have one job, aiding your respiratory system. It doesn't do anything else. Now you put all these organs together and they have a program attached to them. They will perform one function only, but you— the core of which is your thoughts—will simply follow whatever you say. The free agent to you is your thinking and not your body, and yet we live our life as if the body runs us.

Often the focus of healing was not the physical manifestation, which was only a symptom of the problem. Instead, the concern was with the thought patterns that created the illness. One person asserted, "The reason why people get sick in the first place is because of—it's an outward manifestation of the universal law which we are all in tune with even if we're not aware of it, which is a real cause and effect. The thought produces an action. Every thought produces an action."

According to some respondents, the thoughts of others may also cause illness. One woman commented, "Many in the world today are victims of the thoughts of others, even thoughts from other eras, which endure because mankind has fed their attention and their energies into them."

The role of the mind and emotions is a dominant focus for members of psychic healing groups. They consider psychic healing approaches far more advanced than modern medicine. According to them, the medical establishment is only now beginning to understand and to validate what they have known all along. One respondent said, "I think emotions are really some of the biggest causes of imbalances. Thought patterns with a lot of emotional overload . . . fear I think is what is the basis for everything else that draws us away from peace and therefore perfect health." Psychic and occult adherents favored scientific and pseudoscientific terms to explain this relationship between illness and emotions. One healer said, "I take the stand that emotional situations will cause perturbances in the energy field which makes up your consciousness in the same way that it will cause disturbances in your soma, in your body tissues."

Stress was commonly cited as a disease-causing factor. A respondent explained, "Stress is the number-one killer. It is the only cause. Because stress will create an imbalance in the body. Stress is imbalance, and therefore manifests in the body as imbalance. How, where, what organ gets affected by stress is a matter of degree, is a matter of how much stress." One member called the resulting illnesses "combat diseases." Recommended solutions, however, were not changes in a stress-producing society, but relaxation exercises to help the individual cope with the existing social situation.

These groups were generally less concerned with environmental issues as social concerns than were most other groups studied. Pollution was mentioned but often in a symbolic sense (e.g., polluting the earth spirit) rather than a literal concern that, for example, breathing polluted air leads to lung cancer. Physical environment was far less important to psychic adherents than to other alternative healing groups. Some psychic adherents downplayed environmental causes of illness because they believed that it is relatively simple to psychically transmute dangerous substances to harmless ones.

Psychic healing adherents also mentioned the medical profession's role in causing illness. They emphasized that overmedication masks symptoms that one should be noticing and addressing rather than covering. They were concerned about the harmful effect of pharmaceuticals on the natural balance of the body.

Overall, however, these external illness-causing factors were deemphasized. Psychic and occult groups asserted the individual's responsibility for illness. In contrast to other groups studied, they denied the influence of chance or accident; all events have a specific cause and meaning.

Diagnostic Approaches

Psychic healing adherents often used doctors for diagnosis but did not necessarily accept resulting therapeutic recommendations. Instead, frequently they merely sought doctors' reassurances that they did not have a dreaded disease. At the same time, these believers also utilized psychic methods of diagnosis or corroboration of the medical diagnosis.

One approach to diagnosis was to have a healer evaluate the individual's condition, based on "knowledgeable reading" of the person's skin color or posture, characteristics of the iris of the eye, or sensitive points on the feet. One respondent, who worked in a hospital, explained, "Sometimes patients would come into the hospital for routine tests. . . . And I'll think they have cancer, and they're going to die, and they would . . . I don't know what it was about them. The only thing I can pinpoint it to is color and I know that sounds weird, but color is vital."

A few respondents used astrology as a tool or technique for understanding an illness. A healer claimed, "I use astrology basically to diagnose people. I calculate charts for specific periods of time, analyze the charts and getting inside into what are the unconscious processes that are going on in the personality and how that might be showing up in the physical body."

The most common diagnostic approach in this type of healing was analyzing the individual's aura, or energy field. Psychic healing adherents generally believed that illness manifests in the energy "body" before the physical body. Thus, one could treat the problem before it developed into physical symptoms. This assessment was made on the basis of "visual observation" of the energy field for size, color, and clarity, or by a more tactile approach, sensing with the hands the aura's density, congestion, or temperature. Most practitioners emphasized that these methods of aura assessment are not mystical and can be learned by anyone, with practice. Sometimes psychic healers used pendulums, crystals, dowsing rods, and other "technical" aids to locate problems in the body's energy field. Overall, these practitioners considered any extreme condition of the aura to indicate a problem in that area of the body. The body requires balance of energy for health, so any perceived imbalance (such as extreme heat or cold) in the aura was interpreted as a more useful symptom of illness than overt physical symptoms.

On the surface, psychic diagnosis often proceeded much as a medical diagnosis might: medical history, examination, elicitation of symptoms, technical "testing," and so on. At the same time, however, psychic healing adherents also relied heavily on intuitive, alternate ways of knowing to reach a diagnosis. One healer stated, "It's purely intuitive. There's no logic or rationale connected to it. I just get a sense in myself as to what the person needs and I operate on that and I trust that. And I've found it to be accurate."

Sometimes, these healers demonstrated their psychic skills by making a diagnosis without asking any questions or without the physical presence of the sick person. More so than any other type of group studied, these adherents believed that certain highly developed healers had the skill to "know"—even at great distance—what a person's problem was. One teacher explained, "You could be given the names of people that you didn't even know and you could psychically tune in on their problems, just the way radio and TV waves are transmitted. Your human body has an energy field and you can transmit."

Most healers who utilized these techniques felt that they were useful in generating the confidence of the client, but not necessary. In their efforts to become acceptable to an educated clientele, they have developed scientific-sounding language to describe such processes. One healer, for example, called her diagnostic procedures a "body scan."

Adherents of this type of healing often relied on others (a healer or healing group) to make a diagnosis and effect a healing, in contrast to

Eastern and traditional metaphysical healing groups where *self*-healing was the norm. Most healings described by respondents in this study were done by fellow members of a healing circle or association. Some respondents also reported using the services of a paid psychic healer, but this was less common.

According to some followers, diagnosis by another was important. It was theoretically possible to read one's own aura by looking in a mirror or running one's own hands over one's energy field. Getting a "second opinion" (i.e., preferably the diagnosis of a skilled psychic healer) was recommended, however, because of the difficulty of being objective about one's own health.

Diagnostic skill also depended on other kinds of knowledge. Knowledge of nutrition, anatomy, and herbs, for example, were valued adjuncts to psychic diagnosis. One respondent noted, "Many doctors and nurses take this [psychic] healing course, as well. They're especially good diagnosticians, because they're so knowledgeable about the body, so that they're much more specific than the lay person might ordinarily be." Psychic adherents respected professional judgment highly, but their definition of "professional" included psychic "professionals" as well as medical doctors.

Psychic diagnosis does not require the sick individual to be present. Even with the person present, psychic diagnosis relies heavily on non-physical means of assessment. One psychic healer explained, "What I would do is I would tune into her in meditation, visualize her as clearly as I could possibly see her, picturing her as clearly as I could get. And then I would pass through her outer body into her inner body and, in sort of a visionary state, see what was wrong with her."

This use of visualization to interpret others' illnesses contrasts with Eastern and traditional metaphysical groups' use of visualization primarily as a self-healing or energy-focusing process. While some Christian healing groups mentioned the possibility of "discerning" the causes or nature of illness through visualization, usually their "discernment" was a more direct knowledge from God. Psychic healing adherents put much more emphasis upon techniques of diagnosis, and visualization was one of the primary approaches used. One woman described how visualization led to diagnosis: "And you'll see [the illness] in your visualization as maybe red. . . . You know, somebody might have a bandage on their head and to that person you'd know there's something wrong with the guy's head. And somebody else might have a flashing red light around the brain. For each person, it's a different thing and you have to kind of find your own point of reference."

Psychic skill can be improved through practice, according to most respondents. For example, some group sessions included gamelike practice through which ordinary members honed their psychic skills. From the group they received immediate feedback about the accuracy of their diagnoses. Skills rehearsed included sensing what type of energy a group member was transmitting or psychically discovering details about each others' concrete everyday experiences—notions that could be judged as clearly accurate or not. These practice sessions occurred in an extremely safe environment. If a described event had, indeed, already occurred, the member got immediate confirmation. If, however, the event had not occurred, the member was not considered incorrect, but instead was foreseeing some future event. Indeed, the event might never occur and the person could still be considered correct, since one can avert future events if forewarned.

Like Eastern meditation groups, several psychic healing groups sought to "diagnose" the symbolic identity of the illness, as well as the physical significance. Location of symptoms, symbolism of body parts, and other interpretive categories were employed in determining the larger significance of a malady. For example, one woman explained:

> I hurt myself very badly skiing, and I was going through a situation in my life where I felt I could shoulder no more. And it was my shoulder that I tore up. It was very ironic the fact it was my left shoulder. The left side is the female side . . . I was having a lot of indecision about the female role in life and I felt I can't take this anymore! It was like, I can't shoulder any more of this responsibility.

The symbolic significance of specific diseases was exemplified by another adherent, who stated, "Okay, now I've got a fever blister on my mouth; now that's supposed to be related to not speaking up . . . related to having problems with your love life or never being loved as a child."

Source of Healing Power

Psychic and occult healing adherents' ideas about the source of healing power varied widely, since their belief systems were eclectic and individualistic. Most respondents in this category believed that healing power was available to all, who had but to tap it. Even when associated with the concept of "god," this healing power was not described as particularly holy or sacred. Instead, believers treated it as one type of universal energy at their disposal. One woman said, "It's not like sitting back and saying, 'Oh, God help me' or 'heal so-and-so,' which is perfectly fine and I do that too. But I think we're power beings. We really are. And we're much greater and have much more control over our lives than we give ourselves credit. . . . And I think it's just like saying, 'All right God, you gave me this ability; all right, I'll do it.' "

While many psychic adherents attributed healing power to a god, they used a very broad definition of this supreme power. Theirs was not the personal God of the Christian healing groups. One respondent suggested, "I think [the source of healing power] is yourself and yourself is part of God. I think it's ultimately from—you could say 'God,' or 'divine intelligence' or 'divine order' or 'supreme being' or whatever you want to call it. I say 'God' because I was raised in a tradition where you say 'God,' but I'm equally comfortable with the other things." Another person stated, "The source is the source that runs through the universe. Some call it 'God.' Some people call it 'cosmic consciousness.' There's just an energy that connects all of life, that feeds and grows from life itself."

Other adherents preferred to identify the source of healing as light. White light, in particular, was frequently invoked to heal. One respondent said, "I would have to describe it as rather intense light energy. It's almost like having a rainbow with an electric current running through it. It's a very vital kind of feeling."

Whatever the source of this energy, the role of the healer is to mediate these energies, which then enable the body to heal itself. A healer observed:

> You are a channel, and this energy is flowing through you. And it doesn't have to be religious in any sense of the word. You can think of it in terms of universal energy and know that you are connected to everything around you and that you can draw on this source of infinite energy and use it and modulate it to help someone else. . . . I think his own body is what heals itself. All we're affecting is—we're kind of boosting his own regeneration ability . . . getting him in touch with that innate sense of order within him that will produce healing.

Another psychic healer explained, "What I'm doing there is balancing the energy field of the person to allow the natural healing processes of their own body to take over. It's almost like putting a Band-Aid on the physical body so the body can heal itself. . . . I see the auric field as a kind of shield, like skin to the physical body."

The role of the healer, accordingly, is "relaxing the person so that their body takes over," and "the healer sets the process in motion, but the actual healing is done by the body of the individual."

Healing, according to psychic adherents, involves transmitting energy from a universal source to where it is needed. One man described it: "The energy can be transferred from person to person in the way sound is transferred from person to person through the vocal chords. . . . All these energies, whether it's vocal, sound, or sight, have an effect on somebody else."

Figure 6.1 depicts the psychic image of healing power and its mediation. Like adherents of Christian healing, these groups envisioned an external, transcendent healing power. By contrast, however, psychic and occult adherents generally did not think of that force as a personal deity who gave healing power to humans; their image was of an impersonal force that knowledgeable persons could tap for themselves or to transmit to others.

In contrast to Christian and Eastern healing groups, psychic healing groups emphasized the technical rather than spiritual qualities of this mediated energy. A member of a healing circle attributed healing power to:

> Just energy, like I said, with plugging in of energy, like plugging in an electrical current. People to people. People like that care in sending their love, and I think the hands play a very important part in that process. To send energy from one person to another through the current, that a connection is there. We know, I have seen it on ultraviolet light they put on the camera, pictures of the healing lights that come from your hands, and nurses know about this, and touching, touching and closeness of other people are very important in the process of healing because you do send a lot of energy out from yourself.

Even the images they invoked were more likely to be drawn from technology (e.g., "emits," "zaps," "plugs in," "electrifies," "magnetically forces"). One respondent suggested, "It is just like getting an extra charge from the battery. Your battery is running down, so you need a little extra charge. You plug into someone else . . . just a matter of plugging in and it can give you back the energy that has been zapped from you. . . ."

FIGURE 6.1   Concepts of Healing Power in Psychic Healing

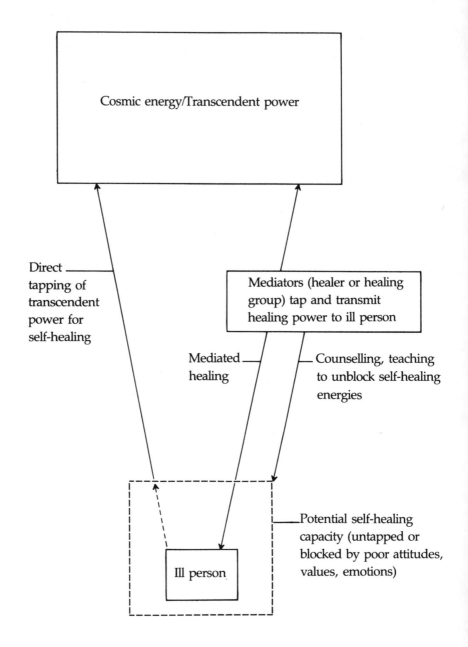

This technical, mechanistic approach is appealing because it seems scientific—not religious "mumbo jumbo," but a practical skill. Healing is simply utilizing natural laws. Members saw nothing particularly mystical or holy about the process. One respondent described belief in healing techniques as analogous to the use of a phone: "I always think about what might an alien think of as I pick up this hunk of plastic and talk to it, you see. My belief says that works. . . . So I use it. If I didn't believe it, I wouldn't use it, but it doesn't mean that the phone would not be working. Okay, same thing. Healing is there, the same as that phone is there. If I believe it, I will use it."

Healing and Health Practices

There were few, if any, limits to what psychic and occult healing groups considered acceptable healing practices. Generally, they used an eclectic combination of practices borrowed from diverse nontraditional, nonmedical approaches; no single method predominated.

When members asked for help with a problem at group meetings, they would receive a wide range of therapeutic suggestions: changes in diet, herbs, flower remedies, wearing certain colors, applying pressure to various body points, special words to say, and so on. The group would typically also lay on hands and mentally send energy to those in need. There was a wider range of experimentation with techniques and healing approaches in this type of group than in other alternative healing groups. Members listened to the options suggested and selected the approaches that had the most personal symbolic significance or were simplest to try.

Virtually no healing method was categorically excluded; various adherents tried ingestion of various vitamins, herbs, teas, specific food combinations, manipulation of various body points, laying-on-of-hands or channeling energy, use of crystals, electromagnetic chairs, exposure to the sun, special breathing techniques, laughter, special words, sounds, colonics, poetry, fasting, studying dreams, t'ai chi, counseling, yoga, Feldenkrais, and so on. The transfer of energy was the predominant underlying explanation of all modes of healing used in these groups.

Respondents emphasized that psychic healing typically was employed in addition to medical treatment. One individual noted, ". . . a broken leg—you'd have to get it set. . . . If you did just [go to the doctor] it would probably heal but . . . I really feel that mental intent, the juices that you secrete into the body through your thinking—your own visualization about healing yourself will actually help you heal faster, if not better."

Since one of the main causes of illness is thought, according to these groups, using thoughts or changing mental patterns is a primary healing method. This approach is similar to that of traditional metaphysical healing groups. Indeed, some of the same mental healing patterns, such as the "I Am" affirmations, were adopted by some members of psychic healing groups. A respondent commented:

> I realize that true healing comes from something deep in the subconscious. And when I clear up some pattern of thought, I sort of deal with that and just affirm the truth that I'm already perfect, and I'm already well, that there is within me a perfect pattern, and somewhere I've gotten off the track . . . I just recognize that the specific symptom is related to a specific belief. And when I deal with that and heal the thought pattern, there is no physical symptom.

The healing process usually began with some type of relaxation and attention-focusing, or "centering," activity. Breathing techniques or other exercises were frequently used to help the individual relax. Adherents held that, like any other skill, the more frequently one performed these relaxation exercises, the easier it became to reach the desired mental state. Many members referred to this state of relaxation as the "alpha level" or the subconscious. One member urged:

> Let us think healthy thoughts for the body. Let us affirm. Let us constantly project mental images that are positive both for the self and someone else. . . . Alpha connects mind to mind, soul to soul, heart to heart. . . . At the alpha state, health occurs naturally. You do not have to work for it. . . . If I direct my light thinking through my brain, through my body, because of the way I've already been created, my body will heal.

Most psychic healing adherents believed that, in this meditative state, one could tap healing and other powers more effectively. They preferred technical images for describing this process, which they believed was essentially an acquired skill—nothing extraordinary. One woman described her routine of healing meditation:

I get myself into a state of alpha where you're in a pure state of awareness. I would ask for guidance in an area if I needed assistance from universal consciousness or God consciousness. . . . I would then visualize a green glowing healing light encircling my head . . . and I would get into a vibratory state where I felt like I was getting beyond the sense of the physical. It was almost like there was a difference in time and space. At the time I had very many visions. . . . Many past visions in my life and previous situations that were clearing up, just in the process of these meditations. . . .

Meditators frequently used nature scenes. Nature is both a depiction of the calming images and a symbol of energy and power. Most frequently, these adherents used images of light and color. Through visualizations, adherents experienced healing light and color vividly. One member said, "You're meditating on this light energy passing through every cell in your body and you're radiating it, just letting it glow. And you get in touch with this energy; you almost start to sway. You think you're swaying—like this—and you open your eyes and you're still."

In healing others, psychic adherents "sent" that light and color to others. One man said, "The white light is actually the energy of God. . . . You focus a silver white light on that part of the body that's achy or that's sick. And the brightest lime green color you can think of." While Eastern healing adherents also sometimes used the image of sending light or color to another person in need, they placed less emphasis upon this as a healing method, because—in contrast to psychic healing adherents— they focused more on self-healing than on healing others. In the parlance of psychic and occult groups, the image of "sending light" or "sending energy" was analogous to the Christians' offer of assistance through prayer. For instance, upon hearing another member's fears of a forth-coming event, a member might say, "I'll send you some light," much as a Christian adherent might say, "I'll pray for you."

Many psychic healing adherents urged using certain colors for specific ailments: blues to cool down inflamations, yellows and oranges to send warmth to arthritic joints and sore muscles. Green was, by far, the most commonly used healing color, because it represented a balance between cool blue and warm yellow. Some healers recommended using only secondary colors, because the primary colors were too intense and could cause harm.

Psychic healing adherents resembled some Christian healing adher-ents in their belief that healing power could be transmitted through objects. Cloth, especially cotton, could be infused with healing power and, later, applied as needed. Food and drink could be similarly used as mediating devices. Gemstones were favorite power-laden objects, and certain metals were used together with gems or separately for their own power-conducting properties.

Like other types of group, these adherents used visualizations and other symbolic manipulations in healing. Accordingly, the more vivid and precise the imagery, the more effective the technique was. One member urged:

> If you know there's a particular ailment such as arthritis and you "see" the bones deformed and calcium deposits, be as imaginative and creative as you want—visualizing a brush and scraping the calcium deposits off . . . but make it practical and very specific in terms of visualization. See the fingers straightened out and healed. See bone marrow being supplied as needed and calcium being properly distributed through the body.

Whereas other types of healing group used visualization mainly for self-healing, psychic adherents described it mainly for healing of others. Psychic healing took place in both group and private situations. Adherents held that healing is an ability all persons can acquire, but some persons become more talented than others. In one group-healing setting, members had been provided with several sick persons' names; some persons' ailments had been identified and others' unknown to group members. The group sent energy into the "communal pot" and to one another. The pooled energy was psychically sent to all sick persons named. The sharing of healing energy was described by one participant: "It's more of a breathing feeling; you're inhaling. I think it comes through your pores in your skin too. But the feeling is one of inhalation. You're breathing it in. And it's coming to you also through the hands that you're holding or through the shoulders, because you're feeling the energy of the other people as you're sitting as part of the circle."

Therapeutic Success, Failure, and Death

Psychic respondents were divided as to whether belief was necessary for healing to occur. Some adherents felt that the healing process was simply a matter of energy transferral and rebalancing. Belief on the part of the persons being healed was irrelevant. One healer stated, "Healing can be accomplished without the person realizing that you're doing it. . . . I have helped people who have been virtually in a coma so they wouldn't have any really conscious knowledge of what was going on."

By contrast, other members observed that belief was important, although perhaps not essential. One adherent said, "The person doesn't really need to believe that the healing can take place, but it may help." And still other psychic adherents felt that, although belief was not a requirement, the recipient did need to be open to the prospects of healing occurring. A man explained, "Some people say 'I don't believe in that,' but they hope it works. That's different. But if somebody is really saying, 'This is a bunch of baloney and I'm not going to allow this; I'm not going to allow this in,' that's different. You're blocking it from entering your body."

Most members, however, felt that, while healing could occur without belief on the part of the recipient, belief was necessary in order to remain well or to develop maximum healthfulness. A member suggested, "When you go to a healer and their energy overrides the patient's energy, but it generally is temporary . . . many of the public go to doctors and get themselves healed. But they come down with the same condition, or another condition of dis-ease again [because they have not been] dealing with themselves holistically, and clarifying the situation from the source, because they created it."

This attitude is consistent with the psychics' emphasis on discovering and addressing the "real" cause of the problem. It is essential to understand why one got a particular illness at a given time. Long-term health requires treating the real cause, as one adherent suggested: "The most important thing is to get to the cause of the illness, not to just think about removing the illness itself, but to get to the cause of the illness. Because if you don't get to the cause and you heal one area of the body, it will break out in another area."

This belief is related to psychics' idea that change or growth is essential for full healing to occur. Failure to change is why healing seems to fail sometimes. For example, one respondent explained, "And sometimes you get people who don't really want to heal themselves because they are not interested in changing. They just want to keep going over and over the same old ground. They are really not interested in healing; they are not ready to be healed." Resistance to change is particularly strong if the sick person "needs" the illness—as a crutch or to get attention, for example. A psychic practitioner commented, "Healing doesn't work sometimes, because it's not accepted by the person who is involved in the healing process. For one reason or another, the person needs the particular illness or will not accept the loss of their illness for many different reasons."

The greater the blockage, the more psychic power the healer must have to overcome it. One believer asserted, "If a person does not want to get better, it's going to take an incredibly powerful healer to get them better, and what might happen is they get better and they get some other disease. But if a person wants to get better, they will more likely find a way to get better, whether it's some method or another of healing."

This belief contrasts with the way other healing groups explain blockages and therapeutic failures. In traditional metaphysical and Eastern approaches, with their characteristic emphasis on *self*-healing, a person's blockage is a virtually absolute impediment to healing. The most another person could do would be to help the person notice the blockage in order to remove it. By contrast, in Christian and psychic healing groups, there is a greater possibility of the healing power being mediated by a healer or healing group, even without the sick person's knowledge and cooperation. Accordingly, that external force could overcome the blockages. Yet, in all groups, full healthiness requires the individual's participation in dealing with underlying causes of illness.

Other members of psychic groups, however, felt that some kind of belief on the part of the recipient was essential to the success of a healing. One man stated, "They have to believe in themselves. They have to know that they are strong enough to have the will to overcome their illness. And then it doesn't matter whether the healing comes from outside or inside."

While doubt might not be a total impediment, a strong negative atmosphere would be. One healer said, "There are some people who dare you to heal them, dare you. . . . If they're going to sit there with that attitude, they're going to block it in some way."

The requisite belief is not necessarily faith in a supernatural being or god; it is more a belief in the power of healing energy and the decision to get well. Several respondents suggested that this faith explained the "placebo effect." Exemplifying this, one woman described the necessary attitude of belief: "They [doctors] could give you a sugar pill and say, 'Now this is just the thing, it's just come out on the market; I've had wonderful results; it's the perfect thing for you.' And if you have confidence in that doctor, and he or she generates the energy and love to you—'I care about you, I want you well'—this will do it for you."

Overall, for psychic healing adherents, healing requires the effective channeling of energy and a general openness to that energy. Since, more than most other types of healing groups, they emphasize the powers of the healer, some adherents believe that healing does not require the recipient's knowledge and cooperation. At the same time, full healing and sustained healthiness require the individual to decide to be well and to make the necessary life changes to fulfill that responsibility.

Thus, therapeutic failure is typically attributed to the lack of awareness and will to change on the part of the recipient. Some such "failures" were, however, only apparent, and not real. The "real" healing was the personal growth process resulting eventually in full health; sometimes, in early stages of growth, pain or other symptoms were still present as residues of the old way of life.

Since psychic healing groups were more technique-oriented than most other healing groups studied, they often explained some apparent failures (or healings that were very slow to manifest) as the result of ineffective use of healing techniques. One group, for example, had worked fervently to send healing energy to a member who was undergoing surgery. Although her surgery was successful, she was hospitalized longer than expected because of a secondary infection. The group claimed a successful healing, but attributed the negative developments to their inexpertise in modulating the large amount of energy they were sending.

Despite this emphasis upon technique and expertise, most psychic and occult groups recommended trying healing practices, even when one was uncertain or inexpert. One woman said, "If you're not real sure of what you're doing and you send them too much energy, you work on them a little too long or something, they'll sleep it off and you're not going to hurt them in any way." Other adherents, however, cautioned about possibly dangerous practices. One person advised that inexperienced healers should not work on the head, since it was more susceptible to damage than other parts of the body. Yet others cautioned that persons who had not yet learned to modulate healing energy should use visualizations with less extreme colors, such as orange and green, rather than stronger colors of red and blue.

Furthermore, these respondents believed that some psychic healers were much more powerful mediators of healing energy than others. Thus, a slow or failed psychic healing may be due to the insufficiency of that particular healer's or healing group's psychic powers. Even an insufficient power, however, was not considered utterly ineffective; believers sometimes held that the recipient had been "helped," but perhaps not enough to show dramatically.

Psychics' general belief in reincarnation, or some other form of spiritual continuation after death, made the question of death relatively unimportant. Death to them was primarily an intermediate situation between this life and the next one. Respondents expressed very little fear about death, nor did they have grand expectations of wondrous worlds awaiting. Instead, they believed that one's postdeath experience might be as a more advanced spiritual being or a lesser one, but it would not be drastically different from this existence. Thus, life after death is different, but also a continuation.

Members of this type of healing group reported the most near-death experiences of all respondents. Thirteen respondents in this type of group gave vivid descriptions of near-death experiences. Although a near-death experience was very powerful and moving, it was treated as one among many extraordinary events in believers' lives. No one reported changing spiritual or everyday priorities after a near-death experience. Extraordinary events, such as precognition, telekinesis, extrasensory perception, or other valued psychic experiences merely confirmed members' existing beliefs and practices.

Adherents did not view death as a barrier or separation from loved ones. Dead individuals were not "lost" or gone; rather, believers could still maintain contact and communication with them. Thus, death was not defined as therapeutic failure, but merely as the fulfillment of karmic circumstances or the result of the individual's own choice and decision. Indeed, healing might consist of learning to accept death as a transitional stage, rather than as something to be feared or overcome.

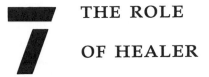

THE ROLE
OF HEALER

Who *does* the healing? Nearly all types of healing studied involved a conception that healing power was accessible to anyone—including the ill person him- or herself. In many groups, individuals were encouraged to exert control in their own lives and, by extension, over their health and healing. The healing process itself involves many forms of empowerment of all members.

At the same time, however, in most groups there were individuals who engaged in healing activities more than others. Some persons were considered to be more effective in healing activities than others. Others were sought as models or teachers of healing approaches. Thus, although the power to heal was generally democratized, there were still specialized roles for "expert" healers.

This chapter examines how these healers contributed to the healing process. When an ill person seeks out the help of another person to work on this transformation process, what does the other person do? What contributes to a person's relative efficaciousness in helping with another person's healing process? What are the diverse patterns of linkage between status as an "expert" healer and available economic and social rewards?

We need to keep in mind that various alternative "healers" are just some of numerous resources utilized by these middle-class persons for health and healing. As the analysis of help-seeking processes in Chapter Eight shows, virtually all adherents used medical doctors in addition to alternate healing. Most believed that doctors were limited in their healing capacities, and they viewed alternative healing approaches as a necessary adjunct to allopathic medicine.

One Healer's Work

Most studies of healing in this and other cultures have focused on "expert" healers in specialized roles. Our evidence, by contrast, shows that healing is actually practiced by *all* involved adherents—expert and non-expert alike—in a variety of roles and social contexts.

The popular image of specialized healer is generally shaped by TV "faith healers" who proclaim special healing powers before a vast, anonymous audience. This image also includes the notion that healers reap substantial financial benefits from their roles. This image does not mirror the healing observed in these middle-class groups. Relatively few healers studied received any money for their efforts; indeed, typically most healing in these groups was done informally by fellow believers for one another.

The role of specialized healer is better exemplified by the following composite portrait of one member of a psychic healing circle. Marge[1] is a forty-eight-year-old pediatric nurse employed full-time in a large hospital in a nearby community. She is successful in her career, with the appropriate advanced degrees and experience for high-level positions, although she has not chosen to leave active nursing for administration. Her husband is a senior partner in a law firm in a nearby city. The couple has four grown children, one of whom still lives at home while attending college. Neither her husband nor her children are particularly sympathetic toward Marge's alternative healing activities, and she avoids discussing these activities at home. She does, however, apply her healing efforts for her family; for example, she selected a gift for her daughter with its "healing properties" in mind.

Marge is involved, with varying degrees of commitment, in several groups using alternative healing. She personally utilizes some Eastern methods; for example, she practices t'ai chi fairly regularly and obtains occasional shiatsu massages, but she does not teach these methods nor is she affiliated with a group in which Eastern spirituality is a focus. As a nurse, she has used Therapeutic Touch for about three years. She uses her psychic healing methods to "get in touch with" the pain and suffering of the children in her ward; patients do not need to know that she is "sending" them healing energies. Privately, she has been practicing psychic healing for about six years; her methods are eclectic and she tries new "modalities" as she learns about them, discarding some approaches, keeping others.

Her main support group is a psychic healing circle that meets each week in members' homes. She learned about the group from a member who also belonged to her professional women's club. When she seeks healing for herself, she usually turns to the members of this group. In addition, she attends the monthly or weekly meetings of three regional holistic health and metaphysical societies. These meetings are important sources of new ideas and techniques. She has also taken numerous workshops and short courses on various alternative methods: Therapeutic Touch, foot reflexology, rebirthing, and crystal and color healing.

Marge's role as a healer exemplifies the complex mixture of specialized and nonspecialized, formal and nonformal healing roles in many alternative healing groups. Figure 7.1 illustrates the variety of Marge's healing roles. As this diagram suggests, Marge does healing almost any time, any place, and with anyone—even many people who do not know she is "sending" them healing energy. For Marge, as for most adherents of alternative healing, the process of healing is something that occurs regularly throughout each day and in many situations. It is not confined to the group meetings or to encounters with healers. Marge described working on healing herself and others even while doing the dishes or in the elevator at work. Sometimes she engaged in it deliberately; other times, she believed, it was simply a part of her being. She stated, "I believe that in every moment of my life I release energy to those around me. I think everybody needs it every moment. . . . I feel that whoever makes connection with me or I make connection with them, I'm using my energy to heal."

There are no neat distinctions between many of her informal healing roles, although her paid roles with private clients and conducting classes on healing methods are separate. Healers like Marge typically receive healing as much as they give it; healing is normalized as a way of dealing with all "troubles," including one's own.

Marge is also a good example of the general lack of clear financial motivation on the part of many "expert" alternative healers. She charges private clients only a nominal fee (from $15 to $30, depending upon ability to pay) for a thirty- to ninety-minute session, and she earns about $100 to $150 (depending upon number of registrants) for teaching a day-long workshop. These services are, however, minor sources of income for Marge. Her professional salary, combined with that of her husband, supports a high standard of living; Marge views her paid work as healer as a sideline, done mainly as a service.

FIGURE 7.1   Healing Roles of One Healer

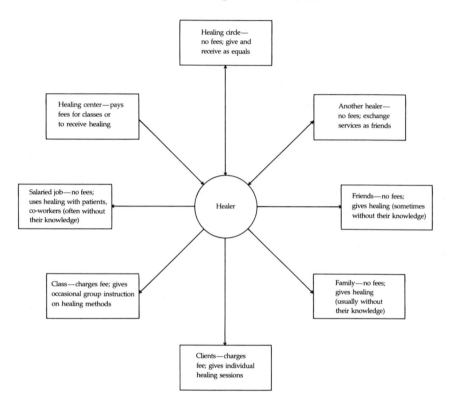

Healers and Self-Healing

If we are to understand alternative healing among middle-class Americans, it is misleading to emphasize healing that comes from *outside* the person needing healing—typically from an "expert" healer. Very little of the healing described by respondents in this study was performed by specialized, "expert" healers. Rather, most groups believed that healing was mainly endogenous—a transformation process within the person.

As shown in earlier discussions of these diverse belief systems, very little of their healing process involves purely mechanical treatment of a passive recipient. Some healing consists of healer and recipient participating together in a ritual activity. Often the healer and recipient work together to "understand" the illness and its causes and to practice mental, physical, or spiritual exercises to overcome the problem. Thus, we need to examine the interaction between the healer (when there was an identifiable individual "doing" healing) and an active recipient/participant.

The healer or leader contributes to the efficacy of a healing situation, primarily, by helping to produce order or understanding, conveying a sense of empowerment to the person seeking healing, and/or addressing the suffering of the person seeking healing.

Order

One aspect of a healer's role sometimes involves mediation of a cultural explanatory model. Both medical and nonmedical healers frequently interact with their "patients" to negotiate an interpretation of the illness, its etiology, its course, and its appropriate treatment. As the preceding chapters show, different belief systems imply very different understandings of illness. Participants draw upon these cultural models to give meaning and order to the inherently disordering experiences of illness, suffering, and death.

Explanatory models are specific to each illness episode. They explain: etiology (i.e., cause, origin, or source); time and mode of onset of symptoms; pathophysiology (i.e., some understanding of the physical conditions and changes accompanying a particular disease); course of sickness (severity and duration); and treatment.[2]

Indeed, much of the preliminary interaction between doctor or healer and "patient" may consist of the co-construction of a satisfactory explanatory model. Doctors and "expert" healers often utilize different explanatory paradigms from those of their "patients," so some interaction may be devoted to trying to convey an understanding from one perspective to a person with another perspective. In Western "scientific" medicine, encounters between doctor and patient typically involve less attention to explanatory matters than in many non-Western medical systems.[3]

Reaching a useful explanatory model for an illness episode does not necessarily require interaction with a healer or doctor. A sick person could find satisfactory meaning by introspection, discussion with family and friends, or in interaction with non-"expert" healers, as many of the respondents in this study in fact did. Talk is not the only way for a doctor or healer to address the need for order, however; ritual actions, such as arranging symbols of illness and healing in a prescribed pattern, also contribute to the reordering process.

Producing order in illness situations is not necessarily or solely a cognitive process. Nor are the cognitive operations used necessarily linear, "logical" thought.[4] There are different modes of thinking and interpreting. For example, many respondents in this study used "intuition" as a source of understandings of illnesses they encountered. The creation of order is not always by "rational" discourse. Ritual action and evocation of symbols are also used to produce order, as described further in Chapter Nine. Even the "explanatory models" themselves have elements of affect and motivation.[5] They often include moral evaluations of responsibility and right-and-wrong.

Questions of the meaning of illness are central to much concern for order: Why me? Who is responsible for my suffering? Why does God allow this bad thing to happen to a good person (or why has this bad thing not happened to that bad person)? What must I do to free myself from this suffering? How am I going to endure and pull my life together in the face of this? Western medicine does not generally address such questions of meaning, so ill persons and their families may be simultaneously obtaining Western medical treatments for their biomedical conditions while seeking meaning and order from their alternative healing approaches.[6]

Beyond the role of explanatory models in shaping a course of therapy, there is also the extent to which the assertion of order is, itself, therapeutic. Sometimes, for example, the diagnostic process constitutes the healing.[7] Without order or meaning, the individual cannot act or effectively plan action.[8] Applying order to an illness episode implies that the situation is predictable, controllable, and less threatening. Some respondents indicated that merely naming the illness relieved their anxiety and enabled them to go on in everyday life.

While the reordering aspect of therapy applies to all medical systems, it is central in this study, because, as previous chapters illustrate, many respondents identified disorder as illness itself or as a cause of illness. In identifying "disordered" aspects of life, many of these respondents described larger social situations: interpersonal relationships such as marriage or parent-child relationships, community, society, the world.

Reestablishing order, thus, is intended to affect not only the sick individual, but also often the larger social group. The resolution of the illness episode often involves communicating and legitimizing changes in social relations in the family and community. The very articulation of illness etiologies compels participants to reflect on important aspects of the social order. In many respects, then, these interpretations resemble socially important myths.[9]

Power

Anthropological studies have documented the healer's role in using power on behalf of the ill person, either to enhance the power of the ill person or to counteract the power of illness-causing entities. The restoration of the balance of power is a common theme in medical systems.[10]

Several researchers have noted parallels between psychotherapy, on the one hand, and shamanism, folk healing, or faith healing, on the other. They suggest that both involve a high degree of expectancy on the part of the patient; the healer's perceived power contributes to this expectancy.[11] Although the healer's representations may serve to build this level of expectancy, the actual transformations may often be endogenous processes within the ill person.[12] Chapter Eight documents attitudinal changes linked with healing; Chapter Nine describes the function of symbols in such transformations.

Thus, the role of the specialized healer is to facilitate these endogenous processes; indeed, some individuals may not need the help of a specialized healer but may accomplish these endogenous healing actions by themselves. In most of the groups studied, the primary healing roles were focused on helping the individual needing healing to reach such a personal transformation. The following discussion describes how adherents conceptualized healing power and its uses.

Source of Healing Power and Role of Healer

The role of healer was very different in groups that believed healing power to be transcendent and external, compared to those that believed it to be immanent and tapped from inside oneself. The specialized role of healer was found primarily in those groups believing the healing power to be external; healers were the channels or conduits by which healing energy was transmitted from the external source to the person needing help.

Even in groups where some persons were believed to be powerful or gifted healers, there was still an emphasis that *everyone* could engage in healing. Group settings typically encouraged all members to participate. For example, in many Christian healing groups, a specialized healing ministry might pray over and lay hands on a person needing healing, while the rest of the prayer group formed almost a human chain of concentric circles of persons channeling prayer forward to the healing ministers.

Christian and psychic healing groups were especially likely to accept the notion of specialized healers who channeled healing power from a transcendent source. They generally believed that, while everyone could heal, some persons were especially gifted.

Christian Groups

The predominant notion of healing power implied ministry of God's healing power, especially by prayer, but also by teaching and admonishing. The healer was viewed as an intercessor between the ill person and the healing God.

The stereotypical role of "faith healer" performing before large, anonymous audiences was deemphasized in all but one Christian healing group studied. Although several members of these groups had attended large healing services of itinerant faith healers, they viewed those as an occasional adjunct to the ongoing, ordinary healing ministry within their groups.

Christian adherents generally believed that persons with strong faith, humility, and commitment to the Lord were especially likely vehicles for God's healing power. At the same time, however, they emphasized that God could heal through anyone—even an unbeliever or sinner. One priest who led a healing ministry explained, "God uses anyone that He desires. . . . Various people have acknowledged that He's working through them in a unique way. . . . Every Christian, perhaps everyone who follows God, has some unique gift and service in ministry."

Psychic Healers

Persons involved in psychic healing, likewise, felt that some healers were especially gifted, and they often told stories of how they first discovered their gifts. One prominent "gift" was the ability to intuit a person's "real" problems and have a sense of "direction" about how to proceed with healing. Even intuition, however, was potentially a resource anyone could use. One man explained:

> It's [intuition is] a sensitivity that everyone has. It's just a matter of getting yourself to focus on it. . . . There are ways to develop it; there are ways to enhance your intuition; there are ways to learn to listen to yourself or to sense it. . . . If you can tune into your primary ways of knowing the world and processing the world, then you can begin to enhance the intuition.

Another "gift" was ability to focus or channel strong energy to another. For example, one psychic healer said:

> Usually, I'll ask for energy, to be used as a channel for healing. . . . You don't have the energy naturally; you're channeling in to the other realm and it comes from above and through you. Some people are better channels than others. . . .
> Supposedly everyone has the power, but some people have a special gift and have more, but anyone can learn to heal.

Several respondents described this special role as that of catalyst: the source of energy and direction that sets another process (in this case, self-healing) into action.

Most "expert" psychic healers emphasized that they did not do healing *to* another person. They asserted that ultimately all healing was self-healing, but that another person could assist by channeling energy or by leading the sick person to self-healing. Thus, the healer role also often involved teaching, counselling, offering information about a variety of practices to try, and serving as an exemplar of higher levels of psychic development. One woman emphasized, "I do not heal anymore. At one point it became very clear to me that all healing is self-healing, and so I have been teaching the art of self-healing."

Traditional Metaphysical Groups

There was no role of healer in the Unity churches observed. Consistent with their individualistic notion of immanent healing power, leaders were—at most—counsellors, instructors, and sources of encouragement and inspiration toward self-healing mental work. There is no sense of "doing healing"; all healing is totally from within. One long-time member of Unity explained, "I believe that there's a state of consciousness that we call God . . . and through prayer and meditation . . . one tries to reach that state of consciousness. And it's in that state that healing happens. I don't think people can say that they are healers."

Even in Christian Science, with its more specialized healing roles of qualified (i.e., Journal-listed) "Practitioner," or Christian Science nurse (and even in institutional settings of Christian Science sanitariums), the emphasis was still upon self-healing. One member explained the relationship between the practitioner and the person doing "work" toward self-healing:

> The Christian Scientist has all the tools at hand; he can pray for himself and heal himself. And if he's not healing himself, he can call on a practitioner or someone else. . . . The practitioner doesn't give advice. A practitioner doesn't say "you do this or you don't do that." . . . The practitioner prays. The practitioner might, in talking with the patient, detect something there that needs to be corrected in the thought. And . . . the practitioner will go to the Bible for

inspiration or go to the Christian Science textbook and find what he or she needs to direct thought and prayer.

Eastern Meditation Groups

Because of their emphasis upon immanent sources of healing power, these groups generally gave little emphasis to transmitting healing energy. Rather, they focused more upon teaching methods for or creating situations conducive to self-healing. Unlike the traditional metaphysical approach, however, most of these groups did not hold purely mentalistic notions of how self-healing occurred; instead, they emphasized working toward mental, emotional, and bodily changes to produce healing. For example, some taught body techniques (such as breathing, yoga, or t'ai chi poses), and many emphasized physical settings and symbolism (such as music, incense, candles, chanting mantras and other sounds, dance).

Typical healing roles included teacher, exemplar, and guide (for example, by leading meditation). Leaders offered encouragement and suggestions of healing methods to try. Although these groups were highly eclectic and individual healers often practiced numerous healing methods simultaneously, the foremost healing function was that of teacher, showing adherents many possible paths to self-healing.

Thus, the "expert" healer in many of these groups frequently does not *do* the healing. Rather the role includes teaching, leading ritual actions, counselling, serving as a role model and exemplar, introducing and demonstrating various techniques, and encouraging others in their beginning efforts at self-healing. Several persons explained that, at most, the healer was a catalyst, promoting the healing within the individual. One professional holistic healer stated, "Healing is . . . helping people discover in themselves other alternatives. . . . So I see [being a] healer as the same as an educator . . . to bring a person to a place where they are more conscious about what the problem is, what the ramifications are and what they are getting from it, what it is keeping them from doing."

Technique Practitioners

The notable exception to the emphasis on endogenous healing was among practitioners of isolated therapeutic techniques. Several of the

alternative technique practitioners emulated the medical profession in its
professional distance and charges for services rendered. Although some
of these practitioners involved their clients extensively in the healing
process itself and shared their specialized knowledge informally or in
classes, others merely sold their expert services (as chiropractors, naturopaths, homeopaths, colonic irrigationists, reflexologists, and so on).

Many studies of "alternative" or "holistic" healing equate these
nonmedical practitioners with the entire alternative healing movement.[13]
Certainly practitioners such as chiropractors, homeopaths, acupuncturists, and naturopaths appear to be the main professional alternative
healing competition to medical doctors. For example, chiropractic, which
received limited acknowledgement by the AMA in 1979, had over twenty
thousand licensed active practitioners (just under one-tenth the number of medical doctors).[14] With the limited approval of the practice of
acupuncture in many states (usually with the qualification of doctor
supervision), acupuncture has also become increasingly successful and
professionalized.[15]

The range of alternative beliefs and practices promulgated by these
various technique-practitioners is enormous. Even among chiropractors,
for example, there is considerable variation as to the range of ailments
considered appropriate for chiropractic therapy. Chiropractors differ also
as to how extensively they use other alternative approaches, such as
nutrition counselling, kinesiology, ultrasound, biofeedback, and so on.[16]

Respondents in this study were typically aware of these technique
practitioners and often preferred their services for many ailments. Perhaps because of the way our sample was drawn, however, there were
relatively few respondents who considered technique practitioners their
main form of alternative healing. Rather, they generally viewed the
practitioner as providing a limited service.

Several respondents in all four other types of healing group used
chiropractors as their primary health care professionals; however, they
were critical of their practitioners for some of the same reasons as other
adherents were of their M.D.'s: They failed to address the real underlying
causes of illness and did not treat the whole person. This criticism was
based on the fact that these adherents did not share (or necessarily even
know) chiropractic's understanding of the causes of illness. Their view of
illness came from their primary belief system. The ministrations of the
technique practitioner were valued, however, because they seemed to

work and were not as drastic or unpleasant as the surgery and powerful medication often recommended by doctors.

A few respondents considered technique practitioners their primary form of alternative healing. Because there were relatively few of these and because they represented such diverse methods (e.g., homeopathy, kinesiology, straight chiropractic, macrobiotics), it is difficult to generalize about these adherents.

Furthermore, because they downplayed the notion of healing knowledge vested in a small number of "experts," most alternative healing groups in this study generally promoted sharing of knowledge and techniques. Thus, the important healing activities were often democratized and available to the entire group. While they might value the expertise or personal manner of their rolfer or reflexologist, for example, they typically viewed those services as adjuncts to the central healing process.

Using Healing Energy

A significant part of respondents' sense of empowerment derived from the experience of "healing energy"—either from within or without. Thus, the role of healer involves using energy and varies according to the images of the healer's own energy, the energy of the ill person, and general (e.g., "divine," "cosmic," or "universal") energy. Both "expert" and non-"expert" healing roles involve "working" with energy.

Images of healing energy figure importantly in how people describe what it is to engage in healing. These images are not necessarily used literally; they are, rather, attempts to put experiences into words. Furthermore, since many of these images are part of a shared group vocabulary, they are not particularly unique or original to each healer.

Many of the images used reflect the technological thrust of American culture; healing energy was treated as analogous to technical energy-producing devices. These images were especially common among psychic and occult adherents, with their awe of scientific legitimation, but were occasionally used by Christian and Eastern groups, as well. One Christian adherent, for example, recommended visualizing Jesus' love as a laser beam that could be directed to where it is needed in healing. A psychic healer described healing as using "a rather intense light energy.

It's almost like having a rainbow with an electric current running through it."

Electricity was the main image of healing energy, which was likened to an electric current, charges, electricity flowing through a conductor, lightning, an electric shock or spark, an electric battery, or a magnetic field. Electrical appliances were used as examples of how such a non-visible energy source is used. Some respondents even referred to becoming "plugged in" to the energy source or being "zapped" or jolted by it. Radiation was another frequently invoked image. For example, several persons referred to healing energy as being like x-rays; some referred to "psychic emissions" that worked like radiation to reach parts of the body where they would heal.

The role of the healer in groups using "expert" healers was often interpreted in terms of these technological images. Psychic healers spoke of becoming "charged up," of "tuning in" to the person needing healing and of "finding what frequency they are on." Similarly, the healer's energy was transmitted "like radio or TV waves." One psychic healer expanded on this imagery:

> . . . [T]here is only one energy in the universe. . . . It comes through me. It's almost like a *television set* that the *impulses* have to come into the set. Now you have to have a finely *tuned* set that has a really great *antenna* to let the energy come in and have powerful *tubes* and have everything right in order for that picture to come through. And that's how I feel about the being of the healer.
>
> For the person who's doing the healing, the person should be a *high energy* person in good balance in order for the energy to *flow* through them and be able to be *transmitted* effectively to the person. So I see myself as a kind of *sending and receiving station* for cosmic energy to come through [emphasis added].

The other major approach to imaging energy is with nature analogies. Indeed, the same sensations might be described in technological or natural terms. For example, the idea of energy pulsing could be imaged as "surges of electrical current" or as "ocean waves rhythmically surging on the sand." These nature images often were more multisensory than the technological analogies. They often involved music or other sounds, sensations such as a cool breeze on the skin, visual images like light or color, and even taste (e.g., a sense of nectar). The following quotation illustrates how one psychic healer tried to articulate the qualities of healing energy (its texture, malleability, and subtleness):

> It's like taking a piece of cloud. There's something there. You can feel it in your hands. And you can mold it. . . . For instance in the Bible, it says about being made from clay. That's it. It's like a clay out there in the universe that you can just kind of pick out of the air. It's like cotton; you can just pick a piece off and mold it and put it in where you think the person needs it.
>
> It's not physical. But also remember you're not working even with your physical hands and your physical body. So it's a very fine vibration. It's not coarse, it's not dense. It's very fine. But still when you're working with very fine vibration, it's just a little less fine than you are so it feels like something in your hands. [This energy is] all over. I've never had a problem finding it. When I need it, I just take it. It's there.

People's experiences of doing healing are often expressed in vivid, but not necessarily literal, images of healing energy. Doing healing usually consists of "transmitting" or "sending" energy. Other actions include "balancing" energies to allow an even flow, or "transmuting" negative into positive energy.

In groups that attributed illness to blockages of energy, healing might consist of "releasing" energy, leading to self-healing. Either in transmitting energy or in helping other persons tap their own energies, several healers described "focusing" and "modulating" the energy. A nurse who used primarily Eastern forms of alternative healing emphasized that all energy is one and that this interconnectedness broke down the usual distinctions between the healer, person being healed, and source of healing energy. She said:

> It's when you see the interconnectedness, when you think in terms of energy, when you know you don't stop at your skin, and that there's all kinds of levels to yourself that are interpenetrating, actually affecting the people that are around you that you are healing or even just being with. . . . It's an ability to be able to focus and to maintain that focus and to know that it's not *your* energy.
>
> . . . You can think of it in terms of universal energy and know that you are connected to everything around you and that you can draw on this source of infinite energy and use that and modulate it to help someone else resonate, if you will, in a more healthy pattern.

In describing how they used healing energy, healers show how the endogenous healing processes are evoked in the person seeking healing. One woman, whose highly eclectic healing methods she described as "Jewish spiritual healing," explained:

> . . . [As] a healer, I can feel healing energy coming through me. I can see the energy moving around my hands or the energy coming through me or [through] the vitamin that I'm giving a person or the meditation that I'm giving them or the breathing exercise, telling them to visualize or [use] guided imagery—whatever I'm telling a person to do, I can feel that that's going to work and that's going to help. . . . I'm doing it *and* I know that this person is healing themselves. . . . both the healer and the receiver heal, do it completely . . . essentially it's both working in partnership together.

Protection and Purification

Several "expert" healers described "dangers" they considered to be inherent in the healing situation. Some of the more dualistic Christian and occult groups believed that persons involved in healing were closer to both good and evil forces; mild ritual exorcisms were routinely used in several of these groups. One psychic healer used the following purification rituals:

> So you know the illness will not settle in your body, you wash your hands (which are a great emanating and absorbing point of energy). . . . Your aura replenishes right away after you are done with the healing. After a short time you feel already the energy coming back in, because you are a receiver at all times. As a matter of fact, you have to protect yourself from negative energy by putting the yellow light around you like a circle. Then only the good energy goes through.

Several healers considered purification necessary to protect the healer from taking on the other person's illness. For example, one woman explained, "It's sort of a protection. I cleanse my body first and heal myself. The source is infinite and you're not going to run out of energy, so you might just as well take it through your own body first and allow it to flow freely. That way you lessen any danger of taking on a condition yourself."

Other healers recounted "dangers" of depleted or misguided energies. Persons from Christian, Eastern, and psychic groups mentioned the importance of selflessness; if a healer had impure intentions, the healing would not be as effective. One Eastern healer stated, "Sometimes it's because the person doing the healing gets on an ego trip and says like, 'Hey, look what I can do.' And then ego gets in the way and then the love doesn't flow. Then you're not giving anything. You're going through the physical motions, and maybe chanting or whatever you're doing, but the energy is not flowing, because your pride is blocking it."

Improper use of healing energies could also result in feeling drained oneself, according to several healers. One member of an Eastern healing circle said, "The harm is that I could deplete my own energy. If you become too intensely involved with 'let me help this person,' you drain yourself emotionally. . . . If you are not grounded and centered, you will find yourself being just drained by other people's problems and needs. . . . So I try always to stay centered, clear and connected with the earth."

By contrast, using energy properly should be invigorating, according to several respondents. A psychic healer explained, "It's a very vital kind of feeling. Some people I know . . . said that healing makes them feel drained. And I often wondered why, because it seems to me when you're allowing the energy to flow through you, it's not coming from you personally, and it's just going through you. So I don't feel drained if the energy is flowing."

One man theorized that doing healing did not take his energy, because "instead of a transfer of energy, it's a transfer of information which has no quantitative component. I transfer a pattern, as opposed to an actual energy jolt to this person."

Altered States

Studies of "expert" healers in other cultures frequently emphasize the extraordinary states of consciousness and unusual actions performed to heighten the sense of energy and power during healing rituals. Use of dance, hallucinogens, rhythmic instruments and other music, chanting, and fasting are all believed to contribute to the effectiveness of the healer. In particular, many such healers achieve dramatic altered states of consciousness, such as spirit possession and vision-quests, to tap healing power in the ritual process.

By contrast, extraordinary states of consciousness appear to be relatively unimportant in the forms of alternate healing studied among
middle-class Americans. Even specialized healers in these groups rarely
described trance states, although many respondents (healers and ordinary participants alike) described a quiet, meditative state of consciousness. For both healing oneself and working with others, one woman
suggested, "I think any holistic modality has at its base the ability to
center, the ability to go into that quiet place. . . . The key to it is how well
you can center yourself."

This image of using energy is in stark contrast to notions of frantic
activity, bustle, excitement, frenzy, and agitation. Instead of frenetic
outward displays of energy, respondents in this study emphasized
healing energy in experiences of inner calm, intensity, and control. Thus,
even the altered states used were very mild, undramatic, and accessible
to all. For this reason, adherents emphasized the ordinariness of healing:
One could achieve such a "centered" state any time, any place, without
any ritual action, and without anyone else being able to observe any
change in one's behavior or appearance.

The only ecstatic, emotional buildups observed were in some of the
Christian groups, especially in their large healing services: singing,
clapping, swaying, and expressive exhortations from the service leader to
heighten the sense of effectiveness and expectancy. There were also
some mild forms of altered states of consciousness, such as "slaying" or
"resting" in the Spirit, in which a person "touched" by God's power fell
to the floor and lay there peacefully for a short while. These experiences,
however valuable, do not typify the regular healing done in most of these
groups. Most healing in Christian groups, by contrast, occurred in
ordinary settings, without specialized "faith healers," and with little or no
emotional buildup. Altered states of consciousness, thus, were clearly not
prerequisite to "successful" healing.

Performances and Power

Healers do, however, enhance the sense of empowerment through
effectively orchestrating the performance of healing actions. Whether cast
in the role of teacher, exemplar, ritual leader, or "expert" healer, these
performance aspects contribute to a successful healing session.

Many of the persons considered especially effective in their group's healing roles were able to create and sustain an appropriate mood for that type of healing, successful at connecting the healing actions with the group's core beliefs and values, and capable of maintaining a personal presence that conveyed valued personal qualities. For example, persons considered particularly effective as leaders of healing meditations were those who had a soothing tone of voice and paced their phrases to keep the guided meditation moving without intruding too much on members' personal meditations. They chose images that "worked" for that group or that did not jar with the mood, and they selected images that flowed together without disruption (for example, held together by alliteration). Effective meditations seemed smooth and spontaneous, no matter how carefully orchestrated.

"Successful" healing sessions were also promoted by skillful use of space, lighting, music, clothing, and various other sensory devices. While these aspects alone could not "bring off" a healing performance, healers found it necessary to attend to performance aspects. Some care was also necessary to prevent distractions from the performance and to disrupt the "centering" of healing energies. "Successful" healers controlled these aspects as much as possible.

Suffering and Empathy

One of the foremost features of respected healers in several groups studied was their ability to get in touch with the feelings and needs of the person seeking healing. Adherents typically sought out "expert" healers who were especially compassionate.

Effective healers were typically good at communicating personal warmth and concern. In contrast to most medical relationships, there was very little distance between the persons doing the healing and recipients. Respondents described their sense of well-being and warmth and strength from healers' simple acts of caring. One recipient of several different forms of psychic and occult healing described how she felt being healed: "A sense of being cared for. It's a warm, almost aromatic sense. . . . What I feel is an aura of light around my whole body which is like a big sponge, absorbing all this love and warmth and caring. And it's almost a transfer of energies, . . . spiritual electricity. And you can feel in your body. I mean it's a physical embrace without a physical presence."

Several healers emphasized that their own personal experiences with suffering or pain have made them more sensitive to the needs of others. One woman stated, "If I had had a very strong body, I would never be able to empathize with the people that I have to heal. . . . If I had never experienced any of the stuff that I have gone through—like a bad marriage when I was young—I think it would be a little bit harder to feel what these people feel."

Another person described how she tried to become sensitive to her own daily experiences of pain or fear or worry: "Like, when I was working with this troubled kid, I tried to get in touch with how I felt when I was lost in a scary part of the city last week." She emphasized that as a healer she cannot become so involved that she loses her own sense of balance and centering, but she also avoided becoming remote or callous toward people's pain. She added: "Even if they bring it on themselves, it still hurts. And I have to respect that and care about them as people anyhow."

Thus, the healer shares with the "patient" not only the interpretive framework but also some of the same experiential world.[17] This connection reduces the distance between them. The patient feels that his or her suffering is being taken seriously and addressed in the healing relationship. The "successful" healer treats the suffering person—not only the illness, however broadly defined.

Economic Arrangements

The example of Marge, the psychic healer, shows some of the diverse economic arrangements between a healer and persons seeking healing. The vast majority of healing encountered in this study involved non-"experts" and no exchange of money whatsoever.

Some "expert" alternative healers, however, did charge for "professional" services rendered, especially to individual clients. These healers included some psychic and occult healers, a few eclectic healers using Eastern approaches, psychotherapists who incorporated alternative healing methods, and virtually all technique practitioners. With the exception of psychotherapists, chiropractors, and some massage therapists, these services were not covered by third-party payments (i.e., health insurance). Fees for uninsured services were generally quite modest (i.e., about equal to the prevailing price of a woman's haircut) and adjusted according to the person's ability to pay.

Concomitant with the fee-for-service model, these healers also emphasized a professionalized image, including such qualifications as certificates of training, academic degrees, and credentials from parent organizations. The professional image was further enhanced by some level of formality in arranging appointments, presenting bills, keeping files, and the organization and presentation of an appropriately professional-looking office.

More variable were fees charged for the teaching services of alternative healing groups. Often individual healers or leaders offered to teach or to arrange a teacher for inexpensive short courses or workshops, whenever enough members indicated an interest. For example, at one "holistic health center," members expressed some eagerness to learn shiatsu techniques. The leader (a yoga, meditation, and Therapeutic Touch practitioner/teacher) located a teacher for some shiatsu classes; the fee charged was calculated to pay the teacher $200 for the series of three classes, if at least five persons registered. When seven persons registered, the additional money went to the center toward its expenses.

In general, the fees charged by local teachers for their services were only slightly higher than fees charged by the municipal adult school for comparable courses. For example, a series of eight t'ai chi lessons was $80. A weekend workshop on music and dance therapy was $120 and included two light meals.

By contrast, training sessions through nationally promoted or franchised therapeutic organizations were often relatively expensive. Groups such as Silva Mind Control, Transcendental Meditation, Arica, and Neuro-Linguistic Programming charged a significant sum for the initial training sessions and typically encouraged participants to further commit themselves (and their money) for advanced training. At the time of this study, the average introductory training sessions of these national programs cost about $350.

Interestingly, many respondents were introduced to alternative healing through participating in these nationally promoted programs at the expense of their employers. For example, one woman had become involved in psychic healing after the pharmaceutical company where she worked had offered a Silva Mind Control course to employees. She considered the SMC approach a fascinating but insufficient introduction to healing and now, through participating in a regional psychic and occult association, she has learned many modes of healing and practices them regularly.

Prestige and Authority

Money is not the only reward that healers may receive in exchange for their services. In many healing systems (including Western biomedical systems), healers receive considerable prestige and related social rewards. The extent of these rewards within the alternative healing groups studied presented a complex pattern.

Healing roles and leadership roles[18] were seldom coextensive. Persons respected as good healers were often unobtrusive, ordinary members in healing groups. The group leaders were generally appreciated for their organizational skills, whether or not they were also effective healers.

At the same time, however, a certain amount of honor regularly went to healers. They were respected for their compassion, their spirituality, and their dedication to helping others. They were the epitome of group ideals and, typically, elevated as exemplars for the whole group.

Healing roles do not appear to be disproportionately women's roles in most groups studied. Women were, however, predominant in volunteer or minimally paid healing roles. Overall, there was about the same proportion of women "doing" healing as there were women members of these groups. The main exception was in Christian groups, where a larger proportion of members were housewives; women's presence in the healing ministries of those groups was a function of their roles in the home and freedom from the time constraints of paid employment. As in the example of the psychic healer, Marge, most of the women "expert" healers did not need prestige or honor from their healing roles to "compensate" for lack of successful or honored roles in their work, family, or social lives.

The ideologies of virtually every group emphasized that the "expert" did not "do" the healing, but was merely a vehicle. Thus, groups distrusted healers who took personal credit for healings wrought. The entire healing process was essentially democratized. All persons could heal, and no one healer performed an essential service that others could not in principle also accomplish.

Conclusion

While some individuals in alternative healing groups did serve as leaders, teachers, counsellors, exemplars, and other specialized roles, they generally viewed themselves as guides. They emphasized that *all* were capable of accomplishing what they did. This deemphasis upon the role of experts is consistent with a major feature of most of these alternative healing groups: Individuals were encouraged to take control over their own lives and, thus, their health and healing.

One aspect of the healer's role was the production or restoration of order and meaning for the ill person and the entire social group. Another aspect that contributed to a healer's effectiveness was empathy and addressing the person's suffering. The healing process involved many forms of *empowerment* of all members. Many healing rituals, for example, were specifically rituals of empowerment. Some groups believed their healing power was from an outside, transcendent source; others found it within themselves. All, however, spoke strongly of their experience of that power in their lives. Rather than promote the image of the passive, disempowered "patient," those who do the healing in alternative healing groups encourage all individuals to see themselves as active, empowered participants in their own healing.

8

HELP-SEEKING,

BEYOND THE MEDICAL

MODEL

Through the mass media, we sometimes get an image of faith healing and other alternative healing practices as being an all-or-nothing phenomenon: Either people use professional medical assistance or they reject it completely in favor of faith healing or some marginal medical cure. This image is further enhanced by stories of court cases in which intervention is sought to prevent the person from possibly harming him- or herself or a dependent by refusing legitimate medical attention. The data, however, show that this picture is not accurate for middle-class adherents of alternative healing and may be an oversimplification of others' practices, as well. Virtually all respondents in this study used nonmedical healing in conjunction with medical treatment. Because of their beliefs about healing, however, the way these adherents use medical help differs somewhat from the usual model of medical help-seeking.

Before turning to help-seeking itself, however, it is useful to examine the extensive ways in which the beliefs and practices described in the preceding chapters affect adherents' everyday lives, especially their health and illness experiences.

Healing Practices in Everyday Life

Alternative healing beliefs and practices are integrated into the routines of most believers' everyday lives so thoroughly that these persons are only occasionally conscious that they are specifically doing healing. Similarly, healing is seldom distinguished from prevention; an entire approach to life is involved, not merely a response to a particular illness.

A typical day of one representative eclectic adherent included a short round of yoga exercises ("sun salutations"—believed to be energizing) before her morning shower. Her meals were selected for particular nutritional benefits; she used mini-meditations during her hectic moments at the office, applied acupressure and visualization to counter a headache before an important meeting, and employed breathing techniques and visualization at each stoplight to handle the stress of a difficult commute home. At home, she used a mantra, crystal, and visualization to "center" herself during and after an argument with her teenage daughter.

Most days she spent one hour on exercise, with special attention to flexibility and aerobic exercises, followed by stress-reducing visualizations in the sauna, after which she applied vitamin E to a troublesome skin condition. Later she had a cup of herbal tea and meditated for half an hour at bedtime. In addition, this woman attended weekly meditations with her group, received biweekly shiatsu massages from a friend, consulted a nutritionist about three times a year, and utilized regular medical doctors for checkups and acute conditions.

Despite the extensive amount of time and energy she devoted to her alternative health and healing practices, she was hardly aware of them because they were so pervasive in her everyday routine and way of thinking. She made no neat distinction between what she did for her physical, emotional, or relationship problems, on the one hand, and what she did as part of her preventive care and lifestyle, on the other.

Most respondents were surprised at how many healing practices they actually used when they began to list them in response to interviewer probes. Seemingly minor responses and ways of thinking were used constantly throughout the day. One psychic adherent said, "For instance, at an athletic event, if there's a kid who got hurt or something, I'd go like this [gestures] and I visualize these rays coming out of me and making like a rainbow shape dropping onto the person."

Similarly, several Christian healing adherents described a steady flow of conversation every day with God, in which requests for healing of every little aspect of life were regular themes. They often tucked in brief blessings for healing of their children with routine touches. For example, one woman always prayed that her children be protected from sickness as she dressed them, and each time she bathed her daughter, she "soaked" the child's eczema in prayer.

Many respondents with particular illnesses had created their own personalized healing meditations or other practices. One woman humorously referred to her arthritis as "Arthur" and regularly talked to it, commanding it to behave. Depending upon how the arthritis was "acting" that day, she might add a series of little mental exercises (such as imagining Arthur doing a frolicking dance).

Another woman described a gradual "healing" of epilepsy through meditation. Her daily routine involved, among other things, an extensive meditation:

> I bring myself down to a deeper level where the—everything slows—where you're in the alpha level . . . and you're in a meditative state. . . . I use that state for programming, for replacing parts of the body visually, rebuilding the brain—a new one—symbolically, or opening up the healing. This is all inside, with imagination, creative imagination, and scouring it [the brain] and polishing it and making it brand new. And then [I use] positive affirmations: "I am free _____." And then filling in the blanks whatever it is I want to be free of: "I am free of symptoms of epilepsy; I am free of the discomfort that is so terrifying and I am free of losing consciousness; I am free of unstable brain waves; my brain waves are functioning perfectly and nor- mally." Positive directions and positive affirmations at the alpha level, where I believe the computer lies—that which governs our whole functioning.

Even when seeking help from others, such as fellow members of a healing group or a more specialized alternative "healer," these respon- dents typically viewed their actions as a regular part of routine health care. For example, several members requested healing at each meeting of their group; they would simply mention, as needing healing, whatever particular problems they experienced recently: a sore throat, painful shoulder, sleeplessness, lack of energy—old or new, recurring or newly experienced. Seeking healing, in these contexts, was not viewed as exceptional or requiring any major decision (as perhaps the decision to see a doctor might). Rather, seeking healing was often a routine part of participating in the group and engaging in its beliefs and practices.

In seeking healing, most respondents made no clear distinctions among physical, emotional, relationship, or other problems. Healing was the appropriate response to virtually every problem; holism reduced the boundaries and made it meaningless to segregate, for example, emotional from physical healing.

In the context of group-mediated alternative healing, seeking help often taps group resources for a network of support and mutual care. The extent of mutual care varied widely. Most Christian healing groups were committed to a model of mutual care and concern, but there were variations in success in implementing this goal. Also, some individuals were more closely linked with care networks than others. Group responses to help-seeking included teaching and guidance, home or hospital visits and other expressions of concern, and child care and related "neighborly" help, as well as the healing practices themselves. Some other kinds of healing groups also offered close networks of mutual help, but typically they were more loosely knit groups. Help and concern were typically proffered more on an individual rather than group basis.

Nevertheless, in all settings, adherents described a sense of concern and care from members and healers. Several respondents contrasted this caring with the more perfunctory "tending" that they believed characterized medical help-giving.

Thus, beliefs and practices of most adherents of alternative healing are thoroughly interwoven into everyday life, not so much as a response to illness per se but as a gradual but comprehensive change in their entire approach to well-being.

How Healing Works

People who use nonmedical healing alternatives are adamant that these *work*. Accordingly, it is a fully rational option to use alternative healing beliefs and practices. To understand the efficacy of alternative healing, however, it is necessary to appreciate that it "works" for adherents in many ways, only one of which involves purely biophysical developments. There is some evidence suggesting that alternative healing may, indeed, have such biophysical effects. Before discussing that issue, however, let us examine some of the other ways in which alternative healing "works" in the experience of these respondents.

For most respondents in this study, alternative healing involves more than merely alternative "techniques"; rather it entails an entire belief system. In addition to whatever biophysical effectiveness they may have, these alternatives "work" by shaping the illness experience and by giving believers cognitive tools for managing the illness experience and for handling death.[1] Thus, the provision of meaning is central to how these (and other) forms of healing "work."

By shaping the meaning of a bodily experience, these belief systems affect whether that experience will be defined as problematic for health and, thus, whether it will be considered important for healing or medical attention. If a particular "hurt" is considered to be "normal" or "good" pain, it is not likely to be viewed as "needing" medical or alternative healing intervention.

Indeed, since many of the groups studied influenced their participants' self-awareness of body and emotions, they probably increased the likelihood that members would even perceive physical or emotional conditions. This heightened awareness, however, rarely resulted in participants feeling overwhelmed by how many problems they perceived, because it usually went hand in hand with an increased sense of control. For example, one man explained:

> As I got to understand my body better and better, and as I got more in touch with it—what's normal or not—I got better at knowing what my body needed. I used to push myself—my body—too much, causing strain and sometimes injury. Now I know when doing something is okay or when it's too much. I know how to really relax, how to take care of myself when my body needs it, how to choose the foods or whatever that my body needs just then.

A bodily experience has no inherent meaning; meaning must be applied, drawing upon a range of culturally available explanations. Alternative healing systems give their adherents a repertoire of possible meanings to apply to their sensations. Some of these interpretations had implicit normative content: a pain could be "good" or "bad," a symptom from "evil" or "good" sources, and so on.

Not only are these alternative healing systems effective in providing meaning, but they also provide empirical proofs in support of their explanations. Participants have a sense that their healing system "works" when a sickness episode is consistent with their expectations.[2] For example, some adherents had learned to expect that an accumulation of toxins in the body needs to be purged from time to time and that a fever is nature's way of accomplishing that purification. If such a believer then experienced a short period of fever, treated the illness experience as a purification process, and subsequently felt a sense of restored energy, his or her faith in the larger explanatory system would be strengthened.

Insofar as these alternative healing systems adequately match adherents' expectations with their experiences, they "work."

Evaluation of the Medical Establishment

The decision to seek nonmedical healing alternatives might result, in part, from the evaluation that orthodox medical treatment does *not* "work" in some important ways. Respondents were asked how well they thought the medical profession was meeting people's needs. Further questions asked what were some of the good things and some of the bad things about how medicine was practiced in America. Although these questions focused upon the medical profession primarily, they also elicited comments about hospitals, other health-related institutions, medical insurance systems, the AMA, drug companies, and health professionals other than medical doctors.

Interestingly, the respondents who were most negative about the way medicine is practiced were adherents of practitioner-type healers and the persons in the control group (i.e., those not using alternative healing systems). By contrast, members of Christian, Eastern meditation and human potential, metaphysical, and psychic and occult groups were less negative; they balanced positive and negative comments, and had some—albeit qualified—respect for the medical profession and medical institutions.

Much of the positive and negative evaluation of the medical profession and institutions appeared to be based upon concrete personal experiences—good or bad. Certain types of medical experiences are linked disproportionately with positive or negative evaluations. Persons who had sought orthodox medical treatment for chronic back pain were, for example, overwhelmingly negative about their experiences; by contrast, those who had had joint-replacement operations for severe arthritis were dramatically more favorable toward their experiences. One older woman whose hip joints had been replaced exclaimed, "Well, let me tell you this. I have regained my respect for doctors since I had this surgery. . . . I couldn't believe it—they were just fantastic!"

Likewise, negative evaluations were often a result of the loss of faith in orthodox medical treatment through particularly bad experiences, such as serious misdiagnoses, "unnecessary" surgery, extended or unpleasant—yet "unsuccessful"—treatments, and so on. Loss of faith in medical approaches was especially pronounced in cases of debilitating chronic illness and pain. Women's experiences with unpleasant, callous, or medically unsatisfactory treatments related to their reproductive system were also often the bases for such "loss of faith." For example, one psychic healing group devoted much of one of its sessions to help a member deal with her feelings about the medical problems that her daughter was developing due to the mother's use of DES during that pregnancy. The mother cried, "We're all just human guinea pigs!"

Most respondents' criticism of medicating and other treatments stems largely from their belief that medical treatment addresses the symptoms of illness, not the cause. They differed among themselves in their interpretation of the true causes, however. For example, one member of a Christian healing group stated:

> What they [doctors] are doing is they're treating symptoms. There is something physical—say something here on your skin—and they're treating it—say with medicine—but what they're doing is treating the surface. It's superficial. See, the sickness on the outside of the skin is a superficial thing—the result of something else. And it's a spiritual problem—all the way to the core of the person. It may be that they're Christian, but they just don't know that healing is theirs. But most people that are sick in the world, they don't know God.

According to this perspective, although it is not inconsistent with a Christian approach to seek medical care, real and long-term solutions must begin by tackling the spiritual causes of illness.

Generally, adherents of Christian faith healing reflect one of three basic approaches:

■ Doctors are vehicles of God to accomplish healing (for example, one woman described doctors' skill and training as a "gift of God," adding that they were "anointed to do that kind of thing").

■ Doctors can heal the physical part of the person, but the deeper (spiritual, emotional) part requires healing by God (as exemplified by one man's assertion that " . . . a doctor can heal you out[side] in, but God can heal you from the inside out").

■ Doctors cannot really heal, but they can ameliorate the symptoms (for example, one group leader exclaimed, "Medicine is not healing, and operating by doctors is not healing. They only treat the symptoms; only God can heal and treat the real cause").

Adherents of the other types of nonmedical healing studied tended to be more critical of the actual practices used by the dominant medical system. These respondents strongly criticized overreliance on drugs and medication, overreliance on or premature use of surgery, excessive use of x-rays, and excessive use of or overreliance on laboratory testing for diagnosis. Like adherents of Christian healing, these respondents felt that orthodox medicine treated the symptoms, not the root causes of illness. Many of them linked this problem with the overuse of drugs; they believed the drugs masked the illness by ameliorating the symptoms but not actually curing the basic disease. Several respondents felt that such medication often made problems worse by upsetting the balance of the body and further weakening natural defenses.

These respondents were adamant about lifestyle factors in healing; they were strongly critical of the medical profession's inattention to these factors. Like Christian healing adherents, these respondents criticized orthodox medicine's failure to treat the whole person, although their definition of what treating the whole person means differed from the predominant Christian definition. A nurse stated:

The medical profession has kind of gone off the deep end with this whole germ theory of disease—that for everything there's this one specific cause and we'll treat that regardless of who has the disease—everyone gets treated the same way, and that we can break the body down into little parts and just treat one part separately from the rest—and it hasn't worked. Our hospitals are filled, and the people keep coming back. And what they've done is good, but they've gotten lost; they've forgotten how to look at the whole person.

Unlike adherents of Christian healing, other respondents were disturbed that doctors were not truly healthy themselves. One woman exclaimed, "Doctors abuse themselves and I don't think that people who can't take care of themselves can take care of other people." It is not merely a criticism of hypocrisy; rather, the ideal healer is someone who strives toward and approximates these respondents' holistic images of real health—physical, emotional, social, and spiritual. Traditional Christian faith healing adherents focused upon God as the healer. By contrast, other alternative healing adherents were more likely to believe that real healing power is possible for *any* individual and that those who were truly healthy were more likely to also have power to heal others.

Thus, numerous respondents in these categories distinguished between doctoring and healing. They suggested that, while some doctors might also be healers, their technical skill alone was not the necessary quality. For example, one person stated that doctors are "not healing persons. A doctor is a diagnostician—someone who diagnoses and treats. That is not healing in my concept of healing." Another emphasized that "doctors don't heal in the real sense of the word, because they don't address the person's way of thinking." He went on to explain that real, long-lasting healing required sick persons to come to a new way of thinking about themselves and their worlds.

Most alternative healing groups hold a very different image of the role of the healer from the typical role of medical doctor. The following comments by a "holistic healer" in one of the groups illustrate this distinction:

> I honestly think that healing is much more of an art than a science. And the best healers are born that way. . . . Now I think that one of the worst aspects of allopathic medicine is that they treat it as a scientific thing, where it's not. . . . I think some of the best physicians or healers—no matter what field they're working in—are those people who go beyond the basics of "this is what it has to be." . . . There's a certain intuitive quality also. You have to try to just open yourself up to listen. . . . And I think all really good healers—including medical doctors who are truly healers—have that [intuitive quality]. . . . Somebody who's very linear, very scientific . . . I don't think they'll ever develop into a good healer. They may become a competent doctor, but I don't think they'll be a good healer. . . . [They can't get] beyond a mechanical saying, "This person has this set of symptoms so we'll give him this drug."

Such attitudes are not limited to those who are actually committed to alternative healing approaches, however. Several respondents in the control group voiced similar concerns. For example, a nurse in that group stated:

> Health needs to involve the whole person. Doctors very often can treat symptoms, treat the disease, but they can't treat the person. They don't see

him in his environment. . . . They don't develop a rapport with patients. They don't want to know any more than what's wrong with you physically. I just feel they have a very inflated attitude toward themselves. They want unquestioning patients.

Help-Seeking Patterns

This study found that very few persons (less than one percent of all respondents) who are involved in alternative healing would reject medical treatment altogether. Indeed, respondents showed considerable respect for (along with criticism of) the medical profession. This finding strongly contradicts the prevailing notion that persons involved in faith healing and other alternative healing systems are so extreme in their beliefs that they endanger their very lives. At the same time, however, respondents did apply criteria in their help-seeking decisions that differed from the approaches of persons who do not believe in alternative healing methods. Both adherents of traditional Christian faith healing and other alternative healing systems revealed complex patterns of help-seeking.

There is no necessary connection between having symptoms of an illness and getting a doctor's assistance. Studies of medical help-seeking suggest that fewer than two out of every three illness episodes are brought to a physician's attention.[3] Awareness of symptoms and decisions about potential courses of action precede a visit to the doctor. It is not only adherents of alternative healing systems who have nonmedical responses; most persons try waiting, self-medicating, resting, eating special foods, and other responses before seeing a doctor for many ailments.

The decision about which network of friends or relatives to consult about one's problems may also shape what kinds of help the individual will seek. All persons' social locations and belief systems enter into the help-seeking process, influencing the interpretations they give their symptoms and the responses they consider possible. The different help-seeking patterns used by respondents in this study illustrate the complexity of this process. These patterns are perhaps more complex than those of the average person (because some adherents explore so many alternative responses), but common to all help-seeking decisions are the aspects of the individual's awareness, interpretation, and response.[4]

Respondents in this study generally believed that most of the time the body would heal itself and that medical intervention should be saved for extraordinary needs. This approach led, understandably, to waiting to allow the body to do its healing. Many persons were genuinely ambivalent about medications. Several described going off medications that they felt were not working. Interestingly, several respondents described going to doctors to get diagnosis or advice, knowing in advance that they did not intend to take any medications prescribed. They acted as though they accepted the prescription, but they had no intention of taking the medicine. They were eager to stay in the good graces of their doctors but did not accept all of the doctors' recommendations. For example, one housewife said, "I still think they give you too much medication, which I accept gratefully and then don't take." By contrast, another woman felt that she had already been healed through Christian faith healing, but was continuing to take medication because the doctor recommended it: "I'm not worried about the medication, even though it's making me fat, my hair is coming out, but the doctor kept me on it, so—I'll stay on it."

The extensive literature examining patient "compliance" with doctors' "orders" shows how complex are the factors underlying patients' decisions about health care. Basic demographic factors, such as gender, socioeconomic status, and education have little or no explanatory correlation with whether or not patients follow doctors' "orders." The very notion of "compliance" implies a normative power differential between doctor and patient.[5] Many of the respondents in this study rejected that model; the doctor was viewed as one—among many—respected sources of information, advice, and help.

Not only did respondents in this study not share most doctors' explanatory models of health and illness, they did not share doctors' definition of the help-seeking situation. Doctors may generally assume that patients come to them in order to receive the full range of their medical help. Many respondents, however, valued part but not all of the doctor's help (e.g., diagnosis but not prescribed surgery). In some cases, they sought diagnosis merely to rule out the possibility of something more serious. For example, one woman was confident of her alternative methods for treating colitis, but consulted her doctor to confirm that her problem was colitis rather than some other more serious or difficult sickness. Getting the doctor's recommendations for treatment was never part of why she consulted him. She noted his recommended treatment, however, and decided she might try his recommendations, if her non-medical approach did not work in a "reasonable" time.

This pattern leads to the comparative question: Might this reason for "noncompliance" be characteristic of a general population as well? How many people consult a doctor, not so much for treatment of problematic symptoms, but rather to disconfirm a feared illness? If the diagnosis points to something less serious and frightening, such patients may decide not to bother with the treatment regimen, unless the symptoms themselves become particularly severe or disabling.

Respondents were asked what they would do if there were a conflict between their doctor's advice and their alternative healing: Under what circumstances might they discontinue medical treatment? This question posed a hypothetical conflict that surprisingly few respondents had encountered or expected to encounter in actual decisions. Adherents of different forms of alternative healing reflected very different approaches to help seeking.

Christian Healing

Adherents of Christian healing groups were more authority-oriented than other respondents. Their predominant pattern was to rely on the doctor's diagnosis and treatment and to use prayer and other faith-healing methods as adjuncts. A large proportion of adherents of Christian healing believed it was especially important to seek a doctor who was also a person of faith. Several specified that the doctor should be born-again.

For some respondents, choice of a doctor was a dangerous dilemma. One born-again Christian expressed this fear: "I'd be afraid to put myself in a doctor's or hospital's hands—because he's into this World—even though the Lord could use doctors. . . . So I seek the Lord's healing first, but if He really wants me to go to a doctor, I will go where He leads me."

Most of these respondents said that they would pray to seek the Lord's guidance as to whether to seek a doctor's help and which doctor to use. One woman explained, "I'd go to the doctor, because I feel that's what I should do. I'd also pray about it. First I'd pray to see that the doctor would handle things right and that I'd know which doctor to go to and how to handle it. I would normally go to a doctor."

Prayer was viewed as an adjunct not only to treatment but also to diagnosis. Adherents of most Christian forms of healing described as "healings" such events as praying before diagnostic tests and later receiving negative results. Several respondents said they routinely prayed before seeing a doctor so that God would guide the doctor to a correct diagnosis. A few respondents also prayed over their medications so that God would bless them, make them more effective and less harmful.

Christian healing adherents typically asked for divine guidance as to when to seek help and whom to consult. They believed that all decisions and actions should be submitted to God in prayer first. They were likely to wait until they were certain of God's guidance. A teacher said:

> If I were ill, I'd pray and go to the doctor. I would say I'd pray first. I can do that at home; I don't have to wait. That would be the first thing I would do. Then I would go to the doctor, rather than wait for a healing, if it were something serious. If it were a lump on my breast, or something like that, I would go to the doctor. I would always combine them. Unless the Lord said, "Don't go to the doctor."

Asked if there were a conflict between their doctor's advice and their alternative healing, under what circumstances might they discontinue medical treatment, most adherents of Christian healing asserted that there would be no such conflict. They allowed, however, that if there were any conflict, God's authority superseded that of the doctor. Nevertheless, they were extremely cautions about recommending discontinuing medical treatment. As one housewife said, "There would have to be a strong leading by the Lord. I would have to have confirmation in Scripture."

In general, adherents of Christian healing greatly respected medical authority. Prayer and other healing actions were done in addition to using medical help. God was the ultimate healer; He guided followers to the "right" doctors, aided the diagnosis and treatment, guided the hands of surgeons, and aided in the evaluation of therapy. Through prayer, Scripture, and other confirmation, adherents could know God's will for them and move toward healing.

Nevertheless, since God's authority was considered superior to doctors', there was always the possibilty of having to choose between them. One group leader stated, "My ultimate authority is Jesus Christ, so it would mean the discerning of what He wanted for me." More extreme was a woman who recounted "taking authority over tonsillitis" and cancelling a recommended tonsillectomy. She explained, "I go by prayer; God tells me which way to go."

Other Healing Approaches

By contrast, adherents of most other healing approaches were less inclined to accept doctors' authority without question. Although they typically respected doctors' evaluations and advice, they were not un-critical. They might be characterized as "contractors" of their own health care.[6] This approach is well illustrated by one man:

> I challenge medical authorities, and I encourage people to give their doctors hard times in the sense of demanding to know why they're making the decision they're making. [Exemplifying this with a description of his interaction with a surgeon, he continued:] "I was wearing my [clerical] collar that day and I was especially not feeling like being treated like a child. And I finally said to him, "Doctor, I'm paying you to be my consultant, so I'm the person who's in charge of this interview. Because I'm paying you to be my consultant, I kindly request that you explain to me in great detail . . . exactly why you are advising this [surgery], and once you give me your advice then I will decide whether or not I want to have the surgery."

Most such adherents view medical doctors as some among many potential sources of health services. They might consult several different sources for help with a given problem. For example, one woman with skin problems used a dermatologist, a nutritionist, a hypnotherapist, and a crystal healer. The patterns of health-seeking for persons who operate as "contractors" of their own health care are, understandably, more complex than those of adherents of Christian faith healing, who are less questioning of authority.

Many of these other respondents emphasized their own skill and self-awareness in making health decisions. Knowing when one needs a doctor's help or when to use another alternative is a skill to be developed through both intellectual knowledge about the body and personal aware-ness of one's own body. Respondents described trusting their own sense and self-knowledge in deciding whether to get medical assistance and which kind of help to seek (in contrast both with Christians' trust in God's guidance and with many laypersons' lack of confidence). For example, one member of a yoga meditation group said, "Basically, I think I know my body more than anybody else. I live in it. I kind of know how it functions."

Although these adherents go to doctors, they frequently consult doctors only for limited purposes. Many respected doctors' diagnostic skills but distrusted some of their therapeutic approaches. One man stated, "If I was sick, I would go to the doctor, specifically to find out what was wrong with me. Now once I found out what was wrong with me, then it [whether I followed the doctor's advice] would depend whether or not I wanted to take medication. . . . I would . . . listen to what he has to say, with what I know, and . . . I'd make up my mind at that point." Similarly, some went to a doctor after they felt they had been healed by some alternative method, in order to confirm that the condition was actually healed.

Many respondents felt that their alternative healing approaches were actually ahead of medical science. They were sure that when it gained the ability to tap such phenomena, medical science would vindicate most of these alternatives. They believed that science was only beginning to discover the truth of what their belief system had told them all along.

Like adherents of traditional Christian healing, however, they were often not well treated when they revealed to a medical doctor their use of alternative methods. For example, one told a story of having a serious rash healed by psychic healing; upon returning to the physician who had previously prescribed a medicated cream, the man told the physician that the improvement was not due to the prescribed treatment but to a psychic healing. He said the doctor got very upset and abusive and told him to go to a psychic healer if he got run over by a car. Similar stories recounted doctors' anger at patients' checking their statements with other authorities, getting a second opinion, or changing doctors.

Faced with physician distrust or dislike of alternative approaches, yet respecting doctors' opinions for some purposes, many adherents of alternative healing simply pretend to go along with their doctors, rather than confront them. They want and need the doctor's future advice and ministrations, but they do not accept all the doctor says or does uncritically. This pattern may lead doctors to overestimate the extent to which their patients are accepting their healing approaches. The vast majority of the respondents' physicians probably have no idea of the extent of their patients' alternative healing beliefs and practices.[7]

Technique Practitioner Adherents

These respondents represent a mixed pattern of help-seeking. Some used their alternative practitioner exactly as they would a doctor; they got their entire diagnosis and treatment from one authoritative source. Our sample included relatively few persons whose use of an alternative practitioner constituted their only nonmedical alternative (although this feature may be due to limitations in how the sample was drawn). Most respondents who used this type of healer also belonged to some other type of healing group and employed that other group's characteristic approach to help-seeking. For example, several adherents of Christian healing used a chiropractor instead of an M.D. for most ailments; they would typically pray for God's guidance in finding a Christian chiropractor who would respect their use of prayer for healing.

Interestingly, respondents for whom a technique practitioner approach was the dominant alternative healing system were the most critical of orthodox medical practice of all types studied. This negative evaluation may be because this type includes the more professionalized competitors of the medical profession (such as homeopathy). Unlike the eclectic adherents of most types of alternative healing, many of these persons believed that adherence to their approach meant total rejection of allopathic medicine.

The Control Group

Control group interviews suggest the extent to which negative opinions of medical doctors and hospitals are not peculiar to those with nonmedical healing beliefs and practices. Respondents in the control group were generally more critical of the way medicine is practiced in this country than were most adherents of alternative healing, except for the technique practitioner adherents, described above. Interestingly, the majority of respondents who urged some form of socialized medicine were also in the control group. This difference is perhaps because their criticism of medical practice focused less on its content and more on its delivery (especially the quality of the doctor-patient relationship and the cost-availability problems in American society).

Control group respondents were also somewhat similar in their selective use of doctors. They too shopped around for doctors before finding some that were satisfactory. Several respondents also emphasized the necessity of developing an active rather than passive relationship with their physicians. For example, one woman described negotiation with her obstetrician:

> My husband and I have both had to be very firm in what our needs were, to not just be placated and rather condescended to. . . . I've learned over the years . . . that I must be very careful to be very explicit and very firm in saying "this is what I need to know and you have the information; please give it to me"—instead of being put off by his "you're going to be okay." . . . You must always press doctors to tell you. [She added that, by contrast, nurse-practitioners have always been helpful—supportive and taken the time to explain things.]

The main points of contrast between control group respondents and adherents of the various alternative healing groups lie in the criteria for a "satisfactory" doctor. Members of Christian healing groups often sought a doctor who was a fellow believer, who would utilize prayer and faith in the medical process. Many control group respondents and most members of other types of healing groups typically sought doctors who allowed them to be more active and informed about their health care. Adherents of alternative healing also sought doctors who were "open" to their various alternative beliefs and practices.

Responsibility, Control, and Help-Seeking

Most alternative healing involves a different concept of the individual's responsibility for health and healing. This concept carries over into believers' notions of their responsibility relative to the role of the doctor. It is also a factor in respondents' strong dislike of the professional dominance of doctors. Taking responsibility for one's health was linked with an active—not passive—role in the healing process.

One woman emphasized, "Doctors strive to create a dependence on themselves or on a type of healing . . . but need the involvement on the patient's part with the healing process." The implications of this active role for the doctor-patient relationship were spelled out by another woman, who said, "I really much prefer going to somebody who'll let me be a colleague in my own healing, and I don't find that kind [of doctor] a lot. Doctors put themselves on a pedestal, and expect patients to play like a child—like, 'take care of me.'"

Thus, many adherents of alternative healing are often advocating a different notion of individual responsibility and are calling for greater physician acceptance of this more active patient role. As such, the health-seeking patterns and attitudes toward the medical profession exhibited by many of the respondents can be understood as a counterassertion of power against the dominance of the medical profession.

The relatively high social status and educational level of persons in this study probably make the power issue between them and their medical doctors even more salient. Patients with greater knowledge or relevant experience are less likely to be passive patients; they are less ready to give control over to the physician.[8] Doctor-patient communication is frequently shaped by issues of power and influence.[9] Control of medical knowledge and physician authority are linked; indeed, physicians can control the communication of information about illness to patients to enhance their power and authority.[10]

Respondents' dissatisfaction with the medical profession is related to a fundamental power issue. These respondents are asserting an alternative model of medical practice—one in which the patient exerts greater power and control. They seek a different quality of doctor-patient communication—a model in which doctors serve as knowledgeable resource persons for self-aware patients. Such communication would, accordingly, consist of much information exchange and mutual respect. It would also be (in the ideal image of respondents) open to nonmedical alternatives, which patients could choose as respectable options in their health-seeking.

Alternate Modes of Healing and the Medical Paradigm

As the title of this chapter implies, it is necessary to get beyond the "medical model" of health, illness, and healing to understand how alternative healing works and why its adherents seek it. In this and subsequent chapters, three broad yet related interpretations are developed: Healing is linked with personal empowerment; issues of meaning, moral order and responsibility; and an alternative understanding of the self in relationship to society.

As Chapter Seven suggests, much of the healer's role in alternative healing groups consists of enhancing the recipients' sense of personal empowerment, allowing transformation from within, or self-healing. Subsequent chapters show how ritual language and action also promote a sense of empowerment. Furthermore, important evidence from contemporary behavioral medicine lends credence to the these groups' assertion that their approach is effective biophysically, as well as emotionally or spiritually.

The following discussion of biomedical and related studies is not for the purpose of legitimating alternative healing by reference to "scientific" medicine. Alternative healing systems and biomedical healing systems should be understood on their own terms as independent belief systems. Nevertheless, it is useful to keep in mind that—even in terms of biomedical criteria—some of these alternative healing beliefs and practices are highly plausible. Coming from a completely different perspective, behavioral and social medicine documents the importance for health and healing of factors such as order and coherence, control and empowerment.

Personal Empowerment and Healing

Medical doctors, using the Western medical paradigm, have had continuing difficulty in conceptualizing human suffering and in dealing with illnesses that are not purely biophysical in manifestation or cause. Labelling such problems psychosomatic has itself been problematic, or even counterproductive. A psychosomatic ailment is treated as less than real. Whether or not the physician intends the implication, the term implies to the patient that his or her problem is "all in the head."

The Mind-Body-Society Relationship

Part of the reason for the medical profession's difficulty in dealing with social and psychological aspects of disease and illness lies in the medical model's assumption that the fundamental origin of illness is within the individual at a microbiological level.[11] Medicine has thoroughly embedded the Cartesian body-mind dualism in its underlying rationale.[12]

Body is considered completely separate from mind, and problems of the body are assumed to be amenable to treatment of the body, without reference to the mind. The professional shift from reliance on patient-presented evidence (e.g., the patient's self-knowledge and interpretation of problems) to clinical evidence (e.g., blood tests), has further distanced the doctor from the person treated.[13]

Because of this paradigm, medicine has emphasized highly specialized expertise focusing on specific biological systems (e.g., cardiology) or disease treatments (e.g., oncology). Considerable effort has been put into developing ever more precise methods of clinico-pathological correlations (e.g., sophisticated x-ray and ultrasound scans, genetic tests, and so on). Proportionately little attention has been paid to disease causes outside the individual (e.g., social, psychological, or environmental factors) or to the "causes" of health rather than of disease.

Even among doctors who take psychosomatic illness seriously, the concept is used mainly to describe physiological conditions, such as colitis or ulcers, with acknowledged sociopsychological components. Referring to some diseases as psychosomatic implies that all *other* diseases have no psychological or social component. The concept of "psychosomatic" is rarely helpful in actually understanding the range of suffering for which there is no physiological basis, nor is the concept particularly useful in comprehending why some persons suffer greatly from physiological conditions that cause others much less suffering. Thus, the very concepts with which physicians attempt to interpret the body-mind-society linkage often serve to invalidate their patients' experiences.[14]

Social Medicine

Increasingly, however, the fields of social and behavioral medicine have documented a wide range of psychological and social aspects of illness causes, preventive measures, and cures or recovery measures.[15] It is beyond the scope of this volume to provide detail about all these fascinating studies, but the following overview emphasizes some of the points on which this growing body of literature provides some appreciation of the potentials of nonmedical forms of healing.

Perhaps the most familiar connection between illness or disease, on the one hand, and psychological and social factors, on the other hand, can be discussed under the umbrella concept of stress. Stress is defined as "the nonspecific response of the body to any demand."[16] Stressors are the agents of these demands upon the body; they include, for example, intense light or sound, bacteria, pain, long periods of excessive work, or a promotion to a responsible position—in short, anything perceived by the body as a demand. Accordingly, the body must make an adjustment in response to the stressor.

Stress is not, in itself, bad. Indeed, life would be boring without the stress of happy and exciting events, challenges, and rewarding work. Furthermore, some bodily stress is a necessary adaptation response; for example, a fever, while itself stressful, is part of the body's ability to cope with an infection. Thus, some researchers find it useful to distinguish between *distress* (unpleasant, potentially damaging) and *eustress* (positive, potentially satisfying).

Stress theorists propose that stress is connected to disease-causation through bodily changes in response to certain stressors. Stress induces pathologies when the body's response to it creates a serious imbalance in bodily systems, mediated through the central nervous system. Some theorists propose that stress itself and the body's patterns of adjustment to stress promote disease through breakdown, wear and tear, and general disequilibrium. Other interpreters emphasize that it is inadequate or even pathological patterns of *coping* with stress that bring on disease.

Various studies have suggested some of the pathways by which the body is vulnerable to stress; they focus mainly on neuro-endocrinological patterns, controlling or influencing virtually all bodily systems (e.g., visceral functions, immune system, hormonal secretions, and homeostats controlling such functions as hunger, sex drive, and sleep).[17]

Beyond stress, as a generic concept, specific emotional patterns have been implicated in the development of specific diseases.[18] One such emotional pattern is the driven/aggressive "type A" personality, linked with coronary heart disease.[19] Similarly, studies of women with arthritis distinguished an emotional pattern (including nervousness, tenseness, worry, moodiness, depression, and denial and inhibition of anger) that was correlated not only with presence of the disease but also with rapid progression of the disease, degree of functional incapacity, and lack of response to medical treatment.[20]

Patterns of emotional or personality characteristics have been proposed for a wide range of other diseases as well, including cancer, asthma, bronchitis, eczema, colitis, diabetes, and tuberculosis. Although these diseases would not occur were it not for agents such as viruses, bacteria, and genetic defects, emotional patterns appear regularly as factors in a given individual's susceptibility to a pathogen. They also seem to play a significant role in the course of the disease, its severity and amenability to cure.

Several studies have correlated the development of a variety of diseases with the quantity and degree of life changes an individual has experienced. "Social stresses" such as divorce, change in residence, job loss, or death of a parent appear to be factors in triggering illness episodes, exacerbating levels of suffering and low response to treatment. Initially, such studies employed a simplistic notion of life change, often merely counting how many changes a person had experienced— regardless of the intensity, duration, or significance to the individual.[21] Recent work attempts a more complex appreciation of the role of social factors in the development of both physical disease and emotional disturbances.

Although some of these factors may vary according to individual personality, social environments strongly shape stress-producing experiences. Studies of individual perceptions of "locus of control" show that certain individuals are more likely than others to attribute events to forces outside themselves; they are, thus, more likely to experience events as uncontrollable. At the same time, social environments determine whether an individual does, indeed, have actual or potential control over important aspects of his or her life. For example, stress produced by work overload is greatly compounded if the workload and time is out of the control of a worker, such as on an assembly line.[22]

The impact of stress is not based solely upon the stimulus/stressor (e.g., a life crisis); rather, it depends mainly upon the meaning or appraisal of that stimulus.[23] For example, the death of one's parent would be more likely to be experienced as a serious stressor by someone heavily dependent, emotionally or materially, upon that parent than by someone very separate and independent from a parent; the dependent person would appraise the situation as a highly threatening loss. Similarly, a person with a substantial network of social and emotional support-givers might appraise the death of a parent as less threatening than would someone who feels all alone in the face of the loss. Emphasis upon the meaning of a possible stress-producing situation is particularly important for our understanding of how nonmedical healing works, because it is precisely through provision of meaning and belonging that the groups studied affected their members' everyday lives—and everyday appraisals and perceptions of life events.

A separate but related line of research has focused on the somatization of suffering and the relationship between a person's body experience and health and illness.[24] These studies suggest some of the cultural and psychological factors in the translation of nonphysical suffering into bodily disturbance and illness. Physical suffering becomes a vehicle for the expression of social and emotional distress.[25]

Especially interesting for our purposes are studies that implicate particular aspects of social or emotional experiences in health or illness. Events and experiences perceived as threats appear to be particularly likely to promote illness.[26] Two related themes stand out: lack of order or coherence, and lack of control or power. At the same time, lack of control or power seems also to be related to the individual's ability to face the perceived threat, for example by developing immunity to prevent the disease or by overcoming the disease after contracting it.

Order, Coherence, and Illness

One component of stress-producing events and experiences is change. The life-events studies described above generally assumed that any change was stress-producing and potentially deleterious to health. Other studies, however, have shown that only certain aspects or kinds of change are particularly stress-producing. Although these researches are not conclusive, they do point to some strong hypotheses.

Undesirable change is more stressful, all other things being equal, than desirable change. For example, getting a much coveted promotion is less stressful than being unexpectedly fired. Ambiguous change appears to be more stressful than unambiguous change. Workers living under the shadow of gradual layoffs and a possible plant closing would, for example, experience considerable stress, at least until the fate of their jobs was clarified one way or the other. Foreseeable change (allowing anticipatory socialization) is less stressful than unforeseeable change. Having one's children go off to college, for instance, is less stressful than having them run away from home. And controllable events are less stressful than uncontrollable events. For example, the pressure and threat created by driving the daily commute to work is less stressful than experiencing an air raid, the timing, severity, or mere fact of which is completely out of one's control.[27]

One theorist in this field hypothesizes that one particularly harmful psychosocial characteristic of modern society is information input overload.[28] Accordingly, a social environment that proffers a surfeit of gratifying, arousing, attractive stimuli—both material and symbolic— bombards the individual with information (implying many options) with which he or she must cope. Furthermore, the important value-related information and options are, in affluent societies, characteristically ambiguous, conflicting, and continually changing. Translated into sociological terms, this means that disease-producing stress is particularly related to problems of social order.

Perhaps the most useful formulation for bridging the findings of behavioral medicine and sociological interpretations of health and illness is the concept of coherence, as proposed by Aaron Antonovsky.[29] With a sense of coherence, the individual has a general feeling of confidence that "one's internal and external environments are predictable" and that life is reasonably under control. Three components of this sense of coherence are identified: comprehensibility, manageability, and meaningfulness. *Comprehensibility* refers to a sense of order; it means that individuals can make sense of their worlds, experiencing everyday stimuli as structured and clear, not chaotic, accidental, and unpredictable. The *manageability* component refers mainly to the sense of competence, control, or power to meet the demands of the situation. And *meaningfulness* goes beyond the aspect of order to include commitment and emotional engagement— a sense of purpose.

Antonovsky suggests that individuals gain a sense of coherence through lifetime experiences, such as making decisions or confronting tasks. While firmly rejecting a conception that puts the responsibility of health or illness solely on the individual, he proposes that a sense of coherence is health-producing, regardless of how sick or well the person may otherwise be.[30] The three components of a sense of coherence, therefore, serve well to link the issue of order with the aspect of control and power.

Control and Power

A number of studies have pointed to the individual's sense of power or lack of it as a factor in health or illness. As Antonovsky suggests, a person's sense of power affects whether he or she feels enabled to cope in a given situation. Two qualities of a sense of powerlessness have been linked with illness and poor recovery from illness: helplessness and hopelessness. Corollary attitudes—mastery, agency, and efficacy, as well as positive expectation of healing and will to fight—appear to be connected with health and successful recovery. Studies corroborating these findings are not conclusive, but they do seem to all point to the importance of a sense of power and control in maintaining health and recovering from illness.

One social source of stress is continual (but not necessarily traumatic) role strain, especially that occurring in important identity-confirming areas of life, such as work or marriage and the family.[31] These strains diminish crucial aspects of the self—mastery and self-esteem—and thus make the individual especially vulnerable to stress and its negative effects.

In both retrospective and prospective studies, helplessness and hopelessness were identified as precursors to the onset of symptoms.[32] In a remarkably high percentage of cases studied, these researchers found that, before developing any sign of disease, persons who were later hospitalized had experienced an actual, threatened, or symbolic loss of some highly valued form of gratification (often in a relationship), with concomitant feelings of either helplessness or hopelessness. They suggest that these two feelings often produce a giving-up process, making the person especially vulnerable to both physical and psychological illnesses.

Other authors have linked the experience of loss of control with stress-related illness and death.[33] Thus, it is the sense of hopelessness in the face of loss or threat—not the life event itself—that produces illness. One interesting line of questioning tries to link perceived lack of personal power or control with objective, structural bases for lack of power and control.[34] Feeling helpless or hopeless could affect anyone, but might those persons who lack social resources for power and control (e.g., women, poor persons, persons of lower occupational status) be more likely to experience hopelessness or helplessness?

An increasingly refined understanding of emotions contributes to the importance of control in health and healing. Popular conceptions of stress, often combined with psychologistic notions of emotional repression, sometimes treat emotional control as if it were in itself a source of illness. Some therapeutic notions condemn "holding in" unpleasant or undesirable feelings; they suggest that merely expressing these feelings is therapeutic.

Several studies of emotions, however, have argued that emotions do not overwhelm people against their will. Rather, emotion is self-regulated. Thus, an individual can build up a desired emotional response or subdue an unwanted response. A person's emotional state is not determined by a stimulus (e.g., a hug), but rather is mediated by an appraisal of that stimulus. For example, does the hug represent an unwanted advance by the boss, or is it a friendly sign of affection and encouragement by a friend? Accordingly, "emotion work" (i.e., the effort that goes into self-regulation) is not the same as inhibiting or repressing emotion. It means controlling the *experience* of emotion.[35]

The element of control is a significant one for many respondents; controlling the quality of one's emotional experiences was a positive goal of several groups studied. Interestingly, when respondents talked about "control," they often simultaneously talked about "release," or "letting go." This dual emphasis suggests that self-regulation of emotions was not geared toward rigid suppression of the emotions themselves but toward a different experience and expression of those emotions. The groups did, however, vary in the kinds of emotional experiences they encouraged. Self-regulation of emotion is not necessarily health-producing. Some authors suggest that a considerable physical and emotional toll is taken by the emotional constraints imposed by conditions in the work world and other social interactions.[36] For example, companies that expect employees to continually manage their emotions to present a "happy, friendly" image to customers may be indirectly contributing to health problems.

At the same time, theories about emotion work suggest that people could learn to manage their emotions—if the social situation allowed—for their own benefit. It appears that some of the groups studied promoted this kind of emotion work, through rituals, social settings, interpersonal norms, and so on. Whether an individual would be able to use these norms and techniques in other settings is essentially a political question, relevant to the issues raised in Chapter Ten.

The obverses of helplessness and hopelessness appear to be important factors in favorable medical outcomes: Recovery appears to occur faster and more frequently for patients who feel able to fight their illness, who are active in their treatment, and maintain strong self-esteem and sense of efficacy and competence in the face of their illness.[37] Rogers argues that the medical profession should reexamine the standard procedures for treating patients, especially in hospital settings, where institutional and professional priorities may unintentionally rob patients of their sense of control and agency. The usual model of active doctor treating passive patient may be medically damaging.[38] And hospital routines that diminish a patient's control (e.g., over time, space, or decision making) and self-esteem (e.g., loss of privacy, inability to look one's best, or being treated with little respect) may, thus, actually harm the patient.

Specific social interactions may, by contrast, serve to empower people, increasing their sense of self-esteem and coherence. A number of studies have documented the importance of "social support" in preventing or recovering from illness.[39] The positive aspect is not due merely to the existence of a social network (which may, in some cases, be more detrimental than helpful). More important is whether the person perceives him- or herself to be supported, loved, and valued by significant others. It is possible that social support functions not only to reduce the impact of stress but perhaps more importantly to empower and strengthen the individual in the face of stressful situations, including illness itself.

The biophysical effectiveness of placebos and nocebos (pharmaceutically inactive substances which, nevertheless, produce positive or negative effects in the person using them) is also related to empowerment. Placebos may be one form of symbolic power; Chapter Nine includes further discussion of the placebo effect.

The twin issue of power and control also figures into the relative ability of individuals to manage various difficult life situations—that is, to cope. Some individuals appear far better able to effectively manage the strains of everyday life. In addition, coping styles make a difference in how a person faces the stresses of illness itself. Coping in this instance refers to the things people do to avoid being harmed by life strains.[40]

Different degrees of success in coping vary from one individual to another depending upon the person's social and psychological resources, as well as on the specific coping responses the individual employs. Psychological resources center upon self-esteem and mastery—that is, the power/control factors described previously. Social resources generally include the aforementioned social and material support of networks of family and friends.

Specific coping responses include ways of modifying the situation (such as by altering the source of strain), attempts to redefine the situation (such as by interpreting something as a positive rather than negative event), and ways of managing stress rather than being overwhelmed by it (such as learning how to relax or to physically work out pent-up strain). Although all coping responses are part of the individual's overall ability to manage life, some strategies are more successful or healthful than others. For example, a relaxing vacation at the beach may be a good way to cope with existing stress, but an employed single parent of young children may not have the financial or time resources to use this strategy successfully. Similarly, coping responses such as drug abuse, fatalistic acceptance of adversity, or withdrawal from all sources of strain may be successful but unhealthy.

The concept of "coping" is useful in understanding how social and psychological factors relate to people's experience of stress. It is closely connected with Antonovsky's broader concept of coherence. At the same time, "coping" implies a reactive rather than active stance toward life. Our data suggest that the world views held by adherents of alternative healing were not merely reactive responses to problematic aspects of life, although they did also imply ways of coping with those problems. Rather, these adherents used their beliefs and practices as an active and comprehensive perspective from which to understand the non-problematic as well as the problematic, the positive aspects of life as well as the negative, and health as well as illness.

Furthermore, as noted in preceding chapters, people were not attracted to alternative healing approaches in response to specific illnesses.

Typically, they were first attracted to the larger world view and then, as problems arose, they applied the group's healing beliefs and practices. Thus, coping, as a reaction, was only a part of their broader stance toward life.

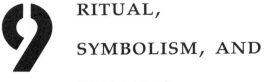

RITUAL,

SYMBOLISM, AND

HEALING

One feature of these healing groups stood out, especially when data were compared across all the types of healing: the extensive use of ritual and symbolism. In everyday parlance, ritual connotes repetition of empty, meaningless forms, but this is far from the experience of those who participated in the healing groups studied. For most respondents, ritual was highly meaningful; ritual actions were typically genuine expressions of important group experiences and meanings, central parts of the healing process in virtually every group studied.

Three aspects of ritual are examined in this chapter: use of language; use of nonverbal concrete symbolic objects; and symbolism in imagery and visualizations. *Ritual language,* in this context, consists of speech events and words that are themselves believed to have special efficacy—that is, power separate from and in addition to their meaning. This belief in the power of ritual language may be central to understanding one of the ways healing is accomplished, and not merely an incidental common feature of these particular alternative healing movements.

Nonverbal symbolic forms include concrete representative objects and mental images of symbolic objects. Like words, symbolic objects can embody or represent power—in this case, the power to heal. A key characteristic of symbols is their multivocality—that is, their capacity to represent many different meanings, indeed many different levels of meaning, at the same time. Thus ritual symbols, verbal or nonverbal, can link the order of one sphere of reality with that of other spheres.[1]

Another key characteristic of symbols is their capacity to link subjective experience (including, at the same time, cognition, emotion, and sensual perception) with a culturally available (i.e., objective) scheme of shared meanings.[2] Throughout this volume we have emphasized the meanings of health, illness, and healing. The individual does not relate to these meanings only in terms of cognition; rather, meanings are subjectively engaged cognitively, emotionally, and by way of the senses.

This chapter examines the thesis that one of the key factors in healing is the mobilization of resources of power—typically by enhancing the individual's sense of personal empowerment from either external or internal sources. Ritual use of language and symbols is a primary element in alternative healing, because symbolism both represents and objectifies power. Symbols significant to these groups shed light on their operative cosmologies—especially their images of power.

Another key factor in healing illness is the ability of language to produce a sense of order, for example by naming the illness and its causes. Likewise, some of the ritual symbols used in alternative healing produce a sense of order and transformation. These two themes of power and order are critical for interpreting the ritual use of language and other symbolism in healing.

Beliefs about Language Use

Virtually every group studied held beliefs about the extraordinary power of some words. In many groups, ritual language was a central part of the belief system.

Christian Groups

The ritual use of words is best exemplified by the traditional faith healer's command, "Heal!" Another example is the ritual use of the name "Jesus" both to heal and to exorcise demons. Exorcism is widely practiced in many groups studied, although it is hardly as spectacular as the media portray it; casting out evil spirits is an integral part of much ordinary Christian healing. For example, one respondent said, "And I just stopped at the sink and immediately went into prayer and I took authority *in Christ's name* over this. And I said, 'I know you've healed me and I will not allow for this to happen *in your name.*' And the spasms stopped [emphasis added]."

Accordingly, words not only cast out evil but also protect one from evil influences. One woman explained, "If he [Satan] sees you're a soldier of Christ, he's going to put something in your way, and you've got to recognize it and say 'I cover this with the precious blood of Jesus Christ. Be gone. Get thee behind me'—anything. But dispel it." Another adherent included in morning prayers some words and a visual image of the Scripture enveloping him like a protective cloak.

Among many pentecostal groups, glossolalic prayer (prayer in tongues) is thought to be more effective in bringing about healing than prayer in the vernacular. One event, observed in several neo-pentecostal groups, illustrates well the image of the objective power of words. Members of the congregation had brought in salt, oil, and bottled water to be blessed for use in healing rituals at home. Just before the leader pronounced the blessing, members hurried to open the containers so the words of blessing could get inside. Similarly, one respondent described the healing power of words of Scripture; she attributed the healing of arthritis in her hands to having spent several days copying Scripture verses as gifts to friends.

In addition to these beliefs about ritual words generally, many Christian respondents emphasized the double-referent of "the Word." This traditional Christian notion dates back at least to the reference of John the Evangelist to Jesus Christ as "the Word" made flesh. "The Word" is also often used to refer to the sacred Scriptures, "The Word of God," which for most Christian groups studied was endowed with a collective power beyond that of the meaning of individual passages.

Without delving too deeply into complex theologies of "the Word," we can appreciate the extent to which Christians might build beliefs and practices using the concept of "Word" literally and metaphorically. One of the most graphic examples is the idea of the "Word of God" as food. One man emphasized, "It's the Word that heals us. The Word of God, as we absorb, as we take it in, as the Spirit makes that Word real to us. It's the Word, the Word, the Word. You gotta eat the Word. You eat that Word like you eat bread for your body, because the Word is the healing of the soul. He sent His Word and healed. It's the Word, the Word, the Word that heals."

Metaphysical Groups

Words have traditionally had great prominence in metaphysical groups, because of their mentalistic conception of health and healing. Instead of praying for healing by supplication, these groups more typically affirm the healing as having happened: "I am whole; I am free of pain." The verbal formulation "I am . . ." is believed to be particularly potent in realizing the condition stated. For example, if one desires to become prosperous, one should regularly say, "I am becoming prosperous." The affirmation is believed to help produce the reality.

Similarly, however, if one has bad habits of thinking and speaking about one's condition, one can bring on undesirable states, too. For example, one man described a chronic neck and shoulder pain that often kept him awake at night. After meditation and study, he realized he had brought his painful condition upon himself by his careless use of the phrase, "That gives me a pain in the neck." Thus, whether used intentionally or not, words and thoughts are believed to have real power to produce the condition they evoke. Indeed, leaders often reiterated that "thoughts are things." Control of one's thoughts is metaphysical "work."

Eastern Meditation and Human Potential Groups

Eastern forms of meditation are often partially stripped of their spiritual qualities in their Americanized versions, but many of the groups studied retain a number of ritual practices. *Mantras* are a form of ritual language believed to be powerful by many of these groups. In Transcendental Meditation, for example, the literal meaning of the mantra is downplayed, but its secret quality and its power for the individual for whom it is personally chosen are emphasized. By contrast, Jain meditation groups utilize numerous mantras, each believed to have special power for certain situations, certain parts of the body, or certain social or emotional needs. Adherents choose which mantras to use, but they believe that specific mantras are related to tapping specific energies.

Since the mantras used were borrowed from Hindu religiosity, however, to many adherents they were nonsense syllables (e.g., "so-hum," "vi-rum," "aim"). In one group, a young man asked the leaders if it mattered on what words one meditated; he wondered if it would make any difference if he meditated on a nonsense syllable that he found pleasurable. Unanimously, the leaders warned him that there is danger in meditating on unknown sounds, since they might have had a negative significance in some language—perhaps an unknown or dead language—and therefore raise negative energies. They advised it is better to stay with tried-and-true mantras that thousands of years have shown to be linked with positive energies.

Psychic and Occult Groups

These groups borrow many of their beliefs from Christian, metaphysical, and Eastern groups, as well as from the Western occult tradition, science and pseudoscience, myth and history. For example, one group taught that certain words or sounds vibrate on positive energies, producing the power to heal; others vibrate with negative energies and can destroy one's aura, weaken the soul flame, cause illness and even death. Rock music, according to this group, is the epitome of sounds that vibrate on dangerous, negative energies. This group also teaches that the English language has an especially high level (positive) vibration compared with other languages. Indeed, the angels speak English. The main healing ritual in this group is "decreeing"—extensive rapid chanting in English, often using the "I am" formulation, borrowed from metaphysical groups. Decrees are believed to purify the body and transmute disease. Unless those negative energies that produce disease are transmuted, any relief from it is temporary—treating the symptoms rather than the cause.

Intent and Effectiveness

Groups' beliefs about the independent power of ritual language varied. Does the effectiveness of words depend upon the intent of the speaker? Does it require an appropriate attitude on the part of healer or person seeking healing?

Christian Groups

These healing groups generally emphasized the necessity of correct intentions. Indeed, they often attributed therapeutic failure to the lack of appropriate faith of the healer, person seeking healing, or prayer community. Some groups felt healing required the faith of the person seeking healing; others believed that the faith of the person(s) praying was critical and that healing could be accomplished without the cooperation or even knowledge of the person prayed for. Nevertheless, most groups emphasized that the result was ultimately a matter of God's will and timing. Prayers without the correct intent were considered worthless, because God judged the intent of those praying.

Metaphysical Groups

By contrast, metaphysical groups considered unintentional words and thoughts to be powerful. For example, one respondent recommended: "So, when you say 'I'm sick and tired' you're actually praying to *be* sick and tired." Nevertheless, these groups prescribed appropriate attitudes and enormous care to one's intentions as the daily path to health. The idea that someone could be healed without his or her cooperation was foreign to their thought; the individual must do metaphysical "work" to accomplish a healing.

Much of this work involves learning habits of thinking and speaking that affirm desired states, such as health, prosperity, positive social relationships, and so on. For example, one respondent explained, "The Bible says our words shall not go void. They shall not come back to us void. Whatever we send out will come back. If you speak words of lack and limitation in your life, then you're going to have lack and limitation." Accordingly, use of mental or verbal affirmative formulations produce the reality they describe.

Eastern Meditation and Human Potential Groups

According to groups of this type, changes in the individual's inner state bring about a healing. Thus, intention and the attitude of the person being healed were very important. Nevertheless, most groups studied also had some variant of a conception of energies that could be tapped accidentally or without the appropriate attitude. Like the metaphysical groups, these groups emphasized the necessity for the individual to gain mastery or control over his or her inner self—however defined.

Psychic and Occult Groups

Like the metaphysical groups, these respondents believed that power resides in words, regardless of the intent of speakers. Many of these groups conceived of healing power as a remote force, amenable to influence by persons who know the appropriate ritual words and acts. Others saw healing as an inner process; their use of ritual language was similar to that of metaphysical groups. For example, the leader of one occult group described an event:

> I said, "Maybe we should do some decrees for _____," because we believe in the power of the spoken word. The Bible says "decree a thing and it shall be." So we sat down and we did some healing decrees, the words of which actually ask for healing and in one of them, you actually call the person's name and ask Mother Mary, Cyclopea, Raphael of the healing angels, to heal this person. I also did some forgiveness decrees. . . . [She added later,] Now with the science of the spoken word, if you add to that [visualization] with decree, it will happen that much faster. Because not only are you holding the image, but you are commanding that it be made whole.

In these and numerous similar instances of ritual language, healing is linked with images of power: the power to cause illness, the power to overcome or counteract negative or evil powers, the mediation of power from sources outside oneself, or the enhancement of one's existing personal power.[3] All of the groups studied hold cosmologies depicting agencies responsive to human communication.[4] Some of the communication resembles talk (e.g., prayer). Other communication takes the form of visualization or meditation, in which abstract energy is believed to be relating to other energy.

The nature of this communication varied according to the groups' cosmological images of power. One image is that of a transcendent power, external to the individual. Accordingly, individuals need to communicate with that power to gain its influence on their lives. The external power may be conceived of as remote or personal. For example, one occult group envisioned a vast remote agency, overseeing beings of various vibration-frequencies on numerous galaxies, but receptive to human energy emanations expressed in the correct formulaic statements.

By contrast, some groups held cosmologies that located all needed power within the individual. Typically, they considered individual power an expression of some greater power, but individuals need not look outside themselves for the source of all the empowerment they need. Accordingly, if they are weak, it is because they are not in touch with their own power. Communication, in this model, is with one's higher self.

Nonverbal Symbols

Some adherents of alternative healing also used concrete objects as symbols of healing power. According to their belief, these objects were vehicles for the transmission of healing power. Some adherents believed that, through some objects, healing power could be sent over distance or time. For example, a piece of cotton could be ritually "filled" or "soaked" with healing power and carried elsewhere to where healing was needed. Similarly, healing power "stored" in blessed oil or salt could be saved for future healing uses.

Christian Groups

Especially in the Roman and Eastern rites of Catholicism, many Christians have traditionally held that ritual objects could serve to transmit God's power (e.g., blessed oil used in anointing the sick). Other objects have served to symbolize important items of faith or reverence: candles, incense, pictures, and pictograms (such as the image of a large eye inside a triangle). While typically less ritually complex, most Protestant traditions also held important symbols, such as the open Bible, empty cross, or use of water in baptisms.

The groups studied were using traditional Christian symbolism, although occasionally borrowing from Christian traditions other than their own. What distinguishes them from mainstream Catholics or Protestants is their intensive everyday use of such symbols and their belief that the symbolic objects were, in themselves, effective—not merely representations.

Metaphysical Groups

Metaphysical groups deemphasized use of concrete symbolism. Their understanding of healing was almost totally mentalistic, so they tended to concentrate on the use of words and imagery. Physical objects were sometimes recommended as an aid to visualization, for people who had difficulty producing imagery unaided.

Eastern Meditation and Human Potential Groups

Meditation groups also generally deemphasized the use of concrete symbols, preferring imaginary symbolic action or visualization. A few adherents did borrow some Eastern symbolic forms, such as the mandala, but most did not find Eastern symbols especially powerful or evocative. What few concrete symbols prevailed among these adherents were drawn mainly from Western traditions, or were idiosyncratic, but compatible with Eastern forms. For example, many respondents described powerful nature symbols. One woman used a tree she could see from her window; several used the sun and/or moon; candles and other light sources served as symbols for some; and color—typically identified with some nature symbol (such as the blueness of clear water)—was also symbolic.

One unique aspect of several of these groups was their extensive use of the human body—indeed, the concrete body of each member—as a symbol. These adherents believed that action—literal or symbolic—upon a person's body simultaneously produced comparable responses in the person's emotional, social, and spiritual life. For example, if a person's body became more flexible, it would produce flexibility in the person's emotional, social, and spiritual life, too. Thus, adherents' bodies, postures, gestures, shape, space, and so on, typically held symbolic significance.

Psychic and Occult Groups

Adherents of these groups used concrete objects as symbols extensively. Crystals, metals, cloths, shapes, numbers, colors, and nature symbols figured prominently in the healing rituals they used. For example, a member of one psychic healing circle described a typical ritual purification:

> [She had described people's problems with "bad energy" that needed balancing or clearing.] We usually do it with our group. . . . You use salt as a cleansing tool; use pure water or water that has been purified, as a cleansing tool. . . . You go through a little ritual whereby, with candles as well—because then you have fire and water and earth (which is salt) and air with the flaming candles. And so you have these, and you do just a little ritual. You first light the candles, try to draw the energy to you. Then what you do is you stick it in the water; any bad energy, you stick it in the water. And then [the leader] will take the water outside and throw it away. Just get rid of it. See, if it will conduct, if we conduct anything negative into that water, then you can get it out of the premises. That has worked in at least three healings I have been part of.

The use of colors, often in combination with crystals, was by far the most common symbolic healing action. Sometimes in group settings members passed around a variety of crystals, each with different imputed healing properties. Or individual members might wear, hold, or display crystals for healing. Amethyst and clear quartz were frequently preferred, combining the color symbolism of purple and white (or crystal-clear), which were supposed to be especially good for general healing purposes, with the energy properties of the rock itself.

Like ritual words, ritual symbolic objects were treated differently by various groups. Some groups regarded the object as powerful in itself, no matter what the user's attitude or belief. For example, some psychic adherents chose presents (such as blue bedsheets, a crystal pendant, or a record with certain types of sounds and rhythms) for nonbeliever friends in hopes that the symbolic qualities would affect the recipients even without their knowledge. Other groups held that the symbols were only powerful insofar as they evoked a special meaning for a given individual; each person should choose his or her own symbols.

Symbolic Action in Imagery and Visualization

Far more important than concrete symbols in most groups studied were imagery and visualization in the healing process. Psychotherapy has long recognized the value of examining the imagery the "patient" deals with, for example in dreams; some therapists also utilize the creation of new images or visualizations in the healing process. Yet few people in dominant medical practice consider imagery and visualization useful in treating or preventing physical illnesses. Some researchers, however, have been experimenting with this approach in the treatment of cancer, chronic pain, and an array of previously recognized psychosomatic ailments.[5]

It is helpful to distinguish between received images, such as in dreams and visions, and created images, such as in guided visualizations or deliberate imagination. Generally, received images were reported mostly in Christian and psychic/occult groups, reflecting these groups' general notion of a transcendent—rather than immanent—healing power. "Created" images were important in all types of group studied.

While frequently used in combination with meditation techniques, active visualization is a separate healing activity involving the creation of a healthy body and mind, a healthful environment, or a healing experience—in the imagination. Many groups studied had extensively elaborated some form of this active use of imagery.

Christian Groups

It was generally neo-pentecostals who used imagery or visualization. The more traditional pentecostal groups, by contrast, were distrustful of imagination, because they believed imagination opened the mind to be a "devil's workshop." In Catholic and some Protestant charismatic groups, one prevalent healing ritual was the "healing of memories."[6] The "healing of memories" consists of the visualization of a past situation that evokes problems that need healing, such as an unhappy relationship, bitterness, envy, anxiety, and so on. One woman, for example, described being healed gradually of her resentment toward her long-dead father. She had felt that he favored her brother and ignored her attempts to please him. This resentment was considered one root of her present physical problems, and her prayer group believed the healing of memories was a necessary step to the physical healing. Through a series of guided visualizations led by the group's prayer ministry, this woman had reexperienced many painful past experiences with her father and brother. The transformation was wrought, however, by the additional image of

Jesus walking through these experiences with her, enabling her to break down the barriers between herself and her family and forgiving her authoritatively for her bitterness.

Metaphysical Groups

Traditional metaphysical groups mildly resembled occult and psychic groups in their use of imagery, their Christian-based terminology notwithstanding. Unlike the psychic/occult groups, however, their focus was totally mentalistic. Long before the popularity of many contemporary meditation movements, groups such as Unity and Religious Science were advocating meditation as a way of clearing the mind. The purpose of meditation in these groups is solely to remove the obstructions of negative thinking and to free the mind to do the positive thinking and speaking that produce health and other benefits.

More active visualization typically involved trying to imagine the product of one's verbal affirmation. For example, while saying or thinking, "My knee is becoming flexible and free of pain," the believer might also imagine himself kicking up his heels at a square dance. The image of healing white light, also used in many other types of groups, was interpreted as the "Christ light" by many of these adherents. One group leader described a personal experience with severe arthritic pain:

> The white light represents the Christ. The Christ light is always envisioned as white. . . . I tried to visualize it and hold it as long as I could. I just tried to visualize the white light, the Christ light surrounding me, just particularly the shoulder area and everything. I did this about forty-five minutes and all of a sudden I didn't have the pain anymore. I knew that it was okay. There was such a warm feeling in the area where I had visualized it, and I got up and was able to move the arm and lift it.

Eastern Meditation and Human Potential Groups

Most of these groups used visualizations for ritual purifications, creating a harmonious environment, and affirming their unity with other people and with the universe. For example, one woman described, "The earth

. . . there is an energy field in the earth; it's the rhythm of the earth, and is involved in the whole rhythm of the universe. By tuning in and just listening to the peaceful sounds of the rain or summer breeze, to bringing myself more to the connection, that rhythm and harmony." Sound/ rhythm images (e.g., rain, wind, leaves rustling, waves breaking, soft bird calls), sensation images (e.g., warmth of sun, refreshing mist, soft fur or feathers, wind, roughness of tree bark), and visual images (especially colors and lights) were all frequently evoked in guided visualizations or described from personal visualizations.

Many members described "space" meditations as among their favorites. In these visualizations, the individual would imagine a special retreat—usually a room or a cozy nook in a garden or forest. Through creative imagery, the person then "furnished" the retreat, choosing items to fill the special space, and imagining in detail their color, texture, smell, and so on. For example, one woman always filled her imaginary hideaway with seasonal flowers but occasionally chose not to have books in the "room," because sometimes books were relaxing but at other times they reminded her of unfinished work.

Each time the meditator returned to the retreat, it could be rearranged, according to the needs of the moment. Another woman explained that her "room" usually was a bright yellow-gold, because that was such a cheery color, but at the moment the "room" was blue, because she needed soothing and relaxation. While these special imaginary spaces were highly symbolic and clearly part of believers' prevention and healing of illness, they were not typically images of action. Most visualizations used in Christian, meditation, and psychic/occult groups involved imagining action or interaction, which produced change.

In groups where body-work, such as yoga or massage, was important, often members were encouraged to imagine their own bodies in the desired state, posture, or shape. Similarly, whenever a person wanted to change a relationship, imagining the desired situation before action was considered an active part of creating the change. In several yoga groups, members practicing cleansing breathing exercises were encouraged to imagine a crystal-clear ball floating the length of their spine and out the top of their head, emptying them of impurities and freeing their energies.

Some action-visualization used by Eastern and some other meditation groups is a form of purification ritual. One guided meditation involved imagining oneself comfortably submerged, with purifying water washing over the entire body, simultaneously relaxing the body and mind, while floating away undesirable emotions or qualities. Another visualization involved wrapping up the illness, pain, or unwanted emotional quality, almost as a gift parcel, and then floating it away in a beautiful bowl on the swift current of a cascading stream. In contrast to Christian groups, whose purification imagery often included warfare with Satan, Eastern and meditation groups typically used peaceful and visually attractive images to ritually rid themselves of impurities.

Psychic and Occult Groups

Characteristically, the use of visualization and imagery among adherents of psychic and occult healing was more diverse than within other types of group. Generally, their meditations and visualizations tended to be active; they explained their approach as a mental channeling of energy or vibrations. More so than in other groups, these adherents believed this mental activity involved the literal manipulation of cosmic energies or forces. One member of an occult healing group explained:

> I believe that there is a transference of love energy. I really do. And a vibra-
> tion. I think it's just as real as TV or radio waves, which are invisible, too. . . .
> We live in an ocean of energy that is around us. When we heal, all we're
> doing is sending energy as a channel.
>
> [Describing her approach to healing, she said she first went "into
> alpha"—i.e., a creative meditative state.] Visualize in pictures, especially if
> you know that there's a particular ailment, such as arthritis. You see the bones
> deformed and calcium deposits. Be as imaginative and as creative as you
> want, visualizing a brush and scraping the deposits off. See the fingers
> straightened out, maybe actually think of the fingers straightened out and
> healed. See the bone marrow being supplied as needed and calcium being
> properly distributed through the body. In other words, see the pictures.
> Whatever makes it a very strong visualization mentally for you is the most
> effective.

Visualization and imagery were prominent in the healing rituals of all these groups. While these practices are hardly new or unique, their appeal in contemporary society is interesting. Especially important is the extent to which these uses of imagery are creative, individualized, and active.

Ritual Language and Power

The centrality of ritual language in the healing process sheds light on some of the ways alternative healing systems work for their adherents. Three specific features of ritual language use will be analyzed: language as an objectification of power; the transformative functions of ritual language; and the performative aspects of ritual language use in the healing process.

Language as Objectification

Power is a fundamental (if not *the* fundamental) category for interpreting healing. As previous chapters have shown, each type of healing group has distinct beliefs about the loci of the power to heal (or to cause illness), as well as different ideas about ways to channel or control that power. Etiologies of illness yield information about the group's ideas of illness-causing power, and therapies embody ideas about how that illness-causing power can be overcome by other sources/kinds of power. From this perspective, the treatment of illness is essentially the restoration of the balance of power—by weakening the antagonist's (disease-causing) power or by strengthening the victim's power.[7]

As preceding examples have shown, many alternative healing systems hold that healing power can be transmitted through ritual language or objects. Two properties of language make it especially potent as an embodiment of power. First, language is a vehicle of communication. In everyday use, words carry thoughts, feelings, or images from one person to another. These healing groups, however, believe that ritual language and ritual objects are vehicles for energy or power. They are ways by which a source of healing energy (either a transcendent source of power or the "natural" power of the healer) can transmit power to ill persons who need it to strengthen themselves.

Second, language is linked with awe-inspiring power through its seeming autonomy as an objectification of human reality.[8] Language is both external to the individual (i.e., an imposed given in his or her social and cultural environment) and internal (once acquired in socialization, it moves individuals while being used by and generated by them). Words are artificial constructs with no necessary basis in external reality.[9] Once adopted by a people, however, a language is perceived as a taken-for-granted object with coercive power.[10] Tambiah states, "Since words exist and are in a sense agents in themselves which establish connexions and relations between both man and man, and man and the world, and are capable of 'acting' upon them, they are one of the most realistic representations we have of the concept of force which is either not directly observable or is a metaphysical notion which we find necessary to use."[11]

The mysterious quality of words may be even further promoted by practices such as secrecy (for example, the belief that one's mantra is uniquely one's own and not to be revealed to anyone) or by unintelligibility (for example, the ritual use of foreign, esoteric, or glossolalic utterances).[12] Thus, when respondents described experiencing power in these contexts—whether they describe it as their own power or some external power—it is probably an accurate perception of feeling stronger and is likely to be influential in the healing process. The experience of personal empowerment may, indeed, effect the healing of illness (the social-emotional-spiritual component) and the curing of disease (the biophysical component)—although the documentation of this latter aspect is outside the expertise of a sociological researcher. (Chapter Eight describes some of the studies pointing to this connection.)

Some researchers link the placebo effect with symbolic empowerment.[13] While a chemically inert pill is not real medicine, the sense of power the individual gains by that symbol is real. The placebo effect may be merely one way of describing an individual's response to his or her society's peculiar symbolization of empowerment—be it an amulet, ritual word, or pill. Medication, especially pills, is a major contemporary symbolization of the power to heal and of the power of modern medical technology.[14] This symbolic empowerment may have concrete physical and psychological effects. Indeed, symbols of power—such as chemically inert pills—may also produce negative physical effects or sickness; this parallel phenomenon has been called the "nocebo."[15]

Believing oneself to be in touch with a great power may literally empower the individual believer to be more effective in daily life. The successful treatment of many illnesses is related to the patient's hope or expectation of getting well. Yet much of this hope is born of the person's belief in the power of the healing agent or agents; if one feels personally powerless, there is hope in allying oneself with the powerful. One respondent said, "It is not enough to hope in hope itself; we have the power of the Lord to count on." Hope engendered by belief in a strong transcendent power may be, for many, more successful than hope in purely human powers.[16] For others, hope and expectation may be enhanced by their special gnosis, knowledge, or technique.

Although the groups studied varied widely in their images of healing power and its transmission to the person needing healing, all encouraged the empowerment of the individual by rituals of the transmission of power. Symbols of power were especially significant in that sense of personal empowerment.

The Transformative Function of Words

Another feature of ritual language that is effective in the healing process is its ability to represent, at one level of meaning, realities from other levels of meaning. Specifically, ritual words' metaphoric and metonymic operations enable them to work at multiple levels in people's lives. Metaphorical usages of ritual words place them as surrogates, having reference both to the original object and to some additional symbolic object. For example, Catholic pentecostals utilized much body symbolism to refer to the social body of the prayer group or family. They used body images, especially the symbolism of healing the body, to represent the cohesion of the prayer group and the incorporation of individual members into the group. Metaphors, such as references to the "head" as proper authority, had meaning at multiple levels. Thus, it was considered a "healing" if the "head" of a family (i.e., proper authority = husband/ father) were brought into proper alignment with the "body" (i.e., the rest of the "members") of the family. These healing rituals are partially explained by theories of health and illness that identify sickness as the eruption of conflict and divisiveness of the social system; the condition of the sick person is only symbolically an individual expression of the problems of the group.[17] Thus, the individual's healing is the symbolic healing of the larger social body. This interpretation is especially salient for Christian and the more sectarian occult groups, where the healing group itself is a focus of commitment.

The uses of metaphor in healing were particularly important for groups that interpreted the "symptoms" as symbolic. As noted in Chapters Three through Seven, several groups attributed symbolic significance to aspects of the illness experience. In some groups, part of the healing process was the determination of what larger meaning these "symptoms" held. For example, adherents said:

> My hearing problem was telling me God had something to say to me, and I needed to listen.

> If you're a hateful person and that hate is eating you up inside, you'd manifest a disease called cancer.

> With my eye problem, there was something that I didn't want to see. I couldn't get well until I opened my eyes to that something.

> When you're clogged up—like with constipation or congestion—you're clogged up in terms of expressing yourself. Some area of your life is not flowing smoothly.

Such metaphorical conceptions of illness are not peculiar to alternative healing groups in this society. Our language is full of vivid expressions implying similar metaphorical usage. For example, at the time of this study, one acquaintance, who had no connection with any alternative healing groups, underwent extremely serious and painful abdominal surgery. Hallucinating in the aftermath of pain and medication, he tried to rid himself of the political corruption he felt stored in his "guts."

Symptoms are, thus, not only (or not necessarily) referents of biophysical realities; they are often culturally understood "idioms of distress."[18] As such, they are readily linked with metaphors of healing.

Another important function of healing metaphors is personal and social boundary maintenance. The social concerns of the group are reflected in their sense of pollution—"matter out of place."[19] Several of the groups studied perceived the world as a place of grave disorder. The illness etiologies they used reflected two sources of pollution: external and internal.

External pollution is from the chaos of the world. In some groups, this chaos was attributed to human causes; in other groups, a dualistic theory of evil forces explained the disorder. In these latter groups, ritual practices protected the groups' boundaries from attacks by these forces. For example, an occult group recited "decrees" at every meeting to protect itself from negative forces; many of the Christian groups practiced exorcism. Through healing rituals, the individual participates in the mythic battle of dualistic forces, allying with Good to fight the powers of Evil.

Internal pollution refers to disorder within the social group—"the system at war with itself."[20] This problem is seen as the result of human imperfection—interpreted as sin in some groups, as underdeveloped consciousness in others. In many groups, conflicts among members were dealt with by healing rituals. Several Christian groups addressed these concerns through purification rituals, such as confession and "inner healing." Most Eastern meditation and psychic/occult groups had important beliefs and practices about pollution and purification. Respondents from virtually every type of group described symbolic purging and purification.

Ritual language evokes these dual meanings. Guided meditations in several groups explicity used metaphors of healing. For example, in one group, members were instructed to envision a triangle of fire in the region of their stomach. After hearing an elaborate description of the qualities of this fire, they were told to see themselves throwing into the fire some personal problem of which they wanted to be free: a fear, worry, anger, bad habit, or other negative quality. Again, embellishing the image of the fire consuming the unwanted quality, the leader told meditators to see the fire grow hotter with this fuel and turn into an intense light—the light of love—a pure white circle of light floating to the heart chakra and radiating love to all.

In this and numerous similar recorded visualization practices, language is used metaphorically to refer both to the body and to other features of hearers' lives—their emotions, their social relations, and their spiritual states. Thus, when believers say to themselves in a healing ritual, "I see myself, wrapped in pure white light, becoming pure and whole," these words evoke multiple meanings: a literal image of white light, a symbolic light cleansing and energizing, an image of purity and wholeness in one's body, social relations, mental state, and spiritual life.

Not only was language about the body used metaphorically but also, in several groups, the body itself was ritually touched, positioned, manipulated, moved, or changed to produce transformations in other areas of believers' lives. Thus, for example, the yoga group practicing their "tree" pose believed that, by putting their bodies in positions of flexibility, balance, and stability, they metaphorically also produced qualities of flexibility, balance, and stability in their social and emotional lives. Action upon the body is a metaphor subjectively experienced even more directly than that mediated by words and other symbols.[21]

The transformative aspect of ritual language is not merely at the cognitive level; it also affects believers' perceptions and feelings. Symbolic actions have the capacity to transform actors' perceptions of the situation and, concomitantly, their emotional connection to that situation.[22] Part of the transformative potential of ritual action is the opening of a sense of possibilities (e.g., "miracle") not otherwise recognized in the situation; the very acknowledgment of alternate possibilities is, thus, a preliminary to change. Ritual language and symbolic action have the capacity to transform the referents to body and person to symbolize other levels simultaneously.

Performative Aspects of Ritual Language

Members of the groups studied typically believed that ritual language had real power—that it could affect the world of everyday life. There has been a tendency for scholars to treat such beliefs and practices as magical compulsion, coping strategies, or otherwise nonpragmatic behavior. For example, Beattie suggests that ritual representation of actions (such as healing) is make-believe control of natural forces: "There exists no adequate body of empirical knowledge which might enable men to cope with these hazards, or even to hope to cope with them, by means of practical scientifically proven or probable techniques. So they must cope with them symbolically and expressively instead."[23]

Although much ritual behavior appears to be explained by this interpretation, considerable counterevidence exists in contemporary societies, where scientifically provable techniques are used alongside alternative, ritual ones. In "modern" societies, it is assumed that "real" medical control exists, obviating the need for magical control. Most respondents in this study used *both* medical and nonmedical means to heal their ills. Some respondents distinguished certain kinds of conditions for which they would seek medical assistance. For example, several persons who suffered severe arthritis thought the surgery enabling them to walk again was wonderful, but they distrusted medical doctors' prescriptions of extensive painkillers for routine management of daily arthritic pain. Instead, they were trying various meditation methods, prayer, yoga, massage, and other nonmedical methods of pain management. Ritual language figured prominently in these respondents' healings.

While the extent of medical efficacy in contemporary Western societies is impressive, in many important areas of people's experience, medical treatment is weak or useless. Respondents who said "The doctor could not find out what was wrong with me," "Doctors could do nothing for me," or "I felt I just wasn't being helped in the hospital," were expressing their own subjective feelings of helplessness in the face of something troubling them. They may have also been objectively describing the powerlessness of Western medicine to deal with the range of healings people seem to require. In contrast with the turn of the century, medical problems today are predominantly chronic illnesses that can be medically treated and sometimes ameliorated, but not cured. Chronic conditions often entail massive rearrangement of the patient's everyday life to cope with the disease and potential crisis or further debilitation—often for many years.

Similarly, a very high percentage of persons seeking primary medical care come with nonspecific complaints, for which no clinical basis can be found. Western medicine has little conceptual capacity to deal with nonspecific complaints, and practitioners are tempted to dismiss patients with these problems as neurotic or mentally disturbed.[24] Thus, when respondents complained of the inability of medical professionals to help them, they were partially correct in assessing the dominant medical system's powerlessness in certain areas.[25] Ritual action need not be seen merely as make-believe control. The ritual assertion of order may, indeed, produce a sense of order and predictability.

Ritual language among the groups studied may be viewed as "performative utterances"; that is, saying certain words is actually an action.[26] Some studies of indigenous healing practices have discovered the performative aspects of ritual language, for example in Navaho prayer acts,[27] African rituals,[28] Sinhalese healing ceremonies, and Thai healing cults.[29] These studies suggest that the very saying of ritual words plays an important part in accomplishing the goals of the ritual utterance: in this case, healing. Ritual language among the healing groups studied may perform similar functions.

The distinction made earlier between "curing disease" and "healing illness" may be helpful in showing how ritual language is performative. Specifically, the data suggest that alternative forms of healing seek to restore a sense of order—of meaning—for both the individual seeking the healing and for the larger group. Most of the groups studied exhibited a serious concern for order, either in external or internal life. Threats of disorder—resulting from rapid social change, personal or group crises, and the like—are often integrated into the group's distinctive sense of order through healing. The very act of reinterpreting the sources of disorder in terms of the group's beliefs is part of "healing." For example, one woman described her enormous relief in discovering that her previously unexplained fears were from external evil forces. The ritual by which her troubles were named (and thus made orderly and manageable) was experienced as real healing. Restoring order and predictability enhances members' sense of being in control.

Especially threatening are experiences of disorder that cannot be readily managed by reinterpretation in terms of the group's belief system. Healing ritual serves as an important part of the group's plausibility structure. For example, the son of members of one psychic/occult group studied was paralyzed in an accident. Regular group healing sessions included his case for many months before his interview. Although the young man frankly admitted that he perceived little physical change since these efforts began, he and his family claimed a healing had already occurred in the sense of tremendous social support from the group, increased family cohesion, and greatly improved coping with the condition. The entire group had articulated an understanding of "why" something so drastic and debilitating should have happened; healing rituals reiterated meaning for the situation.

Reintegration of the experience of disorder into the group's meaning system serves to confirm these beliefs for both the individual and the group. Chaos is transformed into order.[30] Merely naming the problem is one important ordering function of the healing process, reducing anxiety and fear.[31]

Several pentecostal groups, for example, had a process of "discernment" by which the root cause of illness was identified with the help of the Holy Spirit. Similarly, much metaphysical "work" consists of focusing the mind to discover the negative mental habit that allowed the illness to occur. Although much effort went into this identification, members of metaphysical groups typically avoided mentioning the name of their malady or envisioning its possible negative consequences, because they believed that such acknowledgment of illness would make it real and give it power. For example, one respondent said, "A doctor who tells you 'You have arthritis' is hurting you"—by giving that condition a reality in words.[32]

The link between identifying something and the course of action implied is crucial for the individual's sense of being able to change the unpleasant situation (i.e., hope), because it gives the individual a "handlehold" on the problem. Naming the problem may enhance the sick person's ability to mobilize personal resources against the illness.[33] Furthermore, the order asserted by the group's belief system does in fact structure the experience of illness and/or healing.[34]

Nonscientific medical systems "work" because they provide meaning and empirical proofs in support of their explanations. The quality of such proofs is that the sickness episode is consistent with the expectations of the participants.[35] There is a sense of reassurance in knowing what to expect to experience—such as feeling pain when one is supposed to feel pain.[36] Therapy consists of not only the various means for healing illness but also the means by which the illness is named and given cultural form.[37]

The assertion of order is closely linked with power and empowerment. The analysis of shamanism in other cultures suggests important parallels to some forms of alternative healing in this culture.[38] The shaman's role in healing is to mediate power in order to restore balance and harmony. Disorder is dangerous; the shaman must have the power to counterbalance disorder. The shaman is seen as mediating power from a superhuman source to the social system. The basis for the shaman's power is the ability to distinguish key structural symbols and move them into a proper relationship; that is, to create order.[39] This manipulation produces power. Thus, the *power to establish order* is at the root of a healing process.

The shaman's effectiveness is linked with the art of particularizing these symbols for each sick person, so the person values the symbols and attaches emotion to them.[40] Thus, the manipulation of symbols goes beyond the cognitive aspect of the believers' cosmology to the emotional aspects of the experience. The person being healed participates emotionally in the symbolic changes being wrought by the healer. Rather than view contemporary use of ritual words and symbolic objects or images as regression to superstitious practice, it may be more fruitful to examine the appeal to middle-class suburbanites of these ritual forms, in contrast to church-oriented or medicine-oriented practices. Ritual words and objects are not empty or pretend. Rather, they are the *embodiment of power* in believers' experience. Tambiah relates this to charisma, which can be embodied or vested in institutions.[41] An amulet, such as an amethyst healing crystal or blessed healing oil, is like portable charisma.

Groups whose cosmologies locate healing power in a transcendent source allow many ways for that power to be channeled to the individual needing it. The use of ritual words and objects allows believers to tap healing power throughout their daily lives, even when they are distant from the group of fellow believers or in the midst of other activities. While portable charisma may be very useful in other kinds of societies, it seems especially appropriate to modern societies in which individuals typically leave their fellow believers to venture into the worlds of work and political and social interaction with nonbelievers.

This interpretation highlights the potential for ritual words to accomplish the goal of healing: reordering. Healing rituals are directed to healing illness, not merely to curing disease. Illness as a social, psychological, and spiritual entity is indeed amenable to symbolic effects. Therefore, the utterance of ritual words may actually contribute to effecting the healing goal.

Features of Symbolic Healing Action

While in many ways parallel with symbolic healing action in other cultures, some features of symbolic healing actions taken in these suburban middle-class alternative healing groups are interestingly distinctive. One such feature is the emphasis upon endogenous healing.[42] Whereas studies of most nonmedical healing in other cultures and subcultures have found primarily therapies that were mediated by a healer, most of these healing groups emphasized the extent to which the individual being healed was responsible for bringing about or at least participating in his or her own healing.

The degree of emphasis upon endogenous healing processes varied according to the groups' images of the locus of healing power (and, importantly, their beliefs about the disease-causing powers). Thus, Christian and psychic or occult groups—with their images of a transcendent healing power—were more likely to have both self-healing and healing mediated by others (healer or healing group). Eastern/meditation and metaphysical groups tended to address endogenous healing processes almost exclusively.

As shown in Chapter Seven, the very notion of a "healer" is dramatically different in most of these groups: it is only occasionally a specialized role. Rather, healing tends to be a function *all* members theoretically can do. While especially effective healer-members might have somewhat greater prestige or influence in most of these groups, rarely was their role a major source of reward. Very few of the groups studied expected payment for healing per se.

Another distinctive feature is the relatively individualistic and idiosyncratic quality of much (but certainly not all) symbolism and symbolic action used in the groups studied. The extensive use of creative imagery in their healing rituals represents a highly individualistic approach. Rather than an entire group gathered to celebrate its unity and focusing upon central symbols, these groups often gathered to encourage individuals to create and explore their separate symbols and world images.

The individualistic use of symbolism is also connected with the groups' images of healing power. Those groups conceiving of healing power as coming from an external transcendent source envision words, nonverbal symbols, and images as communicative vehicles for channeling that power to where it is needed. By contrast, groups with an image of healing power as being immanent, needing only to be tapped from within themselves, consider words and images to be ways of getting in touch with their own healing powers; these latter groups typically do not use concrete objects as nonverbal symbols, but focus mainly on words and imagery.

This creative and eclectic use of symbolism is consistent with the cultic individualism and type of commitment characteristic of most groups studied.[43] In general, three of the types of healing group studied (Eastern meditation/human potential, metaphysical, and psychic/occult) tended to be highly individualistic. Characteristically, they did not claim to have *the* truth, and were tolerant of other groups' claims. Indeed, many members drew their personal beliefs and practices from several different groups they had attended simultaneously or serially. Cultic individualism means that no clear locus of authority exists beyond the individual member, and there is thus no way to handle "heresy" and therefore not even any clear boundaries between members and non-members.[44]

These qualities of healing rituals in a modern society may be connected with the images of the self held in this society and the idealized images of the self promoted by the different types of healing group. Healing rituals in all types of groups studied tended to be more individual-oriented than comparable rituals elsewhere documented in the anthropological literature. Indeed, the very rhetorics of healing in modern Western societies emphasize individual choice and transformation.[45] The image of the self is that of a flexible entity that can be shaped and re-shaped, almost perpetually, in the healing process. According to the modern Western image, the self can be "realized," "fulfilled," "brain-washed," "born-again," "understood" through insight therapy, and so on, through a theoretically endless set of transformations and redefinitions of self.

The main point of divergence between Christian healing groups and most of the other groups studied is on the relative importance of the self. Healing, in the Christian tradition, emphasizes the self in "proper" (i.e., subordinate) relationship to a transcendent deity. The renewed emphasis on healing in Christian groups may, indeed, be a ritual response to contemporary urges to "free" the self from constraints of roles, norms, and other "hang-ups." Therapy/healing thus realigns the individual with the group-prescribed ways of thinking, feeling, and believing. In contrast, many of the other alternative modes of healing emphasize a flexible self with a different conception of individual role, responsibility and moral accountability.[46] Accordingly, therapy/healing frees the self and the body from many learned constraints, opening new possibilities and potentials for choice and continued "growth."

One hypothesis worth exploring is that much of the "new" therapy offered in many alternative healing groups may represent an attempt at the symbolic creation and socialization of a new kind of identity—a new mode of self-in-relation-to-the-world. The resulting mode of individualism may be one in which the self would have the flexibility to move between constantly changing roles and attachments, able to choose the quality of its emotional and physical experiences.[47] This interpretation is developed further in Chapter Ten.

Summary

The extensive use of ritual language and nonverbal symbolism is not merely incidental to these healing movements among middle-class, well-educated, fully acculturated, middle-aged suburbanites. Rather, it is a key feature in the particular processes of healing employed. Indeed, the production of a sense of order and control together with a sense of personal empowerment may indeed be both physically and emotionally healing. Ritual language and both concrete and imagined symbols are significant aspects of how these groups produce a sense of order, control, and personal empowerment for their participants.

This discussion further raises the possibility that the emphasis upon creative, individualistic ritual uses of language and nonverbal symbolism may represent an approach to healing that differs in important ways from healing in traditional cultures. For some groups in the present study, healing may reaffirm and reinforce traditional group values and beliefs; in other groups studied, however, the healing rituals may embody an alternative, nontraditional conception of the individual role, responsibility, and moral accountability. This latter use of healing ritual may represent an attempt to symbolically create and socialize a new kind of identity, emphasizing a flexible and relatively autonomous self. In Chapter Ten, this hypothesis is linked with the larger social structural location of middle-class ritual healing.

10 INDIVIDUALISMS AND TRANSFORMATIONS OF THE SELF

By emphasizing the self, we come to examine the very human issue of suffering, as well as the more objective conditions of socioeconomic and power relationships within which middle-class modes of alternative healing are located. This chapter examines the importance of alternative healing for the self—each individual's entire social person.

First, disease, illness, curing, and healing affect the self profoundly. Alternative healing approaches run counter to most biomedical practice, not merely in their emphasis upon holism, but also by addressing healing the self. Secondly, various forms of healing involve different kinds of relationships between self and society; alternative forms of healing imply alternative self-to-society connections. Middle-class forms of alternative healing may represent a statement against the rationalization of body and emotions in contemporary society. This chapter examines the social structural location of such rituals of transformation.

The Self and Suffering

We need to appreciate the importance of the subjective, human experience of suffering and its link with the self. How do we understand suffering, distress, pain, or troubles? If we begin with what "afflicts" the individual, what problems are experienced as serious enough to warrant attention or even outside help, we have a far broader picture than if we focus merely upon discrete biophysical conditions that are (potentially, at least) clinically discernible. If we understand the nature of suffering, we can better comprehend the profound impact of bodily and emotional experience upon people's very selves. And we stay grounded in the essentially human aspects of health, illness and healing.

Practically speaking, being unwell means becoming disabled, in the broad sense of being not able to do things one wants or needs to do; it implies reduced agency. It means loss of some control—an especially disvalued and stigmatizing quality in this society. It implies losing one's routines—patterns by which people order their daily existence and often identify with their selves.[1]

Suffering is not linked with disease or pain in any precise causal or commensurate fashion. The pain of childbirth, for example, may be more severe than the pain of arthritis, but it typically causes less suffering, because it is perceived as temporary and associated with a desired outcome. A disease may be incurable but cause little suffering if it does little to damage the person's sense of self and ability to engage in every-day life. Very probably, most people seek help and healing not so much for disease per se, but for suffering and affliction.

The subjective experience of suffering is real. Using a biomedical model, it is too easy to deny the reality of such affliction and to invalidate the very experiences that compelled the sufferer to seek help in the first place. Indeed, certain aspects of the biomedical approach are likely to exacerbate suffering.

This problem is shown in the introspective reflections of one physician who suffered a serious leg injury. He describes the systematic deper-sonalization he experienced in becoming a patient-inmate of the hospital. The admitting physician insisted he limit the "history" of his injury to "salient facts"—particulars relevant only to the physical injury itself. He kept trying to describe a larger story—a highly meaningful set of experi-ences of near death, fear, and being "saved at the last moment." Rational medicine had no time and no place for the patient's need for meaning or order or even recognition as a person (rather than as a case of torn tendon).[2]

This physician's account further illustrates the intimate link between a person's body and sense of self. Reflecting upon his injury, he exclaimed, "What seemed, at first, to be no more than a local peripheral breakage and breakdown now showed itself in a different, and quite terrible, light—as a breakdown of memory, of thinking, of will—*not just a lesion in my muscle, but a lesion in me*."[3] In his experience, not only did the medical system refuse to acknowledge the real sources of his suffering, but indeed the standard medical treatment (as competent as it was) made his suffering worse.

Another physician and critic argues that the medical system has difficulty dealing with suffering, because "suffering is experienced by persons, not merely by bodies, and has its source in challenges that threaten the intactness of the person as a complex social and psychological entity."[4] He suggests that medical personnel cause suffering when they do not validate the patient's pain and when they fail to acknowledge or deal with the patient's personal meanings of illness. Both of these medical responses can assault the personhood of the sick individual. The modern medical system's inattention to suffering can be understood as part of the rationalization process.

Failing to recognize the whole personal context of an illness, medical personnel often do not comprehend the depth of suffering a person can experience, even when he or she is "cured" and free of physical pain. Cassell reminds us that "people suffer from what they have lost of themselves in relation to the world of objects, events, and relationships."[5] For example, one woman still suffered greatly from a hysterectomy she had undergone six years earlier. She explained, "It meant losing a huge part of my future." Unmarried, childless, and only twenty-nine years old when the operation was performed, she lost hopes and dreams for the future. She expressed enormous anger at the insensitivity of the physicians and hospital staff who had treated her "like an ungrateful child, crying over spilt milk." The medical personnel, even if thoroughly well-intentioned, probably felt their only duty was in the correct treatment of the specific uterine problem; the woman's suffering was not their problem or relevant to their tasks.

Whether induced by a physical problem or not, suffering generally results from a threat to the coherence[6] of one's lifeworld. People suffer from the loss of connectedness[7]—links with loved ones, valued social roles, groups with which they identify. Meaning and order in life are threatened, undermining the person's ability to act or to plan.

In contrast to the biomedical model, alternative healing approaches do address the problem of suffering, albeit with varying degrees of success. Alternative healing takes place, generally, through a process in which the ill person's suffering is located in a larger, usually transcendent order. No neat distinctions are made among physical, emotional, social, or spiritual "troubles." Then, the person's condition is transformed symbolically, often through ritual words and actions. This transformation involves reestablishing order or meaning for the disordered situation "causing" suffering.

It also involves symbolically empowering the ill person. These and other healing actions mobilize the person's self-healing processes. The kinds of transformation and growth promoted by many of these groups can create resilience, empowering suffering persons to tap resources within or around themselves. When successful, healing often creates the sense of becoming enlarged—not reduced—by the illness experience.

Respondents spoke of experiences of renewal, new directions, renewed close ties with loved ones, fresh visions or hopes for the future, purification, and insight. Resolution or amelioration of suffering came from understanding its larger meaning, taking control in the face of their problems, gaining insight into how they could change their selves accordingly, experiencing the support of others who empathized with their situation, and perceiving how their lives and suffering were linked with something larger, interpreted variously as God, cosmic energy, universal Mind, and so on.[8]

Self and Society: The Healing Connection

Beyond the interpretation of this evidence is the macro-sociological significance of alternative healing as a social development. What are the larger cultural and social structural contexts of specifically middle-class forms of nonmedical healing?

Some of the widespread interest within modern Western societies in nonmedical forms of healing may be related to a new mode of individualism—that is, the nexus between the individual and society. What, then, is the shape of this new mode of individual-in-relation-to-the-world? Indeed, might there be several new modes? What, too, are some of the links between social class and status factors and this phenomenon? Do the impact and significance of this development go beyond the private sphere?

The evidence reported in this volume suggests that ritual healing among comfortably middle-class, educated members of a modern industrial society is, indeed, closely related to strains and changes in the nature of individual-to-society relationship. Comparable data are needed for a longer period of time and in a variety of geographic areas. We need more information about the actual conditions of people's social and economic lives, including job satisfaction, actual degree of control over conditions of everyday work, and degree of commitment to work or career. A larger sample would permit socioeconomic differentiation to explore why certain forms of healing may appeal to some segments of the middle class more than to others. And we need far more information about the relevant beliefs of the general middle-class populace—both those who are and are not involved in alternative forms of healing.

Our findings do, nevertheless, point strongly to certain cultural and social structural aspects of middle-class alternative healing. Beyond the diversity of the many groups and individual respondents studied, two common features stand out.

First, all were propounding an *alternative world image*. This different picture of the world is reflected in their ideas about the ideals or values defined as "health," causes of illness, sources of healing power, individual responsibility, and the nature of the self and of self-transcendence. These world images were emphatically holistic—beyond the sense of body-mind holism, to an insistence upon the interdependence of all aspects of the cosmos.[9]

In their ideal of holism, many healing groups challenged world images that hold selves to be utterly separate, alien from each other, their social worlds, and the entire cosmos. One minister, who used many different forms of healing, expressed this interdependence vividly: "It's only literally in the level of the epidermis that we can say that we're really absolutely separate. I more and more believe that people's lives are profoundly interconnected." Although adherents' language for expressing the aspect of holism was often not "religious" in any traditional sense, virtually all groups emphasized a spiritual component to this holism.

Second, in all of the groups studied, healing rituals were prominent and typically pervaded by symbols of power and order. What is especially interesting is that, in many groups, members engaged in these rituals collectively, but simultaneously sought privately experienced self-transformation and self-validation.[10] For these alternative healing groups, "health" is an idealization of a kind of self, and "healing" is part of the process by which growth toward that ideal is achieved.

World Images and Individualisms

Weber examined belief systems to understand how ideas shape individual actors' perceptions of their social world, especially during historical points of breakthrough—times when major social structural changes are developing. He considered how these world images shaped the motivation for individual action and the relationship of the individual to the larger society. Weber explained the importance of such "world images":

> Not ideas, but material and ideal interests, directly govern men's conduct. Yet very frequently the "world images" that have been created by "ideas" have, like switchmen, determined the tracks along which action has been pushed by the dynamic of interest. "From what" and "for what" one wished to be redeemed and, let us not forget, "could be" redeemed, depended upon one's image of the world.[11]

Legitimation of the Self

In particular, in his analysis of certain sects, Weber focused on the link between their world image and the creation of a particular kind of individual-to-society connection.[12] Accordingly, this world image produced the motivation conducive to the development of early capitalism. Salvation in that model meant the production of legitimate, "worthy" individuals; the world image created a need for self-legitimation (as opposed to being saved as part of a group). The sects' this-worldly focus meant that self-worth had to be demonstrated in everyday socioeconomic action, thereby contributing to the motivation to achieve in the immediate socio-economic context.[13]

These sects' affinity with economic and political developments in the secular sphere was a significant part of their influence for social change. Are there, perhaps, parallel "affinities" between the world images of alternative healing movements and developments in their adherents' economic and political conditions? There may be, for example, certain conditions of middle-class existence that help account for the attraction to such movements. Do aspects of middle-class groups, such as level and type of education, communication skills, or mobility, make them especially effective "carriers" of these world images? What are the implications of these healing groups' world images and their definition and creation of legitimate, "worthy" individuals?

A parallel theme for interpreting holistic world images is legitimation in a rationalized societal system. Robertson[14] relates the individual-to-society issue to the notion of a contemporary "legitimation crisis," as adumbrated by Habermas. According to this thesis, internal contradictions in the highly rationalized social system have led to a particularly precarious situation of disjunction between the legitimation needs of the system and the motivation and modes of participation on the part of individuals. For example, the functional needs of a business corporation or a hospital, as organizations, may be radically disconnected from their employees' or patients' individual needs or motivations to participate in the system.

Habermas is pessimistic about the prospect of a societal organization that involves such great cleavage between individuals' corporate roles and their inner selves. He asks whether this might portend the "end of the individual."[15] Other observers are less pessimistic.

Moral Order and Responsibility

Ideas about ethics and moral responsibility are a significant part of any world image. Salvation, however conceived, involves the production of legitimate, worthy persons, according to norms specified in the ultimate beliefs of the group. One of the most dramatic ways alternative healing systems differ among themselves and from the dominant medical system is in how they impute moral responsibility and concomitant notions of control and power.

The dominant medical system in this society is highly rationalized, and questions of moral evaluation are neutralized (or hidden or denied) in most discussions of health and illness.[16] For example, physicians generally would not address patients' questions about the meaning or ultimate causes of a serious illness. Biomedicine represents that diseases are morally neutral categories to be rationally diagnosed and treated in a value-free professional context.

The larger culture operates primarily with remnants of two older styles of ethical evaluation. One style is an authoritative biblical morality, evaluated by the norms of orthodoxy and obedience; the other is utilitarian individualism, evaluated by norms of efficient maximization of self-interest.[17]

In most of the healing groups we studied, the moral concerns pertaining to salvation are expressed in the idiom of health and illness: What must I do to be healed ("saved")? Where does healing ("salvific") power come from and how is it channeled to me? What does it require to be truly healthy ("righteous")? While some Christian and Jewish healing groups affirm traditional "biblical" answers to these essentially moral questions, many other groups have either greatly modified Western traditional answers, borrowed Eastern approaches, or developed dramatically different moral responses.

Some observers have suggested that alternative healing movements contribute to the societal trend toward medicalizing moral issues (for example, by defining deviance such as alcoholism, promiscuity, child abuse and gambling as "sickness" to be treated by the medical system).[18] We found, however, that although the groups we studied used metaphors of illness and healing to refer to a wide range of human concerns, they spiritualized rather than medicalized these issues. They delegitimated the dominance of the medical profession in dealing with such issues.[19] Both medical and alternative approaches use idioms of health, illness, and healing, but their implications are different, even opposing. When the medical profession represents that certain problems of everyday living are "illness," it implies that those problems should be submitted to medical professional treatment and control. By contrast, when alternative healing groups consider such problems of living to be illness, they imply an adamantly nonmedical response.

Possibly these other interpretations were based upon the model of "holistic" practitioners, many of whom are medical professionals or paraprofessionals who use the appellation "holistic" to refer to their broader approach. Most of the groups we studied, however, were vehement that the key issues underlying illness were not in the province of medical knowledge and treatment.

The "spiritualization" of moral concerns in illness is exemplified in these groups' notions of the sources of illness and individual responsibility for it. Most Christian healing groups studied considered personal sin a major source of illness, although they differed widely as to how much emphasis they placed upon individual responsibility, as opposed to general sin or diabolical influences. Likewise, Unity and similar meta-physical groups attributed most misfortune, including illness, to the individual's incorrect ways of thinking and speaking, evidence of the person's lack of connection with Truth or Divine Mind.

Eastern and human potential groups were least likely to hold the individual responsible for the causes of illness, and they were more likely than others to emphasize social and individual lifestyle factors, as well as spiritual means, in protecting oneself from illness. Psychic and related occult healing groups were typically the strongest in their emphasis upon individual responsibility for illness and other troubles. Illnesses, accidents, handicaps—even birth defects and homicide—were considered, at least in part, the victim's spiritual responsibility. Indeed, many respondents from these groups asserted that there are no real victims; no one is truly the helpless pawn of adversity. For this reason, while these groups offered ill members much support, warmth, and help, they gave little or no ordinary sympathy.

The corollary of this notion of responsibility for illness is belief in the individual's control. The more responsibility for a problem that one assumes, the more one is asserting control over that problem area. One woman explained:

> Self-awareness and taking responsibility go together hand-in-hand. If I walk around unaware, then I feel like bad things just "happen" to me. I'm a victim! The more I understand myself and my situation, then the more control I have in my life. I realize that I have choices—like I chose not to accept a promotion if it meant sixteen hour days, . . . or like choosing to be an adult and not a little girl to my mother for the first time in thirty-seven years. . . . And I can choose my responses to situations and to other people. Like, I don't have to get caught up in stress or in anger or whatever.
>
> . . . But there's no single right choice that's for everybody all the time. A lot of paths are good paths. Like, I'm a vegetarian these last few years, but that doesn't mean you aren't making the right choice for you if you aren't vegetarian. And maybe ten years from now, [being] vegetarian won't be what I need then. My responsibility is to choose which paths are best for me for now. . . . We keep growing by using that responsibility for ourselves.

One characteristic, then, of these alternative healing groups is that they promote an active adaptation on the part of believers, not merely adjusting to the fact of suffering or limitation, but actively changing one's life.

Being "responsible" does not typically produce victim-blaming, because it is linked with rituals of empowerment.[20]

Some critics have attacked the notion of responsibility for illness on the grounds that it creates a sense of guilt and undeserved blame.[21] Others suggest that it deflects from the sociopolitical and environmental sources of responsibility by emphasizing the responsibility of the individual who becomes sick.[22]

To some degree, this criticism does apply to some alternative healing. By locating health and illness as part of a comprehensive moral order, many of the groups studied intentionally or inadvertently promoted the notion that one was personally culpable for failure to achieve a desired state defined as health. As in the larger culture, many adherents applied negative moral tags to being overweight or addicted to cigarettes, diet pills, or alcohol. Lack of control implied a moral failing, and deliberate "abuse" of one's own or another's body was morally reprehensible.

At the same time, many respondents recognized and criticized the social sources of illness and illness-producing behavior (e.g., hazardous or stressful workplaces, advertising that promotes unhealthy behavior, industrial pollution, poverty). Their typical responses (with the notable exception of several Eastern meditation groups), however, were not political but individual: One should resist the impact of the advertising, refuse to accept stressful and dangerous work, move away from pollution, address social problems with spiritual means. Not only are these responses unlikely to change the social structures that promote illness; they are also responses generally unavailable to many persons lacking the economic resources of the comfortable middle class.

The Christian groups typically identified moral responsibility with sin, which carries not only connotations of blame and guilt but also the possibility of ritual resolution through confession and forgiveness. Many other groups were less direct in their consideration of blame for moral failure. The moral notion of responsibility is, however, an indication of the seriousness believers applied to their values of health and healing.

At the same time, however, many alternative healing groups were remarkable for their lack of judgment and blame of others' "failings." These groups were generally highly pluralistic in their notions of personal responsibility. For example, one man suggested his friend's weight "problem" was not what she "needed to be working on" at that time, even though it was ultimately her responsibility. Her "growth" in another area of her life was more important, so she should not be account-able for weight control until her personal "right time." Likewise, a group leader reminded members that no single approach was right for every-one. He noted that what worked very well for some people caused more harm than good for others. Since "health" was defined by virtually all groups as a gradual progressive development, individual episodes of illness lost some of their sting as "failure." Indeed, such illness was often interpreted as a sign of progress.

Tipton[23] has interpreted new religious and quasi-religious movements as varied attempts to resolve a postcountercultural moral ambiguity.[24] According to this interpretation, the 1960s counterculture was youth's romantic protest against older styles of moral evaluation prevalent in the culture. As protest, however, the counterculture per se was not a plausi-ble alternative basis for a new moral order. Tipton studied a neo-Christian youth group, an Eastern-style religious group, and est. He concluded that each of these groups appealed to their adherents because it offered an alternative moral order that, in different ways, ran counter to the dominant ethical style. Each incorporated some expressive elements of the counterculture, while retaining enough homology with the dom-inant culture to enable members to participate effectively in the larger society.

While this analysis is an insightful point of departure, it is limited. Most healing movements are not primarily youth-culture products, although some had considerable appeal to the 1960s counterculture youth. Our findings indicate that only a minuscule proportion of adher-ents were involved in the 1960s counterculture; most adherents were not of the same age cohort as the sixties youth. Several of these healing groups were active in the 1960s, and young people were a proportion-ately small part of the membership then.

Another and more serious limitation to the applicability of Tipton's interpretation is its overemphasis on cognitive or belief-system elements as explanatory factors. In addition to alternative world views, alternative healing movements propose new ways of experiencing, and extensive transformations of body and emotional life. If we take these aspects of their alternative ways seriously, we must consider the possibility of a larger significance to these movements.

The Limits of Rationalization

We would argue that modern societies are discovering, in different ways, the limits of rationalization. Two arenas point to these limits: first, the legitimation of the structural aspects of the system and, second, individual commitment to and sense of responsibility in that system. Thus, the countercultural rebellion of the 1960s was not the cause, nor even a significant catalyst, but only a partial expression of a larger social change of which these alternative healing groups also represent an important part. Alternative healing is an attempt to counter societal rationalization, as symbolized by the treatment of the body and the self.

The process of rationalization means applying the criteria of formal rationality to social organizations and patterns of social interaction. For example, in the work world, rationalization results in specialization of tasks, efficiency-accountability, and hierarchical structures of employee management. In the sphere of medicine, rationalization results in (among other things) a focus on treating the body rather than the person. Rationalized medicine assumes, as a matter of principle, that the body can be known and treated in isolation.[25] It also produces instrumental relationships between medical personnel and their patients, reliance upon clinical evidence and direct observation rather than patients' expression of their problems, and the narrow specialization and professionalization of medical practice and institutions. This same process resulted in the removal of concerns with meaning and moral order from the treatment of diseases; the problem of meaning is viewed as irrelevant to the medical treatment.

Rationalization of the Body and Emotions

It is not merely ideas about the relationship between the individual and society that are changing, but the very practices by which self is symbolized, shaped, and expressed. Thus, the significance of these movements is to be found in their various responses to the internal tensions in the system itself, in which the limits of rationalization of the body and emotional experience and the limits of rationalization in styles of moral evaluation and legitimation have been approached.

Our sense of "self" is intimately connected to our bodies and emotions. The link between transformations of self with bodily and emotional experiences is neither new nor peculiar to modern societies. What is characteristic of modern societies is the extent to which they try to apply formal rationalization to bodily and emotional experience and expression, concomitant with the internalization of the controls that enforce those rationalized modes.[26]

The "civilizing process" involves the gradual increase of control over bodily expression, as evidenced, for example, by table manners and norms of posture and gesture.[27] Emotional expression, too, is subject to increasing control: anger, mirth, or sorrow, for example, may be expressed only in approved, measured ways at appropriate times in acceptable settings. To be "civilized" implies distancing oneself from the animal nature of one's own body, such as by controlling farts and burps. Such controls are not merely external; through socialization, the individual applies an almost taken-for-granted self control, supported by sanctions of embarrassment, shame, and guilt.[28]

Socially unacceptable expressions are segregated in the private sphere to separate spaces such as the bathroom, and in the public sphere to separate organizations such as hospitals. With the rise of large-scale institutions like factories, hospitals, and schools, further controls over "inmates'" time, range of motion, and use of space also develop as part of the institutional regimen. Other regimens, such as diets and exercise, are often idealized and made into virtues. This "civilizing process" is a necessary product of increasing rationalization in the economic sphere and the rise of complex modern states.[29]

There is considerable evidence, however, that there are limits to the rationalization of body and emotions. Alternative healing approaches may represent various responses to contradictions or tensions within these changing societal forms. In part, the limits may be due simply to the toll exacted by extreme forms of bodily and emotional control.[30] For example, how much tension is produced by the need to constantly live up to an appropriately professional corporate image: dressing for success, projecting precisely the right image to customers or commercial adversaries, no matter how one feels, always on guard lest one's body or emotional expression betray the desired image? Such control involves considerable tension, too, in its implicit but stark dichotomies between public self and private self, self and other, body and mind, physical being and emotional life.

At the same time, older forms of individualism, with their characteristic patterns of self-control, may not fit the experiences (including socio-economic conditions) of many persons in modern Western societies. For example, the persevering, nose-to-the-grindstone, solitary rugged individualist may be ill-suited to a social and economic setting that demands cooperation, communication, and creativity.

The varying conceptions of health, illness, and healing among the healing groups studied suggest that their beliefs and practices are different responses to these tensions. Their rituals produce and maintain very different modes of individualism.

Traditional Norms and Selves

Several healing groups reaffirm, in new ways, traditional moral norms, roles, and social patterns. Obvious examples include the charismatic groups within the Catholic and several mainline Protestant churches. Other (typically syncretic) movements, such as the Great White Brotherhood of Elizabeth Clare Prophet (a dualistic, conservative movement based largely upon the Western occult heritage), also reaffirm many older patterns of moral norms and individual-to-society relationship.

In such groups, illness is identified with sin, and healing is a ritual response of the individual and group to sin. Furthermore, sin itself is identified with contemporary urges to "free" the self from the constraints of social roles and norms, and from guilt from violating them. Healing is also aimed at restoring wholeness in the face of the fragmentation of everyday life in an institutionally differentiated world. Thus, such groups are not advocates of the status quo, trying to apply moralistic brakes against change. Rather, their healing practices express a profound dissatisfaction with the rationalized separation of the important parts of their lives: religion, family, work, education, leisure activities, community, and so on. The tendency of such movements to spawn intentional communities or religiously homogenous schools and workplaces is another manifestation of this counter-rationalization effort.

Christian healing groups, like other types, value "growth" and believe that healing produces it, but they define growth as becoming closer to God and his authoritatively prescribed ways. The healing process in these groups, thus, serves to realign the individual with group ways of thinking, feeling, and believing. It reaffirms culturally threatened moral norms for the entire group.

Alternative Norms and Selves

Healing groups that do not assert traditional norms and selves instead idealize a flexible self, with changing (often multiple) roles and norms. Rather than socializing members to fixed "right" and "wrong" images of self and moral expectations, there is an ideal of experimentation, "growth," and the expectation of continual change. The end of growth is, however, different from tradition-oriented groups. For these groups, "growth" means producing greater understanding of self and others, greater awareness of one's body and emotions, greater balance and harmony in one's relationship to inner self, to others, and with the cosmos.

With varying degrees of success, these groups pursue an ideal of a self that is able to be flexible and adaptable without being determined or overwhelmed by others. "Health" is linked with strong awareness of a core self that is able to choose relations and reactions. The ideal is also a self that experiences a powerful sense of connectedness with others, as well as with the natural environment (or, indeed, the entire cosmos).

Healing rituals, in these groups, serve to free the self from learned constraints and negative effects of guilt and to open new potentials for choice and change. Many of these rituals provide self-validating experiences, without narrowly specifying norms for evaluating self. They proffer energizing experiences, without expecting permanent commitment for the direction of that energy.[31] New religious and healing movements may be attempts at the symbolic creation and socialization of a new mode of self-in-relation-to-the-world. Both traditional Christian and other forms of ritual healing address patterns of identity.

Patterns of Identity in Socioeconomic Context

Successful forms of identity during industrialization were based on the internalization of authoritatively defined values. Such forms were appropriate to the rationalized economic sphere, partly because successful socialization into these forms produced anonymous, self-responsible individuals who could "fit" the bureaucracy.[32] Individuals internalized specific values, such as perserverance, dependability, consistency, integrity, and duty, that were suited to the rationalized economic sphere.[33]

Wexler links newer modes of individualism with what Gouldner[34] calls the "new class," characterized by its high levels of education, information technology, and occupations involving the manipulation of symbols (e.g., talking, writing, computing) and requiring competence in communication and interpersonal negotiation. The respondents in this study do, indeed, generally fit this description.

Whether this "new class" has any real potential for achieving significant power or autonomy is uncertain. Its situation does, however, highlight growing internal contradictions within modern socioeconomic systems. The bureaucratic organization of production frames interaction in concretely rationalized structures with rigid and limited social relations, predicated upon norms of efficient functioning. At the same time, however, increasing reliance upon "symbolic labor" and interpersonal interaction in the economy may mean that older structures of the workplace and related institutions simply will not work.[35] For example, "new class" workers may need greater autonomy, flexibility, unstructured time for communication of ideas, and social arrangements promoting interpersonal ties in which such communication is fostered. The rationalized structures of production may themselves be counterproductive.

This "new class" configuration may include several related status groups. Status distinctions are based upon style of life and relative esteem or prestige; status groups typically hold a common worldview.[36] For example, persons in technical professions (e.g., engineers) may be connected with different modes of self than persons in the helping professions. Indeed, the disproportionate representation of persons from numerous helping professions in the healing groups studied suggests just such a link.

Persons of different status groups would presumably experience affinity with different modes of individualism. Various social movements (such as the pro-life or pro-choice movements) may be expressions of outright conflict between status groups.[37] Evidence about these healing groups suggests a similar link. For example, women involved in groups affirming a traditional, authority-oriented type of self were almost exclusively those in traditional women's roles, predominantly housewives not employed outside the home. By contrast, professional women were clustered in groups promoting nontraditional modes of self.

A new mode of individual-to-society relationship may be highly appealing to "new class" groups. It may represent their genuine assertion against the formal rationalization of the socioeconomic sphere. A new form of individualism is not necessarily, however, a serious or effective challenge to the political-economic structures within which middle-class lives are situated.

The Social Impact of Alternative Healing Approaches

More evidence is needed before the impact of these middle-class healing movements can be evaluated. As carriers of a social ethos or world image, the members of such a "new class" may be well placed at this point in history to effect change. By definition, the "new class" is more educated and more articulate than others, including much of the propertied class. Often ideas and practices that have been present in previous historical periods become significant or potent in a period when they are linked with an ascendent or socially effective group.

Another serious question about the impact of alternative healing approaches is: Do they actually challenge the production sphere, for example by minimizing workers' motivation to sacrifice their health to success on the job? Or are they readily co-opted by the powers that be, for example by incorporating a meditation class into the workweek? Will adherents retain their emphasis on holism in the face of pressures to relegate their concerns to the private sphere? Will they apply their spiritual sense of connectedness to overcome, for example, the alienating pressures of the workplace? Will the sense of connection be experienced only in leisure time social lives and only with their fellow middle-class suburbanites?

Are these movements adaptations to or assertions against features of contemporary production and consumption? On the one hand, they often resemble items of consumption like other lifestyle factors; for example, considerable investment of time and money goes into classes on healing techniques, equipment, and special products for healthiness. At the same time, however, these groups emphasize that enhancing one's self and one's health is not a commodity; they liken health to other ideals and values, such as justice or learning.

Do the groups represent merely the further rationalization and regimentation of body and emotions through techniques of self-management?[38] Some critics suggest that some alternative healing movements are the contemporary version of Puritan inner-worldly asceticism, pressing their adherents to a life of self-denial and self-discipline, which fits neatly into the requisites of the economy.[39]

Or are these forms of alternative healing counterassertions against the extremes of such rationalization, especially in their emphasis on holism and self-transcendence? Much alternative healing promotes a qualitatively different perspective from that of the rationalized dominant culture. Many alternative healing approaches encourage a reflective and reflexive attitude toward oneself, one's body, and emotional and social life.[40] They affirm the right and power of the individual to choose the quality of experience of body and emotions, to choose how to achieve health and healing, to choose and assert identity. They also promote a holistic perspective, a strong sense of connectedness with one's body and with other persons.

If successful, such transformations of self could have far-reaching consequences for the sociocultural and politico-economic spheres in modern society. Institutions of the public sphere themselves may have to change to accommodate these individualisms.

APPENDIX A

METHODS

OF RESEARCH

To understand alternative systems of health and healing, it is necessary to understand adherents' framework of knowledge. What are their fundamental conceptions of health, illness, and healing? How do they make sense of their experiences? What do they define as needing healing, or as a successful healing? How are their healing beliefs and practices related to other meanings they apply to their everyday world and their very selves?

The specific methods employed in such research are important for achieving this level of understanding. This chapter presents some of our experiences and methodological choices made in the course of this research. How does one tap a phenomenon so broad, loosely defined, and—by definition—rather unorthodox? Who should be interviewed, what questions asked, in what style of interview interaction, in what location? For example, other studies chose to interview people about their alternative health practices while they were waiting for a doctor's appointment in a large clinic; not surprisingly, few respondents reported any use of non-medical healing. The quality and depth of our data depend, in large part upon the relative advantages and limitations of these methods, as well as our success in applying these methods.

There were three broad parts to our work: identifying as many as possible alternative healing groups/practitioners/settings in a given suburban area; extensive participant-observation in numerous representative groups settings; and intensive interviews of persons who have been involved with alternative healing.

This is an exploratory study; quantitative, hypothesis-testing research on such alternative belief systems must be preceded by adequate knowledge of the relevant categories of thought and meaning. Without an understanding of the internal meanings of alternative medical belief systems, quantitative studies can measure, at best, only the degree of congruence with the dominant belief system. Many such studies further distort the reality of alternative medical beliefs and practices by assuming the medical model. For example, the very use of the concept "compliance with medical regimen" implies an evaluative bias in favor of doctors' definitions of the situation.

The concept of a "healing belief system" or a "medical belief system" is somewhat complicated, in that many such systems of belief and practice are neither particularly coherent nor internally consistent. Some may, indeed, be highly eclectic and include a seemingly inconsistent assortment of views and values. For this reason, the working definition of "alternative healing belief system" used in this study is deliberately very broad. We began interviews by asking people about experiences in which they felt they "had been healed by any process other than medical treatment." Similarly, in locating groups for study, we investigated any group or practitioner claiming nonmedical healing to be a focus for them—however they defined "healing."

A broad definition also avoids the more general risk in exploratory research of "defining out" relevent items for study. Nevertheless, certain exclusions can be made. The focus of this research specifically excludes any practices that are not related to a larger system of healing beliefs and practices. For example, self-dosing with diet pills would probably not be included, whereas use of blessed salt and salad oil by neo-pentecostals would be included.

Similarly, groups for which health or healing are a purely accidental by-product of a practice would not be included. For example, if consumption of salt were forbidden as sinful, members' health benefits of salt-free diets would not be sufficient reason for including the group in this study. On the other hand, if abstinence from salt were part of the group's larger belief system about health, the group would be included. At the same time, different groups/healers emphasize the health aspect of their beliefs to varying degrees. For some the ideal of health is the single most important value in life; for others, it is the product of seeking some other, higher, value. This study includes several groups with varying levels of emphasis on health.

The research does not distinguish among groups/healers attempting the healing of physical, as compared to psychological, social, or spiritual ills. Professional specialization in the dominant medical system has resulted in these ills being defined as clearly different domains. Among the many alternative belief systems studied, however, no such neat distinction is made; indeed, many groups are adamant that any solution to a person's ills requires a holistic approach. Even groups that distinguish different types of illnesses to be healed use distinctions that are considerably different from those medical specialists would have made.

Groups Studied

The first phase of the research was aimed at identifying as many alternative healers/healing groups as possible in the catchment area. The catchment area was the middle-class, suburban portion of a populous northern New Jersey county. Initially, we expected to limit our study to towns only in this county, but it became increasingly evident that many persons travelled considerable distances to their various alternative healing groups. The final data, therefore, include additional healers/groups in contiguous counties that drew adherents from the original catchment area; they also include adherents who live outside the catchment area and travel to groups or healers there. The study does not, however, focus on groups/healers in nearby large cities. Numerous persons in this suburban area travel into these cities to seek alternative healing opportunities, which are far more numerous and diverse in the cities than in the suburban area itself.

Our initial assessment of the social class identification of the groups studied was based upon the socioeconomic characteristics of the towns in which the groups were centered. These towns comprised fourteen of the twenty-two municipalities in the county but accounted for about one-fourth of the population. They were also the least densely populated towns in the county. The per capita income (as of the 1980 census) in the communities ranged from $9,297 to $19,126. The county average per capita income was $7,538, compared to $12,188 average in these fourteen towns. The percentage of high school graduates was similarly above average: 80 percent in the catchment area, compared to 63 percent county-wide. The median age (thirty-seven) was considerably higher than the county average (thirty-one). The municipalities in the catchment area varied widely in the proportion of nonwhite residents (ranging from 0.3 percent to 45.6 percent); the overall county percentage of nonwhite residents is 46.2 percent. Taken together, though, these fourteen municipalities have about 91 percent white, 7 percent black, and about 2 percent other nonwhite residents.[1]

Subsequent participant-observation and interviewing of members confirmed the selection of these towns for the catchment area with information about income, education, occupation, neighborhood, dress, and other lifestyle factors. Although some groups included a few upperlower-class adherents, all groups reported are generally middle-middleto upper-middle-class.

Many groups studied were easy to locate; less-public groups or healers are probably underrepresented. Many of the groups studied advertise regularly in newspapers, telephone directories, directories compiled by alternative-oriented regional associations, national movement directories, bulletin boards in public places, and so on. Likewise, many public groups offer information meetings or introduce their ideas through public adult school courses. Other groups were established branches of well-known international organizations, such as Unity or Transcendental Meditation.

Contacts with these groups led to further information about other groups and individual healers, through a snowballing effect. Sometimes we learned of smaller, less-well-known groups, such as private healing circles, only after we had gained the confidence of respondents. Such groups had no reason or wish to be publicly known; they did not actively recruit new members or widely promulgate their beliefs and practices. It is reasonable to assume that such groups are underrepresented in this study, whereas groups or healers who aggressively proselytize or advertise may be proportionately overrepresented.

Alternative healing through totally anonymous media, such as magazines or direct mail recruitment, is also underrepresented. Although many of the respondents in this study utilize these anonymous media, some adherents of alternative healing have no contact with other believers except through such anonymous media. Thus, these persons would not be known to any of our respondents and informants, and we could not obtain their names as potential contacts.

We did tap this form of adherence in a limited way when we conducted control interviews; two of the forty-three control respondents were not affiliated with any healing group or healer but used alternative healing methods learned through anonymous media. This type of alternative healing differs significantly from the types studied in this project in that it is not mediated by social contacts; recruitment, belief, and commitment are through anonymous interactions, and there is no group focus for the practice of health and healing. This type probably also lends itself to an even greater degree of eclecticism and incoherence of beliefs and practices, since there is no group of fellow believers to evaluate adherents' beliefs and practices. A different methodology would be necessary to reach adherents of this type of alternative healing; such research would be fruitful for comparison.

In the first year of this study, over 130 different groups or healers were firmly identified. We had also obtained nearly 100 additional leads or contacts with other similar groups/healers, but time constraints made it impossible to verify all of these leads. Since our sources described these additional healers as similar to those we were already studying, we did not confirm or study these additional leads.

We have organized our data in this volume according to the healing beliefs and practices that were the central approach of each broad type of group. While these typologies and generalizations are useful and necessary for handling the volumes of data here, they are also frustratingly inadequate to convey the fascinating complexity of individual respondents' belief systems.

The individuals interviewed very often described dozens of different healing approaches they were using or had used. They connected these diverse approaches with their personal meaning systems, biographies, and health needs in fascinating and sometimes creative patterns. Thus, looking at a list of therapeutic approaches tried by respondents gives an even more impressive array of alternatives than merely a list of groups/ healers we encountered directly. Altogether, our respondents described having used, presently or in the past, the following beliefs and practices related to healing:

Catholic Charismatic Renewal
Transcendental Meditation
various individual Christian faith healers
individual practitioners of psychic healing
Spiritual Frontiers Fellowship
Association for Research and Enlightenment
Christian Science
Full Gospel and Pentecostal churches, Full Gospel Businessmen's Association, Women's Aglow
Arica

psychosynthesis
Erhard Seminars Training (est)
shiatsu and other therapeutic massage methods
acupressure/acupuncture
Unity School of Christianity
yoga (various methods)
Jain meditation
Zen meditation
Order of Saint Luke (Episcopalian)
various local holistic healing associations
Therapeutic Touch
rolfing
chiropractic
foot reflexology
iridology
astrology, palmistry, numerology
homeopathy
naturopothy
Alexander method
Feldenkrais method
t'ai chi chuan
aikido
Reiki
rebirthing
macrobiotics
vegetarianism
various nutritionist therapists
healing circles and self-help groups
Eckankar
Great White Brotherhood
Religious Science
teachings of Bhagwan Shree Rajneesh, Babi Ji, Swami Muktananda, or
    Ram Dass
holistic health communes
Native American Indian healing (several different tribal approaches)
Sufism
parapsychology
crystal healing

polarity
flower remedies
dowsing and other divination
sound or tone healing
kinesiology
Astara
Science of Mind
bioenergetics
biofeedback
Silva Mind Control
Psychometry
color healing
individual or group self-hypnosis
colonic centers
Reichian therapy
Psychointegrity
Psychocybernetics
Living Love (Cornucopia)
Course in Miracles
Johrei
theosophy
Pathwork
Inner Light Consciousness
art and dance therapy
Tibetan meditation
Jewish faith healing
huna (Hawaiian native healing)

Even this lengthy list is not exhaustive. Not all of these groups were represented by recognized leaders locally; all, however, had some following in the catchment area. Although these healing approaches are listed separately, it was common for several therapeutic methods to be used in conjunction; for example, a gestalt therapist also used vegetarianism, color healing, Tibetan meditation, shiatsu, crystal healing, and bioenergetics with clients.

For purposes of a working topology, five broad types of healing were distinguished: Christian healing groups; meditation and human potential groups; metaphysical groups; psychic and occult groups; and technique practitioners. Key criteria distinguishing types include resulting image of the source of healing power and tradition(s) drawn upon as source(s) of beliefs and practices. This volume reports mainly the four belief-oriented healing types, comparing them to the technique practitioner type and a control group, where relevant.

While this typology was useful in choosing groups for more detailed study, subsequent research showed many of its limitations for analysis. On some themes, the differences between groups within a type were almost as great as those between types; indeed, different groups within the same movement were often as dissimilar as groups representing different movements. Nevertheless, since groups within each type derive from similar belief systems, they do generally share broader objectives— including the purposes of healing beliefs and practices—and a common vocabulary for interpreting their actions and their life-worlds.

The two major modes of data gathering in this research were participant-observation and intensive interviews. Additional information was gained from movement literature—especially the literature for potential recruits. A limited experiment with videotaping a group session for analysis was also tried. The videotape provided much interesting information on the detailed interaction of an ongoing healing circle, but time and money constraints prevented more extensive use of this potentially valuable adjunct to participant-observation. The following sections describe the methods of participant-observation and interviewing more fully.

Participant-Observation

Some groups[2] of each healing type were studied intensively by participant-observation for ten to eighteen months; other groups were visited only occasionally. The groups selected for detailed study were chosen for their representativeness of a certain range within a type of healing group, their geographical accessibility, and their willingness to participate in the study. None of the 130 groups identified refused researcher participation in occasional public sessions; two groups, however, were reticent about allowing access to sessions for believers only. In one of these groups, suspicion and hostility toward researcher presence eventually led to the decision not to pursue interviews of individual members and to discontinue observation of sessions. On the whole, however, the groups identified participated in the research project readily—indeed, with enthusiasm.

A total of 255 separate observations (in 31 groups) of group meetings, special healing services, workshops and other programs, study groups, etc., were made and recorded in detail. Detailed notes included observations of content of belief system, leader-member interaction, healing and other rituals, social interaction and networks within the group, witnessing and other commitment activities, recruitment and socialization of new members, group crises, and responses to problems and to public events.

Table A.1 shows the numbers of each type of group that were studied extensively by participant observation. The number of observations in any given group was determined by two factors: how frequently the group met and how readily the group's beliefs and interaction could be comprehended from sessions observed. Thus, some groups whose regular interaction was of a relatively simple and consistent pattern required fewer visits than others. Groups that met infrequently (e.g., once a month) could be observed fewer times during the participant-observation phase of the research.

Data gathered through both intensive and occasional participant observation provided important background information and contributed to better understanding of groups' specific meanings—thus aiding the later interviewing phase. For example, many groups used the word *clear*

TABLE A.1   Frequency of Group Observations

Type of Group	1–3 visits	4–10 visits	10+ visits
Christian	1	3	3
Traditional metaphysical	2	1	2
Eastern/meditation	2	3	3
Psychic/occult	4	4	3

NOTE: Observations include meetings of all kinds, sizes, and purposes. For example, observations in an Eastern meditation group included regular meditation circles, classes, occasional workshops, and a holiday celebration.

to describe a desired state, but they used the word for very different meanings. Some meanings were: to comprehend fully, to be pollution-free, to experience order, to be in an altered state of awareness, to be psychologically free of "hangups."[3]

Participant observation also yielded important information about how members saw their healing beliefs connected with other aspects of their lives. Group sessions frequently included formal or casual periods of sharing, witnessing, or otherwise making public members' interpretations of events in their daily lives. By observing these sessions we were able to discover, for example, that the same ritual words that were used to promote healing in one group were also used to keep a car from running out of gas or to silence a rowdy drunk on a public bus; members witnessed to each other how these words provided a sense of empowerment in all aspects of life. Such experiences were often not mentioned during the interviews because of the interview's focus on healing experiences. Members' participation in group meetings frequently took the form of telling others about healing experiences; these healing tales are an interesting genre in themselves. Through the recounting of healing experiences, the individual and other members collectively develop an interpretation of those experiences—an interpretation that both reflects and further develops the group's distinctive belief system.

The social construction of the healing event or of the interpretation of individual healing experiences was also evident mainly through participant-observation. We noted which specific rituals were used in group settings and by whom. Were certain members of the group designated as healers, or was healing an activity in which all engaged? Where was the healing event located physically, chronologically, and relative to other elements of group meetings? What importance did the healing event have for the larger group, and how did that reflect the stratification within the group? Was there a distinction between problems that were appropriate for public healing within the group, as opposed to those things appropriate to healing at home or individually? Similarly, stratification patterns and leadership styles were more clearly evidenced in group meetings than in individual interviews.

Methodological Perspective

The method of participant-observation was chosen to best meet this study's fundamental objective: to understand believers' actions from their own point of view—seeking their definition of the situation. It means trying to see things as believers see them and use their categories of thought in the organization of experience. It means developing among members of the research staff a personal stance of empathy.[4]

Methodological empathy differs from sympathy in that it does not imply agreeing with a perspective but rather understanding it. Douglas's distinction between "empathy" and "sympathy" is useful: "Empathy is the ability to feel with, to see things from the standpoint or perspective of the individual being studied rather than to identify with or to act from this standpoint."[5] This empathic stance leads logically and naturally to a specific type of participant-observation and interviewing, discussed more fully below.

Methodological empathy is a useful antidote to the tendency to treat a subject such as marginal medicine as a study of "weirdos." Even the strangest behavior observed in the course of this study was perfectly rational and highly meaningful within the believer's frame of reference. For example, a healing service consisting mainly of humming may seem very strange to the outsider, but within a belief system in which humming is seen as a way of releasing and channeling energy, including the energy to heal, a session of humming is a sensible mode of therapeutic action.

The fundamental difference of perspective, however, between sociologist and believer is that the sociologist *as* sociologist does not accept the believer's taken-for-granted meanings as a given, but rather as an object of study. This difference was more problematic for some groups studied than others. The more action believers attribute to supernatural sources, the less easily their viewpoint can be reconciled with a sociological perspective.

The very fact of treating certain interactions, such as the discernment of the "causes" of an illness, as human behavior—and thus as objects for sociological study—is often incompatible with the basic beliefs of several groups studied (especially the more fundamentalist Christian and occult groups). Sociology must necessarily bracket the crucial religious question: To what extent is an action *also* from God, a higher being, or cosmic force? The more important the supernatural base is to the believer as a legitimation, the more upsetting a sociological interpretation will be to that person. We are not saying that the behavior described in this study is merely human; however, we are asserting that, whatever else it may be, it is certainly human—and as such, amenable to sociological interpretation.

The Participant-Observer's Role

While the research was not disguised, researchers did not call attention to their role as participant-observers. For example, we did not take notes during sessions or tape-record meetings unless others in the group did likewise. The goal was to be as unobtrusive as possible, yet to participate as fully as possible in order to gather a full range of information about the group session.

Often a group ascribed a role to the researcher, sometimes making the researcher more conspicuous within the group, but at the same time often creating access to important information. For example, in one study group where note-taking was the norm, the leader noticed the researcher's diligent writing and assigned her the role of "group scribe." The group frequently asked the researcher to read back remarks they considered particularly important so they could comment on or clarify the notes. This development was an unanticipated source of data, for note taking facilitated the understanding of an extremely complex belief system and distinguished those areas the group or leaders felt were of importance. It had the added advantage of reassuring the group that the researcher was accurately recording their beliefs.

This need to ascertain a specific role for the researcher was encountered in most groups observed. Although they were aware that the researcher's primary goal was to explore and understand the group's healing beliefs and practices, many groups persisted in concluding that we had come to them for some greater or transcendent purpose. Although this belief helped insure their cooperation with the research, it created other serious problems. For example, one healing circle concluded that the participant-observer was not merely an uninformed outsider as she presented herself, but an advanced spiritual being, fortuitously sent into their midst. The researcher's routine participation in the group was subsequently given greater significance, and she was asked to stay after the meeting to give spiritual advice to the group leader herself. Fortunately, enough observation and interviewing had already been done in this group that the researcher was able to exit gracefully without further complicating interaction with the group in her newly ascribed "spiritual" role.

A more typical role ascribed to researcher-observers was that of potential convert. Even sociologists could be converted! Our very interest in alternative healing was interpreted as having some special significance; the fact that we were brought into their midst could not be interpreted as a mere coincidence. Many of the groups believed that very few occurrences in life were purely coincidental. Events were attributed to God's will, the actions of evil forces, the results of actions in previous lives, the effects of cosmic forces, and so on. Thus any action of any participant could be and frequently was interpreted as having special significance.

Groups with a strong emphasis upon recruitment and conversion of new members were particularly likely to cast researchers into the role of potential convert. Very early in this research it was necessary for all members of the research group to clarify their personal stance for themselves and, often, for members of the groups. We presented ourselves as interested, empathic, relatively uninformed visitors, with genuine respect for our informants' intentions and feelings. Often, however, the groups wanted to know more of their researcher-observer: Are you born again? Do you meditate? Do you follow through on our practices and advice at home? Do you have sinful or bad habits, like smoking? Is your husband a Christian? Do you have the right political opinions? And so on. We were careful never to profess a belief that we did not truly hold. We were aware, however, that adherents often translated our answers into something more consonant with their own beliefs than we ourselves would have specified; we did not generally confirm or deny their translations.

Part of the problem of having groups treat researchers as potential converts is that there is some methodological truth to that perception. It is a poor participant-observer who remains aloof from the action and never experiences the moods of the group, the periods of fervor, the moments of awe. A key difference between pure "observation" and participant-observation is that the latter requires encountering the group on its own terms and deliberately exposing oneself to the ideas and experiences that lead many other participants to be converted. Nevertheless, the participant-observer is also in the other sphere: recording observations, analyzing actions, and asking questions from a sociological perspective. This kind of marginality means that the sociologist is not likely to be converted, because the sociological perspective does not assume precisely those beliefs and actions that must be taken for granted by the believer. By definition, the participant-observer lacks "faith."

Staff meetings during the participant-observation phase also reduced the likelihood of researchers being converted. The marginality of participant-observers was increased by the fact that each researcher was observing a number of different groups—often of very different beliefs and practices. Whereas the conversion process often involves the recruit becoming increasingly encapsulated within the group, reducing interaction with competing beliefs and practices, the researchers in this project were exposed to numerous and diverse groups and practices. It is hardly conducive to conversion to any one perspective to spend Monday afternoon with a psychic healing circle, Tuesday evening with a fundamentalist occult sect, Wednesday evening with a Catholic charismatic prayer meeting, Thursday morning with a yoga and meditation class, and Sunday morning at a Unity church service.

Within each group, developing the appropriate researcher role involved negotiation and learning. Observers, like new recruits, must learn appropriate patterns of behavior, but the diversity of beliefs and practices made it almost impossible to anticipate group norms in advance. For example, one researcher arrived at one group to discover that everyone in the group wore shades of red. The fact that she happened to have worn a red shirt turned into a focal point, as the group clearly expressed its approval of her choice of what was for them a very spiritual color. The researcher wore the same red shirt to another group on the very night when they were discussing the negative effects of red on the aura. The group was emphatic that red was not a "New Age" color and should never be worn. The participant-observer theatrically covered her red shirt with a sweater and jokingly pleaded that it "won't happen again." The group let the episode slide with light laughter, but the uninformed observer's unfortunate choice of clothing was worse than a mere faux pas, in that, according to their beliefs, the researcher had inadvertently polluted their environment and endangered the auras of all in the room.

Researcher Rapport

Perhaps the most serious difficulty in this kind of participant-observation is balancing the goal of establishing empathy and trust with the need for subject-object distance. As Richardson points out, there is considerable methodological tension in conducting this kind of research with such "loving subjects."[6] Thus, not only the stance of the researcher, but also the stance of the subjects, contributes to the framework in which these data must be considered. For the most part, respondents in this study were warm and friendly toward the researchers. They showed concern and genuine care for the researchers' needs, although they often redefined them. For example, one researcher interpreted the circles under her eyes as the result of sleepless nights with her newborn; a group she was observing, however, saw her problem as the result of an inability to center herself and meditate—a problem with which they would gladly have helped.

Negotiating research roles with each group also entailed working out an appropriate amount of attention to and participation in each group. Groups tended to expect researchers to participate at least as much as other newcomers. Less attendance seemed to connote lack of seriousness on our part; more attendance was sometimes interpreted as commitment to their beliefs and practices. The groups varied—often greatly—in how much participation they expected of their own members and of researcher-observers. In one group, levels of commitment among members were so low that the researcher, after attending only four book discussions and a few public worship services, was asked to become a Sunday School teacher.

By contrast, another group had such high expectations of member commitment that even beginners and researchers were chastised if they attended merely one meeting a week. Despite the fact that her role as researcher was emphatically reiterated, the researcher was pressured to attend at least one additional weekly meeting, to travel to special seminars, and to attend the group's political action campaign meetings. The group was greatly disappointed when the researcher admitted that she did not recite their prayer chants daily or fast at least once a week. As these examples illustrate, negotiating research roles in each group meant dealing with each group's notion of appropriate levels of commitment— even for a researcher-visitor.

The issue of commitment highlights a research dilemma, characteristic of this kind of participant-observation. The dilemma is described well by Schwartz:

> This kind of empathic rapport creates its own problems as well as bestowing its obvious benefits on the student of religious sects. Once the members of the small Pentecostal group discovered that I sympathized with their religious aims and that I could also empathize with their distinctive religious experience, they could not understand why I did not take the next

"natural" step and become a full-fledged member of their group. They simply could not understand how anyone who perceived the "truth," however remotely, could resist the "innate" desire to participate in it with his whole being.[7]

Robbins, Anthony, and Curtis note that an empathic stance on the part of the researcher is especially likely to create problems for members of groups that are highly conversionist, maintain an exclusivist definition of religious truth, and hold a dichotomized conception of humankind (for example, "saved" versus "damned," "good" versus "evil").[8] This observation appears to hold true for the alternative healing belief systems studied here. The more sectarian groups in the sample were more disturbed than were other groups by the presence of a researcher who appeared to understand, yet was not compelled by that understanding to believe and to practice.

This appearance of understanding is partly due to methodological techniques and to the function of language in establishing group identity. The research technique of using people's own words back to them, in conversations and probes, was interpreted as evidence of some level of "belonging." The more accurate researchers became in using the groups' terms and empathizing with the experiences referred to, the more the members assumed that the researchers "really" understood and, therefore, should believe. Since this discrepancy had the potential of undermining their own confidence in the compelling nature of their beliefs, members sometimes increased their pressure on researchers to commit themselves to the group and its beliefs.

By contrast, a number of groups studied were quite uninterested in converting potential members; these groups tended to be more individualistic and loosely organized. Because researchers were less threatening to and less threatened by groups with this less dogmatic stance, they were often tempted to spend more research energies on them. This would have been a serious mistake, because the respective dogmatic or non-dogmatic stances of these various groups are probably central to the appeal of the groups for some of their members. We needed to understand the full range of groups, whether or not their interaction with newcomers was personally appealing to us.

Similarly, several researchers had to overcome their initial discomfort in doing intensive participant-observation in groups whose ideology greatly differed from their own. For example, one atypical group denied the humanness of certain segments of the population and denied the constitutional rights of atheists in our "God-founded country." The participant-observer initially had difficulty objectively observing sessions in which this ideology was spun out in all its implications. By focusing upon the research objectives of understanding the belief system and by relating to members as pleasant individuals rather than as representatives of their ideologies, the research staff generally avoided the potential biases such interaction could produce. Often an additional researcher attended sessions of problematic groups to balance and correct observations.

The Interview Process

After approximately one year of participant-observation in the groups identified, the interviewing phase of the research began. We conducted a total of 356 interviews with 349 different individuals (some persons were visited more than once in order to gather the voluminous information they offered). Of these, 43 were control interviews, using an abbreviated interview schedule with a matched sample (selected by neighborhood and matched for age and gender) for comparative purposes. Only 4 persons approached declined to be interviewed.

Respondents were mainly persons we had identified during the participant-observation phase of the study. We sought to interview members or leaders perceived to have special healing abilities, those who had had experiences as recipients of healing, and members with varying levels of commitment to the group's healing beliefs and practices. In larger groups, we aimed to interview at least twenty-five persons; in several smaller healing groups, we were able to interview all members.

Respondents were promised confidentiality and that, although most responses would be reported in a generalized form, any individual responses would not be reported with identifying information. All persons interviewed were apprised of the potential disadvantages and benefits of participating in this phase of the research, and an informed consent statement was signed by all who agreed to be interviewed.

With very few exceptions, interviews were conducted in respondents' homes. This enabled us to gather first-hand data on lifestyle and socio-economic indicators of our research population. Furthermore, respondents were relatively comfortable and at ease in their own homes. This factor of setting may seem to be self-evident, but many research projects have attempted to ask people about their "marginal" medical practices or their "failure to comply with medical regimen" in the setting of hospital, clinic, or university—contexts in which an adherent is least likely to feel at ease talking about beliefs and practices deemed "deviant" by the larger society.

Control interviews took approximately forty-five to sixty minutes to complete, but regular interviews averaged about two hours, with several lasting three to five hours. The depth of these interviews is impressive. Most respondents shared intimate feelings and memories of experiences, including personal crises and struggles. These interviews document their interpretations of experiences of pain, handicaps, loss of loved ones, suffering and grief, marital and vocational crises, near-death experiences, conversions, and mystical experiences. Reviewing respondents' statements, even many months after the interviews were done, we are still impressed with their openness, thoughtful and articulate responses, and the genuineness of their convictions.

Furthermore, respondents cooperated enthusiastically by giving us many names of further contacts. It was not uncommon for a respondent to spend another twenty minutes after a two-hour interview in order to look up names and telephone numbers of their contacts. They gave or loaned us books, pamphlets, and other literature, as well. Some kept in touch with interviewers after the interview process had ended, informing them of workshops, radio programs, and other events in the area related to alternative healing.

One methodological problem, however, was that of network creation. We had used snowball sampling to discover existing networks, but several respondents perceived us as resource persons and requested names of others involved in particular alternative healing practices that they wanted to pursue. The creation of new networks was methodologically problematic, but their request for assistance seemed legitimate. In order to protect the confidentiality promised of all respondents, we offered to give the requester's name at the end of the study to the other person(s), who might in turn contact them.

Respondent-Interviewer Interaction

The research staff was composed of six women and one man, ranging in ages from twenty-seven to forty, all except one of whom were trained as sociologists or anthropologists. All were white and middle-class—matching the population studied in many visible social characteristics. A number of personal attributes of the research staff seemed to have an impact upon the course of the interview.

Gender was a significant factor. Female respondents of all ages gave longer, deeper, and more thorough answers to female than to male interviewers. Common gender and the assumption of shared experiences greatly enhanced the rapport and openness in these interviews. Male respondents near the male interviewer's age gave him lengthier interviews, whereas older males were less responsive to male and female interviewers alike. No attempt was made to match interviewer and respondent by gender; rather, researchers generally interviewed persons from groups where they had been doing participant observation.

Other features of researchers' personal lives influenced interviews as well. One interviewer was noticeably pregnant during much of the interviewing phase; her condition elicited a large number of respondents' stories of pregnancy and childbirth, along with advice about health during pregnancy. Another researcher's son required a major orthopedic operation; respondents in one group learned of the child's condition and insisted that they wanted to pray for the child.

Another staff member had a highly visible temporary facial paralysis during several weeks of interviewing. Respondents offered explanations of its causes and several proffered their healing method as a cure for her specific condition. The researcher accepted most of their healing efforts (with one exception, which involved ingesting a remedy of questionable safety). Although her doctor had explained that the condition was self-limiting and would gradually disappear after eight to ten weeks, all except the healers were surprised when the condition disappeared in half that time. This course of events was completely consistent with the expectations of these healing groups, who frequently explain that alternative healing works by speeding up the body's self-healing processes; probably all fourteen of the persons who proffered their help claimed this as their healing success.

It was not uncommon for the interviewers to receive demonstrations and be recipients of various alternative healing practices, including offerings of vials of flower remedies, diet recommendations, massages and physical manipulation, psychic readings, astrological advice, laying on of hands, and so on. Although we never presented ourselves as believers, we were honestly interested in and open to respondents' practices. These experiences were highly valuable sources of information. They illustrated how believers ministered to each other, how they integrated their interpretations of what ailed a person with their ideas of therapeutic response. They also gave us some sense of what it was like to be on the receiving end of an admittedly brief healing effort.

In some instances, however, we were less than comfortable with receiving a particular healing method (e.g., sitting in an electrically magnetized chair). A considerable amount of diplomacy was then necessary to avoid trying a method of which we were personally fearful or doubtful, since we also did not want to convey to respondents a judgment of their practices. A related problem occurred when one respondent claiming psychic powers offered to do a reading for one researcher; one after another of her statements were incorrect and, as she asked the researcher for verification, she became increasingly eager to come up with a correct reading. Eventually, the interviewer tactfully suggested that perhaps her cold was interfering with the process, and the interview was fruitfully resumed.

The interviews themselves were frequently emotion-laden and difficult, for both researcher and respondent. The very subject matter—health, illness, suffering, death—elicited during the interview brought forth memories, thoughts, fears, and other serious concerns of respondents. While researchers attempted to maintain professional distance during these interviews, it was also important to show human concern and thoughtfulness. Respondents often recounted experiences with serious illnesses (and several were currently struggling with such conditions), life crises, or other emotionally "special" experiences.

Sometimes these accounts were emotionally moving or upsetting to respondents; we responded as fellow human beings, not merely distant researchers. It is hardly laudable to callously move on to the next question on a schedule in response to a tearful account of, for example, the death of a child. Although our expressions of sympathy and concern resulted in longer interviews, they also created a social situation that produced greater openness and depth. We also became increasingly aware that many beliefs and practices we were studying were closely connected to the human experience of suffering, in many different contexts. For us to be in touch with the quality of that suffering was, therefore, methodologically important.

These interviews represent the building of a temporary relationship, characterized by trust, openness, and flexibility. Although the research instrument was standardized, it was open-ended and encouraged respondents to articulate their own understanding of their practices and their personal beliefs about health, healing, and the illness experience.

The Research Instrument

The broad objectives for the interviews included:

- To discover the personal systems of meaning in which individuals' distinctive beliefs about health and illness are located
- To explore the individuals' actual conceptions of health, illness, and healing
- To understand the place of these beliefs in the individuals' daily life and social interactions
- To examine the relationship between the individuals' alternative health beliefs and practices and their attitudes toward the dominant medical system
- To identify the sources of the individuals' learning about and attraction to their present medical belief system, as well as to find patterns among the various forms of alternative healing
- To gain further information about the individuals' relationships within their alternative healing group as leaders or members

Since a central objective in this study was to discover respondents' own conceptions of health, illness, and healing, it was critical that the research instrument not impose a preconceived vocabulary. The standardized introduction to the interview included the explanation, "We are doing a study of people's experiences with nonmedical healing—that is, the kinds of healing that come about through means other than treatment by doctors, hospitals and regular medical people."

Respondents were also reminded that, because "people have different ways of talking about healing," the interviewer might not use the terms the respondents themselves used. They were urged to tell the interviewer the terms they would use and how they would explain these concepts. Through further probes, interviewers were able to adapt the interview questions to the actual conceptions of health and healing held by the respondents themselves. For example, for some respondents it was necessary to broaden the term *illness* to include a wide range of "problems" for which they believed healing to be the ideal response. Other respondents did not like the term *healing* because it connoted to them the image of the tent-revival faith healer; they substituted such terms as "increasing wellness."

Opening questions elicited the respondents' personal experiences with healing, as well as their interpretations of these experiences. (See Appendix B for the interview schedules.) Most respondents had so many experiences that interviewers had to move on to the subsequent questions after exploring only a few of the most important stories in depth. These voluminous data about experiences with healing do not, however, give us an adequate picture of all health and illness experiences the person dealt with recently. Also, as retroactive accounts, these descriptions were selective memories, invariably omitting many details about the illness-defining and help-seeking processes that researchers would find interesting.

Next, in the interviews, we asked about the nature of healing—what it is, how the respondent believes it occurs, and what is believed to be necessary to produce healing. Subsequent questions located these ideas of healing in terms of the respondents' larger belief systems, seeking their ideas of causality, moral responsibility, theodicies of illness, death, and therapeutic failure, cosmology, and afterlife.

The subsequent section of questions evoked respondents' ideas about healthiness. Respondents were asked to specify their norms of healthiness. Further questions elicited preventive practices and other notions of how to promote healthiness, as well as respondents' opinions about a number of health-related practices, such as smoking, drinking alcohol or caffeine beverages, and taking vitamin supplements and over-the counter medications. A number of questions asked about the respondents' opinions of the dominant medical system. These questions also sought the interface between the use of the dominant medical system and respondents' alternative medical systems. When time permitted, interviewers probed the broader health help-seeking process. Indeed, this is an important area for further research.

The next segment of the interview was devoted to discovering other alternative healing methods/groups with which the respondent is presently or was previously involved. Specifically, we hoped to analyze any patterns of funneling membership from movement to movement, patterns of mixtures among the various healing approaches, and the respondents' opinions of healing methods other than their own.

Respondents were asked about thirty different healing groups or approaches available in the general geographical area (but not necessarily included in the study). For each, they were asked whether they were familiar with the method, whether they had ever been involved with it (if so, when and how long), and what was their opinion of that approach. In addition, they were asked similar questions about other health-related movements, such as the feminist health movement, La Leche League, the natural childbirth programs, and health self-help movements. These latter questions gave some indication of whether respondents saw their own healing approach as linked with self-help or health-awareness movements in the larger society.

Respondents were also asked a number of questions about how they became involved in their present alternative health system and what aspects of it appealed to them then and now. They were also asked how their thinking about health and how their actual health (in their estimation) has changed since becoming involved. They were asked several broad questions about their religious background, the place of religious healing in their upbringing, their present religious involvement and its link with their health-healing beliefs and practices. Several additional questions tapped the extent of their day-to-day involvement with their alternative healing group/practices, their sense of its relative importance in their every lives, their social networks within their group, and their relationship with leaders of the group.

Overall, this line of questioning was highly productive. The open-ended questions elicited lengthy and deep answers. None of the questions failed to produce useful information, although some were more suited to certain types of healing approach than to others. Most of the time, however, the interviewers and respondents were able to adapt the questions satisfactorily, and valuable information was gained in that process alone.

Had there been more time, a useful line of questioning would have been to develop a more thorough appreciation of the respondents' entire network of help-seeking resources. For example, under what circumstances does a consultation with mother, neighbor, or coworker precede decisions to try a given treatment approach? The data suggest that the patterns of health care used by these middle-class suburbanites are more complex than previously recognized. This part of the research instrument was extremely fruitful but not detailed enough to produce an adequate picture of these patterns.

Coding

The interviews were tape-recorded and transcribed verbatim. The average transcript was longer than fifty single-spaced pages. To manage and retrieve this volume of information, transcripts were coded in 315 categories and subcategories. For example, each of the different types of symbolism (e.g., time, water, air, shapes, numbers, color) used in healing was coded separately for future comparison. Very little of this coded information is suitable for quantification, since the interviews were open-ended and variable in scope.

APPENDIX B

INTERVIEW

SCHEDULE

The following is the primary schedule of questions asked of all respondents, except the control group. Additional probes were used but are not listed because they varied according to the situation and interview content. A small number of control group respondents answered affirmatively that they had experiences with alternative healing; in those cases, the interviewer covered the entire schedule for adherents. Most control group respondents were interviewed using an abbreviated schedule (listed below).

After a brief introductory statement identifying the researcher, the goals of the project, and requesting informed consent for the interview to be conducted and tape-recorded, each respondent was asked:

A. First, we'd like to know about your personal experiences.
   1. Have you ever felt you were healed by some process other than medical treatment?
   2. Could you describe to me what happened?
   3. Have you had other experiences with healing? Could you describe to me what happened? [repeat]
   4. Do you use a different healing method for different kinds of illnesses or problems?
   5. Do you think that there are different kinds of healing? (If so, what are they?)
   6. Are there some things people have to do or to believe in order for healing to occur?
   7. Is it necessary for the person for whom healing is sought to be present?
   8. Does a certain person or group usually do the healing?

9. Could anyone do healing or does it require some special quality? (If yes, what quality?)
10. [For persons who do healing] Do you prepare to do healing in any special way?
11. What is the source of healing power?
12. How is healing power released or channeled to where it is needed?
13. What does it feel like when you are being healed?
14. How would you know if a healing you needed had occurred?
15. Could a healing sometimes occur and you'd not know it?
16. What do you think are some of the causes of the illness or problems that people need healed?
17. Do you think people are sometimes responsible for their own illnesses? (If yes, in what ways?)
18. Are there larger problems—not just individuals' problems—that need healing?
19. Do you believe that evil forces play a part in the illness of humans? [If yes, how?; how can these forces be counteracted?]
20. Do you think that illness or problems are sometimes a punishment for wrongdoing?
21. Do you think pain or illness can be good for you? [If yes, in what ways?]
22. Are there some occasions when you shouldn't seek healing for a certain illness or problem?
23. If someone seems near to death, should that person or loved ones seek a healing to prevent death?
24. Do you believe that healing in this life affects a person's situation after this life?
25. Why do you think healing doesn't work sometimes?

B. We'd also like to know your ideas about healthiness.
26. What are the ways people can prevent illness or protect themselves?
27. What do you think are the qualities of a truly healthy person?
28. Do you follow any particular dietary practices for spiritual or nonmedical reasons?
   a. Vegetarianism?

b. Use special water?
c. Do you fast? (How, why?)
29. How do you feel about:
a. smoking?
b. drinking alcohol?
c. drinking coffee?
d. taking over-the-counter medications, like aspirin or cough syrup?
e. vitamin supplements?

C. The next questions are mainly about doctors, hospitals, and other medical assistance.
30. How well do you think the medical profession is meeting people's health needs these days?
31. What do you think are the main good things about the way medicine is practiced in America?
32. What do you think are the main bad things?
33. When you are ill, how do you decide whether to get a doctor's help?
a. What kind of medical help do you seek first?
b. How long do you wait before seeking medical assistance?
c. How do you decide what help to get?
34. Are there illnesses for which you would use only nonmedical treatment?
35. If there were a conflict between the advice of your doctor and that nonmedical treatment, under what circumstances might you stop following the doctor's treatment?

D. A number of groups, practitioners, or movements have beliefs and practices about health and healing that may or may not be related to your own. For each of the named groups or spokespersons, we'd like to know whether you are familiar with them.
36. Have you ever heard of:
[If yes, have you ever been involved with this approach? When? How long? What is your opinion of their approach?]
a. Catholic Charismatic Renewal
b. Spiritual Frontiers Fellowship

   c. Transcendental Meditation
   d. Oral Roberts
   e. Edgar Cayce (Association for Research and Enlightenment)
   f. the feminist health movement
   g. Rolfing
   h. chiropractic
   i. Christian Science
   j. natural childbirth (e.g., Lamaze method)
   k. La Leche League (i.e., breast-feeding movement)
   l. Full Gospel or Pentecostal churches
   m. yoga, yogic meditation
   n. Agnes Sanford
   o. Arica
   p. psychosynthesis
   q. EST (Erhard Seminars Training)
   r. Adele Davis
   s. Silva Mind Control
   t. foot reflexology
   u. iridology
   v. shiatsu or acupressure
   w. Unity
   x. psychic healing
   y. astrology or numerology
   z. Order of St. Luke (Episcopalian)
  aa. homeopathy
  bb. Zen meditation
  cc. Alexander or Feldenkrais method
  dd. t'ai chi chuan or aikido
  ee. Jesus People
  ff. rebirthing
  gg. macrobiotics

37. Are there any healing or health-related groups or movements or techniques not on this list with which you have had experience? [For each: name, when and how long involved, opinion of that approach.]

E. We also need some background information.

38. How did you first get involved in [primary healing approach of respondent]?
    (What were you involved in before that, and what experiences bridged the two?)
39. How long ago did you become involved in _____?
40. Can you remember what was happening in your life at that time?
41. What aspects of _____ first appealed to you?
42. What aspects are most important to you now?
43. Has your thinking about health and healing changed as you have become more involved in _____? [If so, in what ways?]
44. Do you think your health itself has changed since you've been involved? [If so, in what ways?]
45. How would you describe your religious background (identification, degree of involvement, how long)?
46. Did religious healing have a place in your upbringing?
47. How would you describe your present religious involvement (identification, degree of involvement, link with this group)?
48. How important is _____ in guiding your everyday life?
49. How often do you attend the activities of _____?
50. How much do you socialize, outside of meetings, with other people who are involved in _____?
51. What kinds of schools did you attend:
    a. Elementary (public, private, parochial)
    b. Secondary (public, private, parochial) Did you finish high school?
    c. College (how many years, which college?)
    d. Postcollege training (degrees, which schools?)
52. How long have you lived in this town? Where did you live before that?
53. Where were you born? (Have you moved often since then?)
54. Occupation?
55. Family income range (use card with ranges):
    a. Under $10,000
    b. $10,000 to $20,000
    c. $20,000 to $30,000

       d. $30,000 to $40,000

       e. $50,000 to $50,000

       f. Over $50,000

56. Marital status:

57. (If married) Spouse's occupation

58. Parents' occupations:

    Father:

    Mother:

59. Do you have any children? Number? Age range?

60. Own age?

61. Do you know of any groups or practitioners in this area that you would recommend we talk to in order to learn more about alternative health and healing methods?

62. Can you suggest people who have had experience with alternative healing to whom we might talk?

Observed Items

(completed by interviewer)

1. Physical setting, especially social-status indicators

2. Race, ethnicity

3. Events surrounding the interview (e.g., interruptions, problems, social setting)

4. Evaluation of quality of respondents' answers:

    a. Characterize respondent's attitude during interview.

    b. Your sense of of the depth and sincerity of answers.

    c. What specific clues lead to these evaluations?

5. Evaluation of interviewer's relationship with respondent:

    a. Did you feel comfortable with respondent?

    b. Did certain features of respondent make you feel negative toward him or her?

    c. Was there anything said or done by the respondent that influenced your reaction?

6. Any mistakes, omissions, or problems with the interviewing itself?

Abbreviated Interview Schedule
for Control Group

A. The first questions are about healthiness.
1. What do you think are the qualities of a truly healthy person?
2. Do you follow any particular dietary practices, such as vegetarianism?
3. How do you feel about:
   a. smoking tobacco?
   b. drinking alcohol?
   c. drinking coffee?
   d. taking over-the-counter medications, like aspirin or cough syrup?
4. What are the ways people can prevent illness or protect themselves?

B. The next questions are mainly about doctors, hospitals, and other medical assistance.
5. How well do you think the medical profession is meeting people's health needs these days?
6. What do you think are the main good things about the way medicine is practiced in America?
7. What do you think are the main bad things?
8. When you are ill, how do you decide whether to get a doctor's help?

C. Ideas about illness and healing:
9. Sometimes, when you are ill, do you seek help from somebody or something other than doctors? Describe.
10. What do you think are some of the causes of the illnesses or problems that people need healed?
11. Do you think people are sometimes responsible for their own illnesses?
12. Are there larger problems—not just individuals' problems—that need healing?
13. Do you believe that evil forces play a part in the illnesses of humans?

14. Do you think that illness or problems are sometimes a punishment for wrongdoing?

15. If someone seems near to death, do you think that people should try to prevent that person's death?

16. Do you believe that healing in this life affects a person's situation after this life?

17. Why do you think healing doesn't work sometimes?

18. Have you ever felt you were healed by some process *other* than medical treatment? Describe.
    [If respondent mentions alternative healing methods, use all relevant questions from primary interview instrument.]

19. Have you ever had any experiences with:
    [And what is your opinion of it?]
    a. faith healing?
    b. meditation?
    c. chiropractic?
    d. natural childbirth?
    e. psychic healing?
    f. yoga?
    g. Adele Davis's ideas?
    h. astrology?
    i. Christian Science?

20. Do you belong to any groups that practice healing?

D. Background

21. How would you describe your religious background?

22. Did religious healing have a place in your upbringing?

23. How would you describe your present religious involvement?

24. What kinds of schools did you attend?
    a. Elementary
    b. Secondary
    c. College
    d. Graduate or other postcollege

25. How long have you lived here?

26. Where did you live before that?

27. Where were you born?

28. Occupation?

29. Marital status?

30. Family income range [from card]?
31. [If married] What does your husband/wife do? Where does he/she work?
32. What did your parents do for a living?
    Father:
    Mother:
33. Number of children?
34. Age range of children:
35. Your own age?

Observed Items
(completed by interviewer)

Same as for regular interviews

NOTES

1   Middle-Class Use of Nonmedical Healing

1. The concepts *alternative healing* and *marginal medicine* are used herein interchangeably. The term *alternative healing* or *alternative medical system* is somewhat preferable to the concept of *marginal medicine*, because the latter implies only the social-structural status of the medical system and not also the cognitive aspects. This report has avoided using the concept of *holistic medicine*, although this term has also been applied to some of these forms of healing.

2. See Appendix A for a complete list of alternative forms of healing reported by respondents in this study. Capsule (and by no means exhaustive) descriptions of some of these diverse forms are found in: Ann Hill, ed., *A Visual Encyclopedia of Unconventional Medicine: A Health Manual for the Whole Person* (New York: Crown, 1979); Jeffrey S. Levin and Jeannine Coreil, "'New Age' Healing in the U.S.," *Social Science and Medicine* 23 (1986): 889–897; J. Gordon Melton, *A Reader's Guide to the Church's Ministry of Healing* (Independence, Mo.: The Academy of Religious and Psychical Research, 1973); Herbert Otto and James Knight, eds., *Dimensions in Wholistic Healing: New Frontiers in the Treatment of the Whole Person* (Chicago: Nelson and Hall, 1979); *Spiritual Community Guide: The New Consciousness Source Book*, no. 4 (San Rafael, Calif.: Spiritual Community, 1979).

3. E. Cassee, "Uncertified Healers and Their Patients: Deviant Behavior and Health Care," *Sociologische Gids* 17 (1970): 393–410; Cassee, "Deviant Illness Behavior: Patients of Mesmerists," *Social Science and Medicine* 3 (1970): 389–396; Gary Easthope, "Marginal Healers," in R. Kenneth Jones, ed., *Sickness and Sectarianism* (London: Gower, 1985), pp. 52–71; Barnaby Feder, "More Britons Trying Holistic Medicine," *New York Times*, January 9, 1985: C1, 14; Klaus-Dieter Haehn, "Heilpraktikerbesuche chronisch Kranker: Frequenz und Motivation,"*Diagnostik* 13 (1980): 145–146; Thomas Maretzki and Eduard Seidler, "Biomedicine and Naturopathic Healing in West Germany: A Historical and Ethnomedical View of a Stormy Relationship," *Culture, Medicine and Psychiatry* 9 (1985): 383–421; Julius A. Roth, *Health Purifiers and Their Enemies: A Study of the Natural Health Movement in the United States with a Comparison to Its Counterpart in Germany* (London: Croom Helm, 1976); "Attitudes to Medicine: Belgium—Patients' Experience of Medicine— Orthodox and Alternative," *Test Achats* (March 1983): 7–9.

4. Gallup Poll, "Americans Taking up Religious, Spiritual Experimentation" (Princeton, N.J.: Gallup International), reported in *The New York Times*, November 18, 1976.

5. Robert Wuthnow, *The Consciousness Reformation* (Berkeley: University of

California Press, 1976); Wuthnow, *Experimentation in American Religion: The New Mysticisms and Their Implications for the Churches* (Berkeley: University of California Press, 1979).

6. Horacio Fabrega, Jr., *Disease and Social Behavior: An Interdisciplinary Perspective* (Cambridge, Mass.: MIT Press, 1974); Eliot Freidson, *Profession of Medicine: A Study of the Sociology of Applied Knowledge* (New York: Dodd, Mead, 1970); Sander Kelman, "The Social Nature of the Definition Problem in Health," *International Journal of Health Services* 5 (1975): 625–642.

7. Although a number of authors have analyzed faith healing or related therapies, the majority of them have viewed it mainly as a "technique," rather than an entire medical system of knowledge, or they have assumed the criteria of the Western medical paradigm. For example, one researcher attempted a follow-up on claimed healings of Christian and psychic healers; his data were limited to medical records, interpreted solely within the medical paradigm; Louis Rose, *Faith Healing* (Harmondsworth, England: Penguin, 1970).

Few studies take seriously the claims of faith healing to have effect on bio-physical maladies, but several are willing to allow its possibilities in the realm of psychological problems. This perspective gives rise to a number of studies that treat faith healing and other alternative medical systems as potentially effective "folk psychotherapy." See, for example, Kenneth Calestro, "Psychotherapy, Faith Healing and Suggestion," *International Journal of Psychiatry* 10 (1972): 83–113; Jerome D. Frank, *Persuasion and Healing* (New York: Schocken, 1973); Michael Owen Jones, *Why Faith Healing?*, Canadian Centre for Folk Culture Studies, Paper No. 3 (Ottawa: National Museum of Canada, 1972); Ari Kiev, *Curanderismo: Mexican-American Folk Psychiatry* (New York: Free Press, 1968); Kiev, "Psychotherapeutic Aspects of Pentecostal Sects among West Indian Immigrants to England," *British Journal of Sociology* 15 (1964): 129–138; Isaac Lubchansky, Gladys Egri, and Janet Stokes, "Puerto Rican Spiritualists View Mental Illness: The Faith Healer as a Paraprofessional," *American Journal of Psychiatry* 127 (1970): 312–321; Raymond Prince, "Fundamental Differences of Psychoanalysis and Faith Healing," *International Journal of Psychiatry* 10 (1972): 125–128; Lloyd Rogler and August Hollingshead, "The Puerto Rican Spiritualist as Psychiatrist," *American Journal of Sociology* 67 (1961): 17–21; Pedro Ruiz and John Langrod, "Psychiatry and Folk Healing: A Dichotomy?" *American Journal of Psychiatry* 133 (1976): 95–97; E. Fuller Torrey, *The Mind Game: Witchdoctors and Psychiatrists* (New York: Emerson Hall, 1972).

8. Arthur Kleinman, "Some Issues for a Comparative Study of Medical Healing," *International Journal of Social Psychiatry* 19 (1973): 159–165; see also Fabrega, "The Scope of Ethnomedical Science," *Culture, Medicine and Psychiatry* 1 (1977): 201–228.

9. Kleinman, "The Failure of Western Medicine," *Human Nature* 1 (1978): 63–68. See also Leon Eisenberg, "Disease and Illness: Distinctions between

Professional and Popular Ideas of Sickness," *Culture, Medicine and Psychiatry* 1 (1977): 9–24; Fabrega, "Disease and Illness from a Biocultural Standpoint," in Paul Ahmed, George Coelho, and Aliza Kolker, eds., *Toward a New Definition of Health* (New York: Plenum, 1979), pp. 23–51.

10. See, for example: Kaja Finkler, "Non-Medical Treatments and Their Outcomes," *Culture, Medicine and Psychiatry* 4 (1980): 271–310; Vivian Garrison, "Doctor, Espiritista or Psychiatrist: Health-seeking Behavior in a Puerto Rican Neighborhood of New York City," *Medical Anthropology* 1 (1977): 67–183; Alan Harwood, *Rx: Spiritist as Needed: A Study of a Puerto Rican Community Health Resource* (New York: Wiley, 1977); Kleinman and Lilias H. Sung, "Why do Indigenous Practitioners Successfully Heal?" *Social Science and Medicine* 13b (1979): 7–27; Kleinman, *Patients and Healers in the Context of Culture: An Exploration of the Borderline between Anthropology, Medicine and Psychiatry* (Berkeley: University of California Press, 1980); Ioan M. Lewis, *Ecstatic Religion: Spirit Possession and Shamanism* (Baltimore: Penguin, 1971); Mark Nichter, "Idioms of Distress: Alternatives in the Expression of Psychosocial Distress, a Case Study from South India," *Culture, Medicine and Psychiatry* 5 (1981): 379–409; Nichter, "Negotiation of the Illness Experience: Ayurvedic Therapy and the Psychosocial Dimension of Illness," *Culture, Medicine and Psychiatry* 5 (1981): 5–24; Gananath Obeyesekere, "The Idiom of Demonic Possession: A Case Study," *Social Science and Medicine* 4 (1970): 97–111; Obeyesekere, *The Cult of the Goddess Pattini* (Chicago: University of Chicago Press, 1984); Stanley J. Tambiah, "The Cosmological and Performative Significance of a Thai Cult of Healing through Meditation," *Culture, Medicine and Psychiatry* 1 (1977): 97–132; Victor Turner, *The Drums of Affliction* (Oxford: Clarendon, 1968).

11. Some corroborating evidence comes from studies of new religious and quasi-religious movements among middle-class Americans, British, and Canadians, but few of these studies have directly addressed healing beliefs and practices. See: Dick Anthony, Thomas Robbins, Madeleine Doucas, and Thomas Curtis, "Patients and Pilgrims: Changing Attitudes toward Psychotherapy of Converts to Eastern Mysticism," *American Behavioral Scientist* 20 (1977): 861–886; William Sims Bainbridge, *Satan's Power: A Deviant Psychotherapeutic Cult* (Berkeley: University of California Press, 1978); James A. Beckford, "Holistic Imagery and Ethics in New Religious and Healing Movements," *Social Compass* 31 (1984): 259–272; Beckford, "The World Images of New Religious and Healing Movements," in Jones, *Sickness and Sectarianism*, pp. 72–93; Frederick Bird, "Charisma and Ritual in New Religious Movements," in Jacob Needleman and George Baker, eds., *Understanding the New Religions* (New York: Seabury, 1979), pp. 173–189; Joseph Havens, "Gestalt, Bioenergetics, and Encounter: New Wine without Wineskins," in R. Cox, ed., *Religious Systems and Psychotherapy* (Springfield, Ill.: Charles C. Thomas, 1973), pp. 268–283; Edward J. Moody, "Urban Witches," in James Spradley and

David McCurdy, eds., *Conformity and Conflict* (Boston: Little, Brown, 1974), pp. 326–336; Thomas Robbins and Dick Anthony, "Getting Straight with Meher Baba: A Study of Mysticism, Drug Rehabilitation and Postadolescent Role Conflict," *Journal for the Scientific Study of Religion* 11 (1972): 122–140; Donald Stone, "The Human Potential Movement," in Charles Glock and Robert Bellah, eds., *The New Religious Consciousness* (Berkeley: University of California Press, 1976), pp. 93–115; Steven Tipton, *Getting Saved from the Sixties: The Transformation of Moral Meaning in American Culture by Alternative Religious Movements* (Berkeley: University of California Press, 1982); Roy Wallis and Peter Morley, eds., *Marginal Medicine* (New York: Free Press, 1976); Wallis, *The Road to Total Freedom: A Sociological Analysis of Scientology* (New York: Columbia University Press, 1977); Wallis, "Betwixt Therapy and Salvation: The Changing Form of the Human Potential Movement," in Jones, *Sickness and Sectarianism*, pp. 23–51; Frances Westley, "The 'Cult of Man': Durkheim's Predictions and New Religious Movements," *Sociological Analysis* 39 (1978): 135–145; Westley, *The Complex Forms of the Religious Life* (Chico, Calif.: Scholars Press, 1983).

12. Freidson, *Profession of Medicine*, pp. 286ff.

13. See, for example, Gillian Allen and Roy Wallis, "Pentecostalists as a Medical Minority," in Wallis and Morley, *Marginal Medicine*, pp. 110–137; E. Mansell Pattison, "Ideological Support for the Marginal Middle Class: Faith Healing and Glossolalia," in Irving Zaretsky and Mark Leone, eds., *Religious Movements in Contemporary America* (Princeton, N.J.: Princeton University Press, 1974), pp. 418–458.

14. On these older forms of alternative healing, see: Brian Ingles, *Fringe Medicine* (London: Faber and Faber, 1964); Jones, "The Development of Medical Sects," in Jones, *Sickness and Sectarianism*, pp. 1–22; Martin Kaufman, *Homeopathy in America: The Rise and Fall of a Medical Heresy* (Baltimore: Johns Hopkins Press, 1971); Ronald Numbers, "Do it yourself the sectarian way," in Guenter B. Risse, Ronald Numbers, and Judith Leavitt, eds., *Medicine without Doctors* (New York: Science History, 1977), pp. 49–72; William G. Rothstein, *American Physicians in the Nineteenth Century: From Sects to Science* (Baltimore: Johns Hopkins Press, 1972); Walter I. Wardwell, "Public Regulation of Chiropractic," *Journal of the National Medical Association* 53 (1961): 166–172; Wardwell, "Orthodoxy and Heterdoxy in Medical Practice," *Social Science and Medicine* 6 (1972): 759–763; Wardwell, "Towards a Conceptualization of the Process of Emergence and Disappearance of Health-related Professions," paper presented to the International Sociological Association, 1978; Wardwell, "The Triumph of Chiropractic—and Then What?" *Journal of Sociology and Social Welfare* 7 (1980): 425–439. A bibliography of sources on naturopathy, chiropractic, homeopathy, and osteopathy is found in Clair M. Cassidy, Hans Baer, and Barbara Becker, "Selected References on Professionalized Heterodox Health Systems in English-Speaking Countries," *Medical Anthropology Quarterly* 17 (1985): 10–18.

15. Freidson, *Profession of Medicine*, p. 52.

16. Lowell Levin and Ellen Idler, *The Hidden Health Care System: Mediating Structures and Medicine* (Cambridge, Mass.: Ballinger, 1981).

17. Irving Kenneth Zola, *Socio-Medical Inquiries* (Philadelphia: Temple University Press, 1983), p. 236.

18. James H. Cassedy, "Why Self-Help? Americans Alone with their Diseases, 1800–1850," in Risse et al., *Medicine Without Doctors*, pp. 31–48; Freidson, *Profession of Medicine*, pp. 20–21; Regina Markell Morantz, "Nineteenth Century Health Reform and Women: A Program of Self-Help," in Risse et al., *Medicine Without Doctors*, pp. 73–94; Paul Starr, *The Social Transformation of American Medicine* (New York: Basic Books, 1982), pp. 47–59.

19. *Proceedings of the National Congress on Medical Quackery*, cosponsored by the AMA and the FDA, (Chicago: American Medical Association, 1961); Julian Roebuck and Robert B. Hunter, "Medical Quackery as Deviant Behavior," in Frank Scarpitti and Paul McFarlane, eds., *Deviance: Action, Reaction, Interaction* (Reading, Mass.: Addison-Wesley, 1975), pp. 72–82.

20. James Harvey Young, *The Medical Messiahs* (Princeton: Princeton University Press, 1967), pp. 317 ff.

21. This distinction from quackery does not necessarily imply that the various alternative healing methods are medically effective or recommendable; consumers still need to evaluate the effectiveness and safety of what is being done or prescribed (just as they should evaluate the methods and prescriptions of orthodox medicine). This distinction implies only that there is a major difference between the groups studied and "quacks," especially in terms of meanings and motivations.

22. Only two respondents had not completed high school; both were over sixty-five—an age cohort for which high school diplomas were not normative.

23. Those respondents who were under thirty were disproportionately persons suffering from serious, chronic ailments; some had cancer, multiple sclerosis, major orthopedic problems, and paraplegia. It is likely that this underrepresentation of young adults is because for most the body's health and vigor are not problematic and one's youthfulness is taken for granted.

2   Features of Groups Studied

1. Irving K. Zola, "The Concept of Trouble and Sources of Medical Assistance—To Whom One Can Turn, with What, and Why?" *Social Science and Medicine* 6 (1972): 673–679.

2. Peter L. Berger, *The Sacred Canopy: Elements of a Sociological Theory of Religion* (Garden City, N.Y.: Doubleday, 1967), pp. 53–58.

3. Allan Young, "Some Implications of Medical Beliefs and Practices for Social Anthropology," *American Anthropology* 78 (1976): 5–25.

4. *Ibid.*, p. 13.

5. Michael Balint, *The Doctor, His Patient and the Illness* (New York: International University Press, 1964), pp. 21ff.; Thomas Scheff, "Negotiating Reality: Notes on Power in the Assessment of Responsibility," *Social Problems* 16 (1968): 3–17.

6. Note the strong parallels with the social functions of divination, although the underlying belief systems are very different; compare George K. Park, "Divination and Its Social Contexts," *Journal of the Royal Anthropological Institute* 93 (1963): 195–209; Victor Turner, *The Drums of Affliction* (Oxford: Clarendon, 1968), pp. 25–51.

7. Leonard B. Glick, "Medicine as an Ethnographic Category: The Gimi of the New Guinea Highlands," *Ethnology* 6 (1967): 31–56.

8. Marcia Millman, *The Unkindest Cut* (New York: William Morrow, 1978).

9. Meredith McGuire, *Religion: The Social Context* (Belmont, Calif.: Wadsworth, 1987), pp. 241–243; see also Jean Comaroff, "Medicine: Symbol and Ideology," in Peter Wright and Andrew Treacher, eds., *The Problem of Medical Knowledge: Examining the Social Construction of Medicine* (Edinburgh, Scotland: Edinburgh University Press, 1982), pp. 49–68; Peter Conrad and Joseph W. Schneider, "Medicine," in Joseph S. Roucek, ed., *Social Control for the 1980s: A Handbook for Order in a Democratic Society* (Westport, Conn.: Greenwood Press, 1978), pp. 346–358; Eliot Freidson, *Profession of Medicine: A Study of the Sociology of Applied Knowledge* (New York: Dodd, Mead, 1970), p. 208.

10. Comaroff, "Medicine," p. 63.

3   Healing in Christian Groups

1. General references on Christian healing include Jerome Frank, *Persuasion and Healing* (New York: Schocken, 1972); David E. Harrell, *All Things Are Possible: The Healing and Charismatic Revivals in Modern America* (Bloomington, Ind.: Indiana University Press, 1975); Morton Kelsey, *Healing and Christianity: In Ancient Thought and Modern Times* (New York: Harper and Row, 1973); Kelsey, "Faith: Its Function in the Wholistic Healing Process," in Herbert Otto and James Knight, eds., *Dimensions of Wholistic Healing: New Frontiers in the Treatment of the Whole Person* (Chicago: Nelson-Hall, 1979), pp. 203–225; Louis Rose, *Faith Healing* (Harmondsworth, England: Penguin, 1970). A reasonably thorough bibliography of works on various approaches to Christian faith healing by believers/practitioners is found in J. Gordon Melton, *A Reader's Guide to the Church's Ministry of Healing* (Independence, Mo.: The Academy of Religious and Psychical Research, 1973).

There have been relatively few social scientific studies of Christian faith healing, and even fewer researchers have examined middle-class religious groups. See Gillian Allen and Roy Wallis, "Pentecostalists as a Medical Minority," in Wallis and Peter Morley, eds., *Marginal Medicine* (New York: Free Press, 1976), pp. 110–137; Kenneth Calestro, "Psychotherapy, Faith Healing and Suggestion," *International Journal of Psychiatry* 10 (1972): 83–113; Thomas J. Csordas and Steven Cross, "Healing of Memories: Psychotherapeutic Ritual among Catholic Pentecostals," *Journal of Pastoral Care* 30 (1976): 245–257; Csordas, "The Rhetoric of Transformation in Ritual Healing," *Culture, Medicine and Psychiatry* 7 (1983): 333–375; Daniel Johnson, J. Sherwood Williams, and David Bromley, "Religion, Health, and Healing: Findings from a Southern City," *Sociological Analysis* 47 (1986): 66–73; Meredith B. McGuire, *Pentecostal Catholics: Power, Charisma, and Order in a Religious Movement* (Philadelphia: Temple University Press, 1982); Robert Ness, "The Impact of Indigenous Healing Activity: An Empirical Study of Two Fundamentalist Churches," *Social Science and Medicine* 14B (1980): 167–180; E. Mansell Pattison, "Ideological Support for the Marginal Middle Class: Faith Healing and Glossolalia," in Irving Zaretsky and Mark Leone, eds., *Religious Movements in Contemporary America* (Princeton, N.J.: Princeton University Press, 1974), pp. 418–458; Pattison, Nikolajs Lapins, and Hans Doerr, "Faith Healing: A Study of Personality and Function," *Journal of Nervous and Mental Disease* 157 (1973): 397–409; Pattison, "The Personal Meaning of Faith Healing," pp. 105–115 in Claude Frazier, ed., *Faith Healing: Finger of God? Or, Scientific Curiosity* (New York: Thomas Nelson, 1973); Margaret M. Poloma, "An Empirical Study of Perceptions of Healing among Assemblies of God Members," paper presented to the Society for the Scientific Study of Religion, 1984; Raymond Prince, "Fundamental Differences of Psychoanalysis and Faith Healing," *International Journal of Psychiatry* 10 (1972): 125–128.

2. Max Weber, *The Sociology of Religion*, trans. E. Fischoff (Boston: Beacon, 1963), chapter 9.

3. Peter L. Berger, *The Sacred Canopy: Elements of a Sociological Theory of Religion* (Garden City, N.Y.: Doubleday, 1967), p. 24.

4. Some Episcopalian healing groups studied were an exception; they were less dualistic and tended to emphasize only the use of God's power in effecting healing (i.e., the right half of the image of healing presented in figure 3 1).

5. Randy Cirner, "Deliverance," *New Covenant*, April 1974, pp. 4–7, and May 1974, pp. 22–24; Francis MacNutt, *Healing* (Notre Dame: Ave Maria Press, 1974), and *The Power to Heal* (Notre Dame: Ave Maria Press, 1977); Edward O'Connor, *The Pentecostal Movement in the Catholic Church* (Notre Dame: Ave Maria Press, 1971).

6. Compare Csordas and Cross, "Healing of Memories," and Csordas, "The Rhetoric of Transformation."

7. See McGuire, *Pentecostal Catholics*, pp. 139, 169.

4   Traditional Metaphysical Movements

1. J. Stillson Judah, *The History and Philosophy of the Metaphysical Movements in America* (Philadelphia: Westminster Press, 1967).

2. On the growth and development of early metaphysical movements, see Charles S. Braden, *Spirits in Rebellion: The Rise and Development of New Thought* (Dallas: Southern Methodist University Press, 1963); Braden, *Christian Science Today: Power, Policy and Practice* (Dallas: Southern Methodist University Press, 1958); Horatio Dresser, ed., *The Quimby Manuscripts* (Secaucus, N.J.: Citadel, 1961); Alfred W. Griswold, "New Thought: A Cult of Success," *American Journal of Sociology* 40 (1934): 309–318; Judah, *History and Philosophy*; Alice Paulsen, "Religious Healing," *Journal of the American Medical Association* 86 (1926): 1519–1524; Frank Podmore, *From Mesmer to Christian Science: A Short History of Mental Healing* (New York: University Books, 1963 [1909]); Rodney Stark, William S. Bainbridge, and Lori Kent, "Cult Membership in the Roaring Twenties," *Sociological Analysis* 42 (1981): 137–163.

3. Roy Wallis, "A Comparative Analysis of Problems and Processes of Change in Christian Science and Scientology," *Acts of the CISR* (Lille, France: Conference Internationale de Sociologie Religieuse, 1973), pp. 407–422; Wallis, "Ideology, Authority and the Development of Cultic Movements," *Social Research* 41 (1974): 299–327; Geoffrey K. Nelson, "The Concept of Cult," *Sociological Review* 16 (1968): 351–362.

4. See John Richard Burkholder, "The Law Knows No Heresy: Marginal Religious Movements and the Courts," in Irving Zaretsky and Mark Leone, eds., *Religious Movements in Contemporary America* (Princeton, N.J.: Princeton University Press, 1974), pp. 27–52; Walter I. Wardwell, "Christian Science Healing," *Journal for the Scientific Study of Religion* 4 (1965): 175–181; Wardwell, "Christian Science and Spiritual Healing," in Richard Cox, ed., *Religious Systems and Psychotherapy* (Springfield, Ill.: Charles C. Thomas, 1973), pp. 72–88.

5. Judah, *History and Philosophy*, p. 270; also: Braden, *Spirits in Rebellion*, p. 18, 19; Braden, *Christian Science*, pp. 336–355; Podmore, *From Mesmer*, pp. 262–278.

6. For studies on contemporary uses of Christian Science, see: Janice Demarest, "A Sociolinguistic Study of Christian Science Oral Testimonies," *Working Papers in Sociolinguistics* 26 (1975); R. W. England, "Some Aspects of Christian Science as Reflected in Letters of Testimony," *American Journal of Sociology* 59 (1954): 448–453; Margery Fox, "Paradox Lost: The Christian Science Nurse," paper presented to the American Anthropological Association, 1980; John A. Lee, *Sectarian Healers and Hypnotherapy* (Toronto: Province of Ontario, Committee on the Healing Arts, 1970); Arthur E. Nudelman, "Christian Science Conceptions of Treatment and Etiology of Illness: An Empirical Study," paper presented to the Society for the Scientific Study of Religion, 1976); Nudelman, "The Maintenance

of Christian Science in Scientific Society," in Wallis and Peter Morley, eds., *Marginal Medicine* (New York: Free Press, 1976), pp. 42–60; Harold W. Pfautz, "Christian Science: A Case Study of the Social Psychological Aspects of Secularization," *Social Forces* 34 (1956): 246–252; Pfautz, "A Case Study of an Urban Religious Movement: Christian Science," in Ernest Burgess and Donald Bogue, *Contributions to Urban Sociology* (Chicago: University of Chicago Press, 1964), pp. 284–303.

7. Compare Lee, *Sectarian Healers*, pp. 132–136.

8. Charles Fillmore, *Christian Healing* (Lee's Summit, Mo.: Unity School of Christianity, 1979).

9. Published by Unity School of Christianity, July 1981. Schneider and Dornbusch suggest that Unity and other New Thought movements are an important part of the "popular religion" tapped in their 1950s study of inspirational books. They note that in general the theme of prosperity declined in prominence after the Depression, while the theme of health increased dramatically (Louis Schneider and Sanford M. Dornbusch, *Popular Religion: Inspirational Books in America* [Chicago: University of Chicago Press, 1958]).

10. Theodosia Schobert, *Divine Remedies: A Textbook on Spiritual Healing* (Lee's Summit, Mo.: Unity School of Christianity, 1969 [1934]), p. 86.

11. Braden, *Spirits in Rebellion*, pp. 148–150.

12. Although Unity's founder, Charles Fillmore, had recommended vegetarianism, none of the members who practiced it cited this historical fact as part of their own reason for vegetarianism; more typically, they cited ideas borrowed from Hindu philosophies.

13. Quoted in Braden, *Spirits in Rebellion*, p. 163.

5   Eastern Meditation and Human Potential Groups

1. Paul Heelas, "California Self-Religions and Socializing the Subjective," in Eileen Barker, ed., *New Religious Movements: A Perspective for Understanding Society* (New York: The Edwin Mellen Press, 1982), pp. 69–85.

2. Frances Westley, *The Complex Forms of the Religious Life* (Chico, Calif.: Scholars Press, 1983), pp. 59–85.

3. Westley, in *Complex Forms*, separates "cult of man" groups from other new religious groups on the grounds that they locate the sacred completely within the individual. I agree with this distinction but found very few respondents whose beliefs and practices were primarily shaped by such groups.

Several respondents had taken training courses on, for example, psychosynthesis and Arica but had merely tucked some of the exercises and meditations into their prior eclectic Eastern or psychic/occult beliefs. Other respondents had taken Silva Mind Control (SMC) courses; three of these were or became involved in psychic groups and two were active in the Catholic Charismatic Renewal; even though they valued the training, none saw SMC as a primary element of their current beliefs and practices.

Roy Wallis ("Betwixt Therapy and Salvation: The Changing Form of the Human Potential Movement," in R. Kenneth Jones, ed., *Sickness and Sectarianism* [London: Gower, 1985], pp. 23–51) includes as "Human Potential" or "Growth" movements all approaches concerned with individual "development"; these range from Scientology to reflexology, est to gestalt psychotherapy, astrology to martial arts. He presents interesting diagrams (pp. 28, 29) of the eclectic borrowing and other connections among the various strands of this phenomenon.

Wallis's essay provides an interpretation of Stone's observation that in the West Coast human potential movement there was a growing emphasis on Eastern disciplines and self-transcendence in spiritual terms. See Donald Stone, "The Human Potential Movement," in Charles Glock and Robert Bellah, eds., *The New Religious Consciousness* (Berkeley: University of California Press, 1976), pp. 93–115.

We have no longitudinal data to indicate whether there has been such a transition to spirituality among groups in this area. The data do show, however, that virtually all respondents described in this chapter employed primarily spiritual (usually Eastern) beliefs and practices, while other "growth" approaches were eclectically used and subordinated.

4. Robert S. Ellwood, "Emergent Religion in America: An Historical Perspective," in Jacob Needleman and George Baker, eds., *Understanding the New Religions* (New York: Seabury, 1978), pp. 267–284.

5. For a description of the development of the movement in America and Britain, see Wallis, "Betwixt Therapy"; see also Kurt Back, *Beyond Words: The Story of the Human Potential Movement* (Baltimore: Penguin, 1972); and Westley, *Complex Forms*.

6. For an excellent but now somewhat dated bibliography and theoretical framework, see Thomas Robbins, Dick Anthony, and James Richardson, "Theory and Research on Today's New Religions," *Sociological Analysis* 39 (1978): 95–122.

The following sources document Eastern-inspired spiritual/therapeutic groups. These references include, for the purpose of comparison, studies of youth culture movements (such as Divine Light Mission and Krishna Consciousness) as well as the movements attractive to participants in this study (such as Tibetan Buddhism and Jain yoga). See: Anthony and Robbins, "The Meher Baba Movement: Its Effect on Post-Adolescent Social Alienation," in Irving Zaretsky and Mark Leone, eds., *Religious Movements in Contemporary America* (Princeton, N.J.: Princeton University Press, 1974), pp. 479–511; Anthony, Robbins, Madeleine Doucas, and Thomas Curtis, "Patients and Pilgrims: Changing Attitudes toward Psychotherapy of Converts to Eastern Mysticism," *American Behavioral Scientist* 20 (1977): 861–886; Christopher Bache, "On the Emergence of Perinatal Symptoms in Buddhist Meditation," *Journal for the Scientific Study of Religion* 20 (1981): 339–351; Robert Ellwood, *Alternative Altars: Unconventional and Eastern Spirituality in America* (Chicago: University of Chicago Press, 1979); Robert Frager, "Aikido—A Japanese Approach to Self-Development and Mind-Body Harmony," in Charles Garfield, ed., *Rediscovery of the Body: A Psychosomatic View of Life and Death* (New York: Laurel/Dell, 1977); Marc Galanter and Peter Buckley, "Evangelical Religion and Meditation: Psychotherapeutic Effects," *Journal of Nervous and Mental Disease* 166 (1978): 685–691; Ronald Grisell, "Kundalini Yoga as Healing Agent," in Herbert Otto and James Knight, eds., *Dimensions of Wholistic Healing: New Frontiers in the Treatment of the Whole Person* (Chicago: Nelson-Hall, 1979), pp. 441–461; J. Stillson Judah, *Hare Krishna and the Counterculture* (New York: Wiley, 1974); David M. Levin, "Approaches to Psychotherapy: Freud, Jung and Tibetan Buddhism," in Ronald Valle and Rolf von Eckartsberg, eds., *Metaphors of Consciousness* (New York: Plenum, 1981), pp. 243–274; David L. Preston, "Becoming a Zen Practitioner," *Sociological Analysis* 42 (1981): 47–57; Preston, "Meditative Ritual Practice and Spiritual Conversion-Commitment: Theoretical Implications Based on the Case of Zen," *Sociological Analysis* 43 (1982): 257–271; Raymond H. Prince, "Cocoon Work: An Interpretation of the Concern of Contemporary Youth with the Mystical," in Zaretsky and Leone, *Religious Movements*, pp. 255–271; Tina Posner, "Transcendental Meditation, Perfect Health and the Millennium," in Jones, *Sickness and Sectarianism*, pp. 94–112; Robbins and Anthony, "Getting Straight with Meher Baba: A Study of Mysticism, Drug Rehabilitation and Post-adolescent Role Conflict," *Journal for the Scientific Study of Religion* 11 (1972): 122–140; Thomas Sullivan, "Transcendental Meditation: Locus of Control and Social Isolation," paper presented to the Society for the Scientific Study of Religion, 1977; Steven M. Tipton, *Getting Saved from the Sixties: The Transformation of Moral Meaning in American Culture by Alternative Religious Movements* (Berkeley: University of California Press, 1982); Alan Tobey, "The Summer Solstice of the Healthy-Happy-Holy Organization," in Glock and Bellah, *Religious Consciousness*, pp. 5–30; Ernest Volinn, "Eastern Meditation Groups: Why Join?" *Sociological Analysis* 46 (1985): 147–156; Westley, *Complex Forms*; John Whitworth, "From Across the Black Water: Two Imported Varieties of Hinduism—the Hare Krishnas and the Ramakrishna Vedanta Society," in Barker, *New Religious Movements*, pp. 155–172; Stephen R. Wilson, "Becoming a Yogi," *Sociological Analysis* 45 (1984): 301–314; Robert Wuthnow, *The Consciousness Reformation* (Berkeley: University of California Press, 1976); Wuthnow, *Experimentation in American Religion: The New Mysticisms and their Implications for the Churches* (Berkeley: University of California Press, 1979).

7.   On the various forms of the human potential movement, see Earl Babbie and Stone, "An Evaluation of the est Experience by a National Sample

of Graduates," *Bioscience Communication* 3 (1977): 123–140; Frederick Bird, "The Pursuit of Innocence: New Religious Movements and Moral Accountability," *Sociological Analysis* 40 (1979): 335–346; Burton Giges and Edward Rosenfeld, "Personal Growth, Encounter and Self-Awareness Groups," in Max Rosenbaum and Alvin Snadowsky, eds., *The Intensive Group Experience* (New York: Free Press, 1976), pp. 87–110; Regina E. Halloman, "Ritual Opening and Individual Transformation: Rites of Passage at Esalen," *American Anthropologist* 76 (1974): 265–280; Heelas, "California Self Religions"; John Koffend, "The Gospel According to Helen," *Psychology Today*, September 1980, pp. 75–90; Thomas Oden, *The Intensive Group Experience: The New Pietism* (Philadelphia: Westminster, 1972); Anne A. Schutzenbergen and Yannick Geffroy, "The Body and the Group: The New Body Therapies," in Shirley Weitz, ed., *Nonverbal Communication* (New York: Oxford, 1979), pp. 207–219; Stone, "The Human Potential Movement"; Stone, "Social Consciousness in the Human Potential Movement," in Robbins and Anthony, eds., *In Gods We Trust* (New Brunswick, N.J.: Transaction, 1981), pp. 215–227; Tipton, *Getting Saved from the Sixties*; Tipton, "The Moral Logic of Alternative Religions," in Douglas and Tipton, eds., *Religion and America: Spirituality in a Secular Age* (Boston: Beacon, 1982), pp. 79–107; Wallis, "Betwixt Therapy"; Westley, "The 'Cult of Man': Durkheim's Predictions and New Religious Movements," *Sociological Analysis* 39 (1978): 135–145; Westley, "Ritual as Psychic Bridge Building: Narcissism, Healing and the Human Potential Movement," paper presented to the British Sociological Association, 1981; Westley, *Complex Forms.*

Critical evaluations of the movement include: Christopher Lasch, *The Culture of Narcissism* (New York: Norton, 1979); Peter Marin, "The New Narcissism," *Harper's* 251 (1975): 45–56; R. D. Rosen, *Psychobabble* (London: Wildwood House, 1978); Edwin Schur, *The Awareness Trap: Self Absorption Instead of Social Change* (New York: McGraw-Hill, 1976).

8. Compare Wuthnow, "Political Aspects of the Quietist Revival," in Robbins and Anthony, *In Gods We Trust*, pp. 229–243.

9. On the effectiveness of meditation, see: Herbert Benson, *The Relaxation Response* (New York: William Morrow, 1975); Benson (with William Proctor), *Beyond the Relaxation Response* (New York: Times Books, 1984); Patricia Carrington, *Freedom in Meditation* (Garden City, N.Y.: Doubleday, 1977); Carrington, "The Uses of Meditation in Psychotherapy," in Arthur Sugarman and Ralph Tarter, eds., *Expanding Dimensions of Consciousness* (New York: Springer, 1978), pp. 81–98; Daniel Goleman, *The Varieties of the Meditative Experience* (New York: E. P. Dutton, 1977); Claudio Naranjo and Robert Ornstein, *The Psychology of Meditation* (New York: Viking, 1971); Deane Shapiro and Robert Walsh, *Meditation: Self-Regulation Strategy and Altered State of Consciousness* (New York: Aldine, 1981); John Yuille and Lynn Sereda, "Positive Effects of Meditation: A Limited Generalization," *Journal of Applied Psychology* 65 (1980): 333–340.

10. Unlike interviews, field notes are not verbatim, but very close to verbatim.

11. Field notes are not verbatim. Note also that the reference to Atlanta was at a time when a string of children's murders had raised national concern.

6   Psychic and Occult Healing

1. A concise description of many of these historical sources is in Robert S. Ellwood, Jr., *Religious and Spiritual Groups in Modern America* (Englewood Cliffs, N.J.: Prentice-Hall, 1973), pp. 42–128; see also Ellwood, *Alternative Altars: Unconventional and Eastern Spirituality in America* (Chicago: University of Chicago Press, 1979); and Robert Galbreath, "The History of Modern Occultism: A Bibliographic Survey," *Journal of Popular Culture* 5 (1971): 726–754.

2. Early occult and spiritualist groups were particularly fascinated by the image of the "Red Indian" as healer or spirit guide. Some contemporary spiritualists retain such spirit guides. Spiritualists who used such spirits often described them in detail in the stereotypical image of a Plains Indian in full regalia. See June Macklin, "Belief, Ritual and Healing: New England Spiritualism and Mexican-American Spiritism Compared," in Irving Zaretsky and Mark Leone, eds., *Religious Movements in Contemporary America* (Princeton, N.J.: Princeton University Press, 1974), pp. 383–417.

For these early movements, the "Red Indian" was a symbol of esoteric power and knowledge. Contemporary psychic and occult groups are, by contrast, much more likely to attempt to learn actual native practices. For example, during this study some groups invited as speakers or workshop leaders persons practicing curanderismo (Mexican), huna (Hawaiian), Sioux, and Algonquin Indian healing. For a study of a similar American healing group organized around a kahuna's healing practices, see Tanice Foltz, "An Alternative Healing Group as a New Religious Form: The Use of Ritual in Becoming a Healing Practitioner," in R. Kenneth Jones, ed., *Sickness and Sectarianism* (London: Gower, 1985), pp. 144–157.

3. Jane Brody, "Laying on of Hands Gains New Respect," *The New York Times*, March 26, 1985, pp. C1–2; Dolores Krieger, *The Therapeutic Touch* (Englewood Cliffs, N J : Prentice-Hall, 1979); Krieger, "Therapeutic Touch: The Imprimatur of Nursing," *American Journal of Nursing* 75 (1975): 784–787; Stanley Krippner and Alberto Villoldo, *The Realms of Healing* (Millbrae, Calif.: Celestial Arts, 1976); Lawrence LeShan, *The Medium, the Mystic and the Physicist* (New York: Ballantine, 1975); LeShan, "Toward a General Theory of Psychic Healing," in Stanley Dean, ed., *Psychiatry and Mysticism* (Chicago: Nelson-Hale, 1975), pp. 247–269; J. Gordon Melton, *A Reader's Guide to the Church's Ministry of Healing: An Annotated Bibliography* (Independence, Mo.: The Academy of Religion and Psychical Research, 1977).

4. J. Stillson Judah, *The History and Philosophy of the Metaphysical Movements in America* (Philadelphia: Westminster, 1967); see also Charles S. Braden, *These Also Believe: A Study of Modern American Cults and Minority Religious Movements* (New York: Macmillan, 1949).

5. Bryan R. Wilson, *Religious Sects* (New York: McGraw-Hill, 1970), pp. 44–46, 141–172.

6. Useful studies of contemporary Spiritualism in the United States and Britain include: Macklin, "Belief, Ritual and Healing"; Bernice Martin, "The Spiritualist Meeting," in David Martin and Michael Hill, *Sociological Yearbook of Religion in Britain* (London: SCM Press, Number 3, 1970), pp. 146–161; Geoffrey K. Nelson, *Spiritualism and Society* (New York: Schocken, 1969); Vieda Skultans, *Intimacy and Ritual: A Study of Spiritualism, Mediums and Groups* (London: Routledge and Kegan Paul, 1974); Linda Tschanz, "Healing in the Spiritualist World," paper presented to the Society for the Scientific Study of Religion, 1980; Zaretsky, "In the Beginning Was the Word: The Relationship of Language to Social Organization in Spiritualist Churches," in Zaretsky and Leone, *Religious Movements*, pp. 166–222.

7. John A. Lee, *Sectarian Healers and Hypnotherapy* (Toronto: A Study for the Committee on the Healing Arts, Province of Ontario, 1970).

8. More so than other types of healing, psychic and occult healing is individualistic and does not require group participation or membership; our methodology probably tapped only the variants practiced in group settings or learned through group affiliations. For a study of occult and other mail-order teaching, see Anson D. Shupe, Jr., "'Disembodied Access' and Technological Constraints on Organizational Development: A Study of Mail-order Religions," *Journal for the Scientific Study of Religion* 15 (1976): 177–185.

9. Sociological studies of these related movements include Debra Kantor and Meredith McGuire, "Creative Eclecticism: The Great White Brotherhood of Elizabeth Clare Prophet," paper presented to the Association for the Sociology of Religion, 1981; and Melinda Bollar Wagner, *Metaphysics in Midwestern America* (Columbus, Ohio: Ohio State University Press, 1983); a nonsociological treatment of the contributions of the influential ARE and its founder Edgar Cayce is William McGarey, "Edgar Cayce's Contribution to Holistic Medicine," in Herbert Otto and James Knight, eds., *Dimensions in Wholistic Healing: New Frontiers in the Treatment of the Whole Person* (Chicago: Nelson-Hall, 1979), pp. 321–332.

10. On the role of scientism in these and related movements, see Charles Lemert, "Science, Religion and Secularization," *The Sociological Quarterly* 20 (1979): 445–461; Melinda Bollar Wagner, "Spiritual Science: 'Metaphysics' as a Response to 'Rational Culture'," unpublished paper presented to the Society for the Scientific Study of Religion, 1981; also Wagner, *Metaphysics in Midwestern America*; Harriet Whitehead, "Reasonably Fantastic: Some Perspectives on Scientology,

Science Fiction, and Occultism," in Zaretsky and Leone, *Religious Movements*, pp. 547–587.

7   The Role of Healer

1. This description of "Marge" is a composite of three separate but similar healers; all identifying details are disguised.

2. Arthur Kleinman, *Patients and Healers in the Context of Culture: An Exploration of the Borderline between Anthropology, Medicine, and Psychiatry* (Berkeley: University of California, 1980), p. 105.

3. See Kleinman, "The Failure of Western Medicine," *Human Nature* 1 (1978): 63–68.

4. Allan Young, "Some Implications of Medical Beliefs and Practices for Social Anthropology," *American Anthropologist* 78 (1976): 13.

5. Jean Comaroff, "Medicine and Culture: Some Anthropological Perspectives," *Social Science and Medicine* 12B (1978): 247–254; see also Peter L. Berger, *The Sacred Canopy: Elements of a Sociological Theory of Religion* (Garden City, N.Y.: Doubleday, 1967), pp. 53–80; Kleinman, "On Illness Meanings and Clinical Interpretation: Not 'Rational Man,' but a Rational Approach to Man the Sufferer/Man the Healer," *Culture, Medicine and Psychiatry* 5 (1981): 373–379.

6. On theodicies of illness and death, see Meredith McGuire, *Religion: The Social Context* (Belmont, Calif.: Wadsworth, 1987), pp. 245–247; see also Robert A. Hahn, "Rethinking 'Illness' and 'Disease,'" *Contributions to Asian Studies* 18 (1984): 1–23.

7. See, for example, Lorna Amarasingham Rhodes, "Time and the Process of Diagnosis in Sinhalese Ritual Treatment," *Contributions to Asian Studies* 18 (1984): 46–59.

8. Young, "Order, Analogy and Efficacy in Ethiopian Medical Divination," *Culture, Medicine and Psychiatry* 1 (1977): 183–199.

9. Young, "Some Implications," p. 13.

10. Leonard B. Glick, "Medicine as an Ethnographic Category: The Gimi of the New Guinea Highlands," *Ethnology* 6 (1967): 31–56.

11. Kenneth Calestro, "Psychotherapy, Faith Healing and Suggestion," *International Journal of Psychiatry* 10 (1972): 83–113; Jerome D. Frank, *Persuasion and Healing* (New York: Schocken, 1973); Raymond Prince, "Introduction to Shamans and Endorphins," *Ethos* 10 (1982): 299–302.

12. Thomas Csordas, "The Rhetoric of Transformation in Ritual Healing," *Culture, Medicine and Psychiatry* 7 (1983): 333–375; see also James Dow, *The Shaman's Touch: Otomi Indian Symbolic Healing* (Salt Lake City: University of Utah Press, 1986), pp. 135–150.

13. This limited notion of "holistic" or alternative healing is exemplified by Warren Salmon, ed., *Alternative Medicines: Popular and Policy Perspectives* (New York: Tavistock, 1984), and Gary Easthope, "Marginal Healers," in R. Kenneth Jones, ed., *Sickness and Sectarianism* (London: Gower, 1985), pp. 52–71.

Other studies have examined the adoption of alternative techniques or approaches by various "certified" doctors, such as M.D.'s, osteopaths, and chiropractors. Interestingly, these researchers found spiritual factors significant in the decision to employ alternative approaches to healing; see Michael Goldstein, Dennis J. Jaffe, Dale Garell, and Ruth E. Berk, "Holistic Doctors: Becoming a Non-traditional Medical Practitioner," *Urban Life* 14 (1986): 317–344; Goldstein, Jaffe, Carol Sutherland, and Josie Wilson, "Holistic Physicians: Implications for the Study of the Medical Profession," *Journal of Health and Social Behavior* 28 (1987): 103–119; Jaffe, Goldstein, and Wilson, "Physicians in Transition: Crisis and Change in Life and Work," in Cynthia Scott and Joann Hawk, eds., *Heal Thyself: The Health Care Professionals* (New York: Brunner/Mazel, 1986), pp. 134–144.

14. Walter I. Wardwell, "Sounding Board: The Future of Chiropractic," *New England Journal of Medicine* 302 (1980): 688–690; see also Hans Baer, "Divergence and Convergence in Two Systems of Manual Medicine: Osteopathy and Chiropractic in the United States," *Medical Anthropology Quarterly* 1 (New Series, 1987): 176–193; Jane E. Brody, "Chiropractic, Long Ignored as 'Unscientific,' Now is Scrutinized by Health Specialists," *New York Times*, October 1, 1975; David Coburn and C. Lesley Biggs, "Limits to Medical Dominance: The Case of Chiropractic," *Social Science and Medicine* 22 (1986): 1035–1046; James Cowie and Julian Roebuck, *An Ethnography of a Chiropractic Clinic: Definition of a Deviant Situation* (New York: Free Press, 1975).

15. Joseph A. Kotarba, "American Acupuncturists: The New Entrepreneurs of Hope," *Urban Life* 4 (1975): 149–177.

16. John L. Coulehan, "Adjustment, the Hands and Healing," *Culture, Medicine and Psychiatry* 9 (1985): 353–382.

17. Robert A. Hahn, "Between Two Worlds: Physicians as Patients," *Medical Anthropology Quarterly* 16 (1985): 87–98.

18. Two characteristic patterns of group structure led to very different leadership styles. Several Christian and a few psychic/occult groups were highly authoritarian; leaders were believed to articulate Truths received from a higher Source. By contrast, other groups (especially Eastern/meditation groups, as well as many occult and metaphysical groups) were adamantly individualistic and eclectic. Adherents in the authoritarian groups were believers, whereas members of other groups were characteristically "seekers," who eclectically combined particles of truth from many different sources into their personal meaning systems.

Nonauthoritarian groups are inherently fragile organizations, because of three structural characteristics: lack of clear locus of authority; loose and precarious "doctrine;" and a pattern of segmented commitment. For example, in contrast to the total allegiance expected of a born-again Christian, typical Eastern groups were loosely affiliated around a spiritual discipline and outlook. Members belonged simultaneously to other, often competing, groups and felt free to choose elements of any belief or practice. See Roy Wallis, "Ideology, Authority and the Development of Cultic Movements," *Social Research* 41 (1974): 299–327.

Wallis argues that nonauthoritarian groups may adopt strategies, such as sectarianization or increased spiritual focus, to overcome this structural precariousness; see Wallis, "Betwixt Therapy and Salvation: The Changing Form of the Human Potential Movement," in Jones, *Sickness and Sectarianism*, pp. 23–51. Although we observed instances of sectarianization at the national organizational level in at least two movements, we saw little or no change in the relative spiritual emphasis in the local groups studied during the relatively brief period of the study. Since our study focused almost exclusively on these movements at the local level, some of the larger issues of commitment were less evident. For example, virtually none of the psychic or occult adherents held *any* allegiance to a larger movement, but most felt intense personal commitment toward their fellow healing circle members. Nevertheless, local leadership was important for sustaining that commitment and organizing local activities. To the extent that healing was an important activity and contributed to the group's sense of unity, the role of healer was, likewise, important for the whole group.

8   Help-seeking, Beyond the Medical Model

1. Arthur M. Kleinman, "Some Issues for a Comparative Study of Medical Healing," *International Journal of Social Psychiatry* 19 (1973): 159–165.

2. Allan Young, "Some Implications of Medical Beliefs and Practices for Social Anthropology," *American Anthropologist* 78 (1976): 5–24.

3. Irving Zola, "The Concept of Trouble and Sources of Medical Assistance—To Whom One Can Turn, with What and Why?," *Social Science and Medicine* 6 (1972): 673–679.

4. For an illustration of the complexity of pathways in help-seeking, see Robert Dingwall, *Aspects of Illness* (New York: St. Martin's Press, 1977); see also Noel J. Chrisman, "The Health Seeking Process: An Approach to the Natural History of Illness," *Culture, Medicine and Psychiatry* 1 (1977): 351–377; David Robinson, *The Process of Becoming Ill* (London: Routledge and Kegan Paul, 1971).

5. For a useful critique and corrective, see Chrisman, "The Health Seeking Process."

6. Thanks to Steve Warner for this analogy.

7. Haehn's study of the use of nonmedical practitioners in Germany likewise

found that 80 percent of the adherents use both medical and nonmedical prac-
titoners but do not tell their medical doctor of their involvement with nonmedical
practitioners. His data show that, in an urban area of Germany, approximately 30
to 40 percent of patients of medical doctors also use or have used nonmedical
healing practitioners. This impressive percentage does not include forms of
nonmedical healing that are self-administered or in the context of a therapeutic
group or religion. See Klaus-Dieter Haehn, "Heilpraktikerbesuche chronisch
Kranker: Frequenz und Motivation," *Diagnostik* 13 (1980): 145–146.

8. Julius A. Roth, "Information and the Control of Treatment in Tuberculosis
Hospitals," in Eliot Freidson, ed., *The Hospital in Modern Society* (Glencoe, Ill.: Free
Press, 1963), pp. 293–318.

9. Jean Comaroff, "Communicating Information about Non-Fatal Illness: The
Strategies of a Group of General Practitioners," *Sociological Review* 24 (1976):
269–290. Compare W. Timothy Anderson and David Helm, "The Physician-
Patient Encounter: A Process of Reality Negotiation," in E. Gartly Jaco, ed.,
Patients, Physicians, and Illness (New York: Free Press, 1979), pp. 259–271; Thomas
Scheff, "Negotiating Reality: Notes on Power in the Assessment of Responsibil-
ity," *Social Problems* 16 (1968): 3–17.

10. Howard Waitzkin and John D. Stoeckle, "The Communication of Information about Illness," in Z. J. Lipowski, ed., *Advances in Psychosomatic Medicine:
Psychosocial Aspects of Physical Illness* (Basel, Switzerland: Karger, 1972), pp. 180–
215; see also Waitzkin and Stoeckle, "Information Control and the Micropolitics of
Health Care: Summary of an Ongoing Research Project," *Social Science and Medicine* 10 (1976): 263–276.

11. David Hayes-Bautista and Dominic Harveston, "Holistic Health Care,"
Social Policy 7 (1977): 7–13.

12. George L. Engel, "The Need for a New Medical Model: A Challenge for
Biomedicine," *Science* 196 (1977): 129–136; see also the excellent commentary in
Nancy Scheper-Hughes and Margaret M. Lock, "The Mindful Body: A Prolegom-
enon to Future Work in Medical Anthropology," *Medical Anthropology Quarterly* 1
(New Series, 1987): 6–41.

13. Mark Sullivan, "In What Sense is Contemporary Medicine Dualistic?"
Culture, Medicine and Psychiatry 10 (1986): 331–350.

14. Eric J. Cassell, "The Nature of Suffering and the Goals of Medicine,"
New England Journal of Medicine 306 (1982): 639–645; see also Cecil G. Helman,
"Psyche, Soma, and Society: The Social Construction of Psychosomatic Disor-
ders," *Culture, Medicine and Psychiatry* 9 (1985): 1–26.

15. David V. McQueen and Johannes Siegrist, "Social Factors in the Etiology
of Chronic Disease: An Overview," *Social Science and Medicine* 16 (1982): 353–367.

16. Hans Selye, "Forty Years of Stress Research: Principal Remaining Problems and Misconceptions," *Canadian Medical Association Journal* 115 (1976): 53–56.

The following discussion is based upon Selye, "Forty Years," and *Stress without Distress* (New York: Signet/New American Library, 1975).

On the relationship between the symbolic stimulus and the pathophysiological response, see especially Alfred Amkraut and George F. Solomon, "From the Symbolic Stimulus to the Pathophysiologic Response: Immune Mechanisms," *International Journal of Psychiatry in Medicine* 5 (1974): 541–563; James P. Henry, "The Relation of Social to Biological Processes in Disease," *Social Science and Medicine* 16 (1982): 369–380; William F. Kiely, "From the Symbolic Stimulus to the Pathophysiological Response: Neurophysiological Mechanisms," *International Journal of Psychiatry in Medicine* 5 (1974): 517–529; Daniel Moerman, "Anthropology of Symbolic Healing," *Current Anthropology* 20 (1979): 59–66; Rudolf H. Moos, "Determinants of Physiological Responses to Symbolic Stimuli: The Role of the Social Environment," *International Journal of Psychiatry in Medicine* 5 (1974): 389–399; Gary Schwartz, "The Brain as a Health Care System," in George Stone, Frances Cohen, Nancy Adler, and associates, *Health Psychology: A Handbook* (San Francisco: Jossey-Bass, 1979), pp. 549–571; Solomon, "Emotions, Stress, the Central Nervous System, and Immunity," *Annals of the New York Academy of Science* 164 (1969): 335–343; see also overviews by Jane E. Brody, "Emotions Found to Influence Nearly Every Human Ailment," *New York Times*, May 24, 1983; Daniel Goleman, "Strong Emotional Response to Disease May Bolster Patient's Immune System," *New York Times*, October 22, 1985; Steven Locke and Douglas Colligan, *The Healer Within: The New Medicine of Mind and Body* (New York: E. P. Dutton, 1986).

17. Journalistic overviews of these studies are in Goleman, "Relaxation: Surprising Benefits Detected," *The New York Times*, May 13, 1986; Harold M. Schmeck, Jr., "By Training the Brain, Scientists Find Links to Immune Defenses," *The New York Times*, January 1, 1985.

18. For a thematic synopsis and critique of the methodologies of these studies, see Frances Cohen, "Personality, Stress and the Development of Physical Illness," in Stone et al., *Health Psychology*, pp. 77–111.

19. Meyer Friedman and Ray H. Rosenman, "Association of Specific Overt Behavior Patterns with Blood and Cardiovascular Findings," *Journal of the American Medical Association* 169 (1959): 1286; Friedman, *Pathogenesis of Coronary Artery Disease* (New York: McGraw-Hill, 1969).

20. Moos and George F. Solomon, 1964 and 1965, summarized in Solomon, "Emotions, Stress, The Central Nervous System, and Immunity."

21. Richard H. Rahe and Ransom J. Arthur, "Life Change and Illness Studies: Past History and Future Directions," *Journal of Human Stress* (1978): 3–15; see also Rahe, Merle Meyer, Michael Smith, George Kjaer, Thomas Holmes, "Social Stress and Illness Onset," *Journal of Psychosomatic Research* 8 (1964): 35–44; Holmes and Minoru Masuda, "Life Change and Illness Susceptibility," in Barbara

Dohrenwend and Bruce Dohrenwend, eds., *Stressful Life Events: Their Nature and Effects* (New York: Wiley, 1974), pp. 45–70; Robert Markush and Rachel Favero, "Epidemiologic Assessment of Stressful Life Events, Depressed Mood, and Psychophysiological Symptoms—A Preliminary Report," in Dohrenwend and Dohrenwend, *Stressful Life Events*, pp. 171–190; Aron Z. Spilken and Martin A. Jacobs, "Prediction of Illness Behavior from Measures of Life Crisis, Manifest Distress and Maladaptive Coping," *Psychosomatic Medicine* 33 (1971): 251–264; Peggy A. Thoits, "Dimensions of Life Events as Influences upon the Genesis of Psychological Distress and Associated Conditions: An Evaluation and Synthesis of the Literature," in Howard B. Kaplan, ed., *Psychosocial Stress: Trends in Theory and Research* (New York: Academic, 1983), pp. 33–103.

22. Young argues that the social stress literature is fraught with unacknowledged ideological components; he suggests that it illustrates the uncritical use of science to legitimate conventional knowledge. See Allan Young, "The Discourse on Stress and the Reproduction of Conventional Knowledge," *Social Science and Medicine* 14B (1980): 133–146.

For synopses of several studies on stress-producing social environments, see Stewart Kiritz and Moos, "Physiological Effects of Social Environments," *Psychosomatic Medicine* 36 (1974): 96–114; Leonard Pearlin and Carmi Schooler, "Structure of Coping," *Journal of Health and Social Behavior* 19 (1978): 2–22; Pearlin, "Role Strains and Personal Stress," in Kaplan, *Psychosocial Stress*, pp. 3–32.

23. Richard Lazarus, "Psychological Stress and Coping in Adaptation and Illness," *International Journal of Psychiatry in Medicine* 5 (1974): 321–333; Lazarus, "The Self-Regulation of Emotion," in Lennart Levi, ed., *Emotions—Their Parameters and Measurement* (New York: Raven Press, 1975), pp. 47–67; see also Jacques Winnubst, Frans H. G. Marcelissen, and Rolf J. Kleber, "Effects of Social Support in the Stressor-Strain Relationship: A Dutch Sample," *Social Science and Medicine* 16 (1982): 475–482.

24. See Eric J. Cassell, "Disease as an 'It': Concepts of Disease Revealed by Patients' Presentation of Symptoms," *Social Science and Medicine* 10 (1976): 143–146; Cassell, "The Nature of Suffering and the Goals of Medicine," *New England Journal of Medicine* 306 (1982): 639–645; Kleinman, "Depression, Somatization and the 'New Cross-cultural Psychiatry,'" *Social Science and Medicine* 11 (1977): 3–10; Kleinman, "Neurasthenia and Depression: A Study of Somatization and Culture in China," *Culture, Medicine and Psychiatry* 6 (1982): 117–190; Lipowski, "The Importance of Body Experience for Psychiatry," *Comprehensive Psychiatry* 18 (1977): 473–479.

25. See especially Byron J. Good, "The Heart of What's the Matter: Semantics and Illness in Iran," *Culture, Medicine and Psychiatry* 1 (1977): 25–58; Mark Nichter, "Idioms of Distress: Alternatives in the Expression of Psychosocial Distress—A Case Study from South India," *Culture, Medicine and Psychiatry* 5 (1981): 379–409.

26. Harold G. Wolff, "A Concept of Disease in Man," *Psychosomatic Medicine* 24 (1962): 25–30.

27. For a thorough critical review of this literature, see Thoits, "Dimensions of Life Events"; Pearlin, "Role Strains"; see also: Zeev Ben-Sira, "Potency: A Stress-Buffering Link in the Coping-Stress-Disease Relationship," *Social Science and Medicine* 21 (1985): 397–406; Marianne Frankenhaeuser, "Coping with Stress at Work," *International Journal of Health Services* 11 (1981): 491–510.

28. Lipowski, "Affluence, Information Inputs and Health," *Social Science and Medicine* 7 (1973): 17–29; see also Joseph Eyer, "Prosperity as a Cause of Disease," *International Journal of Health Services* 7 (1977): 125–150.

29. Aaron Antonovsky, *Health, Stress, and Coping* (San Francisco: Jossey-Bass, 1979).

30. Antonovsky, "The Sense of Coherence as a Determinant of Health," *Advances* 1 (1984): 37–50.

31. Pearlin, "Role Strains."

32. A. H. Schmale, "Giving Up as a Final Common Pathway to Changes in Health," in Lipowski, *Advances in Psychosomatic Medicine*, pp. 20–40; Schmale and I. V. Iker, "Hopelessness as a Predictor of Cervical Cancer," *Social Science and Medicine* 5 (1971): 95–100.

33. Engel, "The Need for a New Medical Model." For a critical summary of these studies, see Cohen and Lazarus, "Coping with the Stresses of Illness," in Stone, Cohen, Adler et al., *Health Psychology*, pp. 217–254.

34. See William Dressler, "Psychosomatic Symptoms, Stress and Modernization: A Model," *Culture, Medicine and Psychiatry* 9 (1985): 257–286; see also Pearlin, "Role Strains"; Thoits, "Dimensions of Life Events."

35. Lazarus, "The Self-Regulation of Emotion"; see also Gary Schwartz, "Physiological Patterning and Emotion: Implications for the Self-Regulation of Emotion," in Kirk R. Blankstein and Janet Polivy, eds., *Self Control and Self Modification of Emotional Behavior* (New York: Plenum, 1982), pp. 13–27.

36. Peter Freund, *The Civilized Body: Social Domination, Control and Health* (Philadelphia: Temple University Press, 1982), pp. 55–115; Arlie Russell Hochschild, "Emotion Work, Feeling Rules, and Social Structure," *American Journal of Sociology* 85 (1979): 551–575.

37. William R. Rogers, "Helplessness and Agency in the Healing Process," in Rogers and David Barnard, eds., *Nourishing the Humanistic in Medicine* (Pittsburgh: University of Pittsburgh Press, 1979), pp. 25–51.

38. Compare Thomas Preston, *The Clay Pedestal: A Reexamination of the Doctor-Patient Relationship* (Seattle: Madrona, 1981), pp. 66ff.; on how information control is used to maintain a pattern of professional dominance and patient submission, see also Waitzkin and Stoeckle, "Information Control and the Micropolitics of Health Care: Summary of an Ongoing Research Project," *Social Science and Medicine* 10 (1976): 263–276.

39. See Gerald Caplan and Marie Killilea, *Support Systems and Mutual Help: Multidisciplinary Explorations* (New York: Grune and Stratton, 1976); Cassell, *The Healer's Art: A New Approach to the Doctor-Patient Relationship* (Philadelphia: Lippincott, 1976); Sidney Cobb, "Social Support as a Moderator of Life Stresses," *Psychosomatic Medicine* 38 (1976): 300–314; Cohen, "Personality, Stress and the Development of Physical Illness"; James S. House, *Work Stress and Social Support* (Reading, Mass.: Addison Wesley, 1981); Kiritz and Moos, "Physiological Effects;" Lowell Levin and Ellen Idler, *The Hidden Health Care System: Mediating Structures and Medicine* (Cambridge, Mass.: Ballinger, 1981); James J. Lynch, *The Broken Heart: The Medical Consequences of Loneliness,* (New York: Basic, 1977); R. Jay Turner, "Direct, Indirect and Moderating Effects of Social Support upon Psychological Distress and Associated Conditions," in Kaplan, *Psychosocial Stress,* pp. 105–155.

40. This discussion is based mainly upon Pearlin and Schooler, "The Structure of Coping"; for a critique of the assumptions implicit in the stress/coping literature, see Young, "The Discourse on Stress." See also Cohen and Lazarus, "Coping with the Stresses"; William F. Kiely, "Coping with Severe Illness," in Lipowski, *Advances in Psychosomatic Medicine,* pp. 105–118; Lipowski, "Physical Illness, the Individual, and the Coping Process," *International Journal of Psychiatry in Medicine* 1 (1970): 91–102.

9   Ritual, Symbolism, and Healing

1. Victor Turner, *The Ritual Process: Structure and Anti-structure* (Chicago: Aldine, 1969).

2. Nancy D. Munn, "Symbolism in a Ritual Context: Aspects of Symbolic Action," in John J. Honigmann, ed., *Handbook of Social and Cultural Anthropology* (Chicago: Rand McNally, 1974), pp. 579–612.

3. Compare Leonard B. Glick, "Medicine as an Ethnographic Category: The Gimi of the New Guinea Highlands," *Ethnology* 6 (1967): 31–56.

4. John Skorupski, *Symbol and Theory: A Philosophical Study of Theories of Religion in Social Anthropology* (Cambridge, England: Cambridge University Press, 1976), p. 164.

5. Jeanine Achterberg, *Imagery in Healing: Shamanism and Modern Medicine* (Boston: New Science Library, 1985); Carl Simonton, "The Role of the Mind in Cancer Therapy," in Stanley Dean, ed., *Psychiatry and Mysticism* (Chicago: Nelson-Hall, 1975), pp. 293–308.

6. Compare Thomas Csordas and Steven Cross, "Healing of Memories: Psychotherapeutic Ritual among Catholic Pentecostals," *Journal of Pastoral Care* 30 (1976): 245–257.

7. Glick, "Medicine as an Ethnographic Category."

8. Peter L. Berger and Thomas Luckmann, *The Social Construction of Reality* (Garden City, N.Y.: Doubleday, 1967).

9. Stanley Tambiah, "The Magical Power of Words," *Man* 3 (1968): 175–208.

10. Berger and Luckmann, *Social Construction*, pp. 39–46.

11. Tambiah, "Magical Power," p. 184.

12. Compare the uses of glossolalia and prophecy: Meredith B. McGuire, *Pentecostal Catholics: Power, Charisma, and Order in a Religious Movement* (Philadelphia: Temple University Press, 1982); William J. Samarin, *Tongues of Men and Angels* (New York: Macmillan, 1972). Compare also uses of argot: Irving Zaretsky, "In the Beginning was the Word: The Relationship of Language to Social Organization in Spiritualist Churches," in Zaretsky and Mark Leone, eds., *Religious Movements in Contemporary America* (Princeton, N.J.: Princeton University Press, 1974), pp. 166–222.

13. Howard Brody, *Placebos and the Philosophy of Medicine* (Chicago: University of Chicago Press, 1977), pp. 121, 122. Regarding the ideological limitations in biomedicine's inability to deal with the notion of placebo, see also Linnie Price, "Art, Science, Faith and Medicine: The Implications of the Placebo Effect," *Sociology of Health and Illness* 6 (1984): 61–73.

14. Edmund D. Pellegrino, "Prescribing and Drug Ingestion: Symbols and Substances," *Drug Intelligence and Clinical Pharmacy* 10 (1976): 624–630.

15. Jerome Frank, "Mind-body Relationships in Illness and Healing," *Journal of the International Academy of Preventive Medicine* 2 (1975): 46–59; see also Arthur K. Shapiro, "Factors Contributing to the Placebo Effect," *American Journal of Psychotherapy*, suppl. 1, 18 (1964): 73–88; Robert A. Hahn and Arthur Kleinman, "Belief as Pathogen, Belief as Medicine: 'Voodoo Death' and the 'Placebo Phenomenon' in Anthropological Perspective," *Medical Anthropology Quarterly* 15 (1983): 3, 16–19.

16. McGuire, *Pentecostal Catholics*, p. 178.

17. Turner, *The Drums of Affliction* (Oxford: Clarendon, 1968).

18. See Mark Nichter, "Idioms of Distress: Alternatives in the Expression of Psychosocial Distress—A Case Study from South India," *Culture, Medicine and Psychiatry* 5 (1981): 379–409; see also Byron J. Good, "The Heart of What's the Matter: Semantics and Illness in Iran," *Culture, Medicine and Psychiatry* 1 (1977): 25–58; B. J. Good and Maryjo D. Good, "The Meaning of Symptoms: A Cultural Hermeneutic Model for Clinical Practice," in Leon Eisenberg and Kleinman, eds., *The Relevance of Social Science for Medicine* (Dordrecht, Holland: Reidel, 1981), pp. 165–196.

19. Mary Douglas, *Purity and Danger* (London: Routledge and Kegan Paul, 1966); Douglas, *Natural Symbols* (New York: Pantheon, 1970); Linda S. Mai, "The Re-emergence of Body Symbolism in the Catholic Charismatic Renewal," paper presented to the Society for the Scientific Study of Religion, 1978.

20. Douglas, *Purity and Danger*. For an application to new religious movements, see especially Frances Westley, "Purity, Danger and Facelessness: Pollution Beliefs in New Religious Movements," paper presented to the Society for the Scientific Study of Religion, 1977; on ritual purification in new religious movements, see also Frederick Bird, "The Nature and Function of Ritual Forms: A Sociological Discussion," *Sciences Religieuses* 9 (1980): 387–402.

21. Compare Jean Comaroff, "Medicine: Symbol and Ideology," in Peter Wright and Andrew Treacher, eds., *The Problem of Medical Knowledge: Examining the Social Construction of Medicine* (Edinburgh, Scotland: Edinburgh University Press, 1982), pp. 49–68; see also: F.J.J. Buytendijk, *Prolegomena to an Anthropological Physiology* (Pittsburgh: Duquesne University Press, 1982); Nancy Scheper-Hughes and Margaret M. Lock, "The Mindful Body: A Prolegomenon to Future Work in Medical Anthropology," *Medical Anthropology Quarterly* 1 (New Series, 1987): 6–41.

22. Munn, "Symbolism," pp. 593–595.

23. J.H.M. Beattie, *Other Cultures* (London: Routledge and Kegan Paul, 1964), p. 227.

24. O. Von Mering and L. W. Early, "Major Changes in the Western Medical Environment," *Archives of General Psychiatry* 13 (1965): 195–201.

25. Compare Daniel Moerman, "Anthropology of Symbolic Healing," *Current Anthroplogy* 20 (1979): 59–66.

26. J. L. Austin, *How to Do Things with Words* (Cambridge, Mass.: Harvard University Press, 1975); Tambiah, "Form and Meaning of Magical Acts: A Point of View," in Ruth Finnegan and Robin Horton, eds., *Modes of Thought* (London: Faber and Faber, 1973), pp. 199–229; also, Tambiah, "Magical Power."

27. Sam D. Gill, "Prayer as Person: The Performative Force in Navajo Prayer Acts," *History of Religions* 17 (1977): 143–157.

28. Benjamin Ray, "Performative Utterances in African Ritual," *History of Religions* 13 (1973): 16–35.

29. Tambiah, "Magical Power"; Tambiah, "The Cosmological and Performative Significance of a Thai Cult of Healing through Meditation," *Culture, Medicine and Psychiatry* 1 (1977): 97–132.

30. Compare Ari Kiev, ed., *Magic, Faith, and Healing* (New York: Free Press, 1964), p. 8; Kleinman, "Some Issues for a Comparative Study of Medical Healing," *International Journal of Social Psychiatry* 19 (1973): 162; Claude Lévi-Strauss, *Structural Anthropology* (Garden City, N.Y.: Doubleday, 1967), p. 199; E. Mansell Pattison, Nikolajs A. Lapins, and Hans A. Doerr, "Faith Healing: A Study of Personality and Function," *Journal of Nervous and Mental Disease* 157 (1973): 405; Allan Young, "Some Implications of Medical Beliefs and Practices for Social Anthropology," *American Anthropologist* 79 (1976): 13.

31. Compare Pattison, "Ideological Support for the Marginal Middle Class:

Faith Healing and Glossolalia," in Zaretsky and Leone, *Religious Movements*, p. 452.

32. Compare Zaretsky, "In the Beginning," pp. 190–191.

33. See Aaron Antonovsky, "The Sense of Coherence as a Determinant of Health," *Advances* 1 (1984): 37–50.

34. Kleinman, "Some Issues," p. 160.

35. Young, "Some Implications."

36. On the meanings of pain, compare David Mechanic and Edmund Volkart, "Stress, Illness Behavior and the Sick Role," *American Sociological Review* 26 (1961): 51–58; Thomas S. Szasz, *Pain and Pleasure: A Study of Bodily Feeling* (New York: Basic, 1957); Berthold Wolff and Sarah Langley, "Cultural Factors and the Response to Pain: A Review," *American Anthropologist* 70 (1968): 494–501.

37. Young, "Some Implications," p. 8. Compare also Lorna Amarasingham Rhodes, "Time and the Process of Diagnosis in Sinhalese Ritual Treatments," *Contributions to Asian Studies* 18 (1984): 46–59.

38. On shamanic healing, see Mircea Eliade, *Shamanism: Archaic Techniques of Ecstasy* (New York: Pantheon, 1964); Kiev, *Magic, Faith, and Healing;* David Landy, ed., *Culture, Disease, and Healing* (New York: Macmillan, 1977); Ioan M. Lewis, *Ecstatic Religion: Spirit Possession and Shamanism* (Baltimore: Penguin, 1971); Elmer S. Miller, "Shamans, Power Symbols and Change in Argentine Toba Culture," *American Ethnologist* 2 (1975): 477–496; Julian Silverman, "Shamans and Acute Schizophrenia," *American Anthropologist* 69 (1967): 21–31.

39. Miller, "Shamans," pp. 483, 479; see also Young, "Order, Analogy and Efficacy in Ethiopian Medical Divination," *Culture, Medicine and Psychiatry* 1 (1977): 183–199.

40. James Dow, "Universal Aspects of Symbolic Healing: A Theoretical Synthesis," *American Anthropologist* 88 (1986): 56–69.

41. Tambiah, *The Buddhist Saints of the Forest and the Cult of Amulets* (Cambridge, England: Cambridge University Press, 1984), pp. 335 ff.

42. Csordas, "The Rhetoric of Transformation in Ritual Healing," *Culture, Medicine and Psychiatry* 7 (1983): 333–375.

43. Roy Wallis, "Ideology, Authority and the Development of Cultic Movements," *Social Research* 41 (1974): 299–327.

44. McGuire, *Religion: The Social Context* (Belmont, Calif.: Wadsworth, 1981), pp. 165–166; see also note 2, Chapter Seven.

45. Kenneth Burke, *A Rhetoric of Motives* (Englewood Cliffs, N.J.: Prentice-Hall, 1953); Csordas, "The Rhetoric of Transformation"; McGuire, *Religion*, pp. 50ff.

46. See Frederick Bird, "The Pursuit of Innocence: New Religious Movements and Moral Accountability," *Sociological Analysis* 40 (1979): 335–346; Paul Heelas, "Californian Self-Religions and Socialising the Subjective," in Eileen Barker, ed.,

New Religious Movements: A Perspective for Understanding Society (New York: Edwin Mellen Press, 1982), pp. 69–85; Steven M. Tipton, "The Moral Logic of Alternative Religions," in Douglas and Tipton, eds., *Religion and America: Spiritual Life in a Secular Age* (Boston: Beacon, 1982), pp. 79–107.

47. Hans Peter Dreitzel, "The Socialization of Nature: Western Attitudes towards Body and Emotion," in Heelas and A. Lock, eds., *Indigenous Psychologies: The Anthropology of the Self* (New York: Academic, 1981), pp. 205–223; further sources are discussed in Chapter Ten. Whether this individual "freedom" or flexibility would have significant social structural repercussions is debatable. Some optimistic and critical evaluations are presented in Chapter Ten.

10   Individualisms and Transformations of the Self

1. Eric J. Cassell, "The Nature of Suffering and the Goals of Medicine," *New England Journal of Medicine* 306 (1982): 639–645; see also Cassell, "Illness and Disease," *Hastings Center Report* 6 (1976): 2–3, 29–36.

2. Oliver Sacks, *A Leg to Stand On* (New York: Summit, 1984), pp. 45–50.

3. Ibid., p. 67.

4. Cassell, "The Nature of Suffering," p. 639.

5. Ibid., p. 642.

6. See Chapter Eight for a discussion of Antonovsky's theory of "coherence," as it applies to these findings.

7. Cassell, "Illness and Disease."

8. On the importance of transcendence, see Cassell, "The Nature of Suffering."

9. Compare James Beckford, "Holistic Imagery and Ethics in New Religious and Healing Movements," *Social Compass* 31 (1984): 259–272; and "The World Images of New Religious and Healing Movements," in R. Kenneth Jones, ed., *Sickness and Sectarianism* (London: Gower, 1985), pp. 72–93.

10. Frederick Bird, "Charisma and Ritual in New Religious Movements," in Jacob Needleman and George Baker, eds., *Understanding the New Religions* (New York: Seabury, 1978), pp. 173–189.

11. Max Weber, *From Max Weber: Essays in Sociology*, Hans Gerth and C. Wright Mills, eds. and trans. (New York: Oxford, 1958), p. 280.

12. Roland Robertson, "Individualism, Societalism, Worldliness, Universalism: Thematizing Theoretical Sociology of Religion," *Sociological Analysis* 38 (1977): 281–308.

13. Robertson, "Theoretical Comments on Religion and Society in Modern America: Weber Revisited," presented to the International Sociological Association World Congress, Research Group on the Sociology of Religion, 1978.

14. Robertson, "Individualism."

15. Jurgen Habermas, *Legitimation Crisis*, trans. T. McCarthy (Boston: Beacon, 1975), pp. 117–130.

16. Meredith McGuire, *Religion: The Social Context* (Belmont, Calif.: Wadsworth, 1987).

17. Steven M. Tipton, "The Moral Logic of Alternative Religions," in Mary Douglas and Tipton, eds., *Religion and America: Spiritual Life in a Secular Age* (Boston: Beacon, 1982), pp. 79–107.

18. McGuire, *Religion*, pp. 240–243; for examples of widespread medicalization, see Peter Conrad and Joseph Schneider, *Deviance and Medicalization: From Badness to Sickness* (St. Louis: C. V. Mosby, 1980).

19. See, for example, the interpretation proposed by Sally Guttmacher, "Whole in Body, Mind and Spirit: Holistic Health and the Limits to Medicine," *Hastings Center Report* 9 (1979), 2:15–21; further comment by Jean Comaroff, "Medicine: Symbol and Ideology," in Peter Wright and Andrew Treacher, eds., *The Problem of Medical Knowledge: Examining the Social Construction of Medicine* (Edinburgh, Scotland: Edinburgh University Press, 1982), pp. 49–68.

20. Compare Jane Brody, "Self-blame Held to Be Important in Victims' Recovery," *The New York Times*, January 17, 1984, pp. C1, C6.

21. Susan Sontag, *Illness as Metaphor* (New York: Vintage, 1977), pp. 45–46.

22. Robert Crawford, "You are Dangerous to Your Health: The Ideology and Politics of Victim Blaming," *International Journal of Health Services* 7 (1977): 663–679; see also Comaroff, "Medicine." A relevant argument to the contrary is presented by Alfred Katz and Lowell Levin, "Self-Care is Not a Solipsistic Trap: A Reply to Critics," *International Journal of Health Services* 10 (1980): 329–336.

23. Tipton, "The Moral Logic"; Tipton, *Getting Saved from the Sixties: The Transformation of Moral Meaning in American Culture by Alternative Religious Movements* (Berkeley: University of California Press, 1982).

24. Regarding new religious movements and moral order, see also Dick Anthony and Thomas Robbins, "Contemporary Religious Ferment and Moral Ambiguity," in Eileen Barker, ed., *New Religious Movements: A Perspective for Understanding Society* (New York and Toronto: Edwin Mellen Press, 1982), pp. 243–266; Bird, "The Pursuit of Innocence: New Religious Movements and Moral Accountability," *Sociological Analysis* 40 (1979): 335–346; Thomas Robbins, Dick Anthony, and James Richardson, "Theory and Research on Today's New Religions," *Sociological Analysis* 39 (1978): 95–122; and Frances Westley, "The 'Cult of Man': Durkheim's Predictions and New Religious Movements," *Sociological Analysis* 39 (1978): 135–145; Westley, *The Complex Forms of the Religious Life* (Chico, Calif.: Scholars Press, 1983).

25. Robert A. Hahn and Arthur Kleinman, "Biomedical Practice and Anthropological Theory: Framework and Directions," *American Review of Anthropology* 12

(1983): 313; see also Nancy Scheper-Hughes and Margaret Lock, "The Mindful Body: A Prolegomenon to Future Work in Medical Anthropology," *Medical Anthropology Quarterly* 1 (New Series, 1987): 6–41.

26. Hans Peter Dreitzel, "The Socialization of Nature: Western Attitudes towards Body and Emotions," in P. Heelas and A. Lock, eds., *Indigenous Psychologies: The Anthropology of the Self* (New York: Academic, 1981), pp. 205–223.

27. Norbert Elias, *The Civilizing Process*, vol. 1: *The History of Manners* (New York: Urizen Books, 1978); Elias, *Power and Civility* (New York: Pantheon, 1982); see also Mary Douglas, *Natural Symbols* (New York: Pantheon, 1970); Peter Freund, *The Civilized Body: Social Domination, Control and Health* (Philadelphia: Temple University Press, 1982).

28. Dreitzel, "The Socialization of Nature."

29. Ibid.; see also Michel Foucault, *Discipline and Punish* (New York: Pantheon, 1977); Foucault, *The History of Sexuality*, vol. 1 (New York: Pantheon, 1980); Freund, *The Civilized Body*; Bryan S. Turner, *The Body and Society: Explorations in Social Theory* (Oxford: Basil Blackwell, 1984).

30. Compare Freund, *The Civilized Body*; Freund, "Bringing Society into the Body: Some Notes on Socialized Human Nature," *Theory and Society*, in press; see also Arlie R. Hochschild, *The Managed Heart: Commercialization of Human Feeling* (Berkeley: University of California Press, 1983).

31. Compare Bird, "Charisma and Ritual." Because of the characteristic freedom in such groups to choose not only which beliefs but also which experiences, we must methodologically avoid overreliance on what various promulgators teach. Most alternative healing groups have no clear norms of commitment or orthodoxy (cf. Roy Wallis, "Betwixt Therapy and Salvation: The Changing Form of the Human Potential Movement," in Jones, *Sickness and Sectarianism*, pp. 23–51).

We must focus instead on how individuals construct their own world images and alternative experiences using elements from various groups, in the manner of a "briccoleur," as Lévi-Straus suggests: cf. Claude Lévi-Straus, *The Savage Mind* (Chicago: University of Chicago Press, 1966), pp. 16–21.

32. Robertson, "Religious Movements and Modern Societies: Toward a Progressive Problemshift," *Sociological Analysis* 40 (1979): 297–314.

33. Philip Wexler, *Critical Social Psychology* (Boston: Routledge and Kegan Paul, 1983).

34. Alvin W. Gouldner, *The Future of Intellectuals and the Rise of the New Class* (New York: Seabury, 1979).

35. Wexler, *Critical Social Psychology*, p. 92.

36. Weber, *From Max Weber*, pp. 180–195.

37. Compare Kristen Luker, *Abortion and the Politics of Motherhood* (Berkeley:

University of California Press, 1984); for a similar analysis of the Moral Majority, see Thomas M. Gannon, "The New Christian Right in America," *Archives de Sciences des Religions* 52 (1981): 69–83.

38. Beckford, "The World Images," p. 88; Peter Berger, Brigitte Berger, and Hansfried Kellner, *The Homeless Mind: Modernization and Consciousness* (New York: Vintage/Random, 1973), p. 209; Robert Crawford, "A Cultural Account of 'Health': Control, Release and the Social Body," in John B. McKinley, ed., *Issues in the Political Economy of Healthcare* (New York: Tavistock, 1984), pp. 60–103.

39. Some data from this study support this interpretation, and other data refute it. Many groups' sheer pluralistic openness to all kinds of healing approaches suggests an antirationalizing stance; no single health or healing practice was mandated. Other adherents appeared to view healing practices as moral prescriptions. To evaluate this thesis, we would need to learn more about the extent to which adherents reify the discipline of various health and healing practices. Also, to what extent do their beliefs and practices in everyday life support or challenge the requisites of their niche in the economy?

40. Dreitzel, "The Socialization of Nature."

Appendix A: Methods of Research

1. Edith Horner, ed., *The New Jersey Municipal Data Book: 1985 edition* (Montclair, N.J.: New Jersey Associates, 1985).

2. The word *group* is used for convenience in this volume to refer to both actual groups (e.g., a prayer group) and to healer-adherent situations, which often did not meet as groups per se.

3. Zaretsky states that the particular meaning given a term and the rules for its appropriate use are precisely what separates one part of this subculture (e.g., Spiritualism) from another (e.g., metaphysical movements like Unity); Irving Zaretsky, "In the Beginning was the Word: The Relationship of Language to Social Organization in Spiritualist Churches," in Irving Zaretsky and Mark Leone, eds., *Religious Movements in Contemporary America* (Princeton, N.J.: Princeton University Press, 1974), pp. 166–222.

4. John A. Saliba, "The New Ethnography and the Study of Religion," *Journal for the Scientific Study of Religion* 13 (1974): 145–159.

5. Jack Douglas, *Research on Deviance* (New York: Random House, 1972), p. 28.

6. James Richardson, Mary Stewart, and Robert Simmonds, "Researching a Fundamentalist Commune," in Jacob Needleman and George Baker, eds., *Understanding the New Religions* (New York: Seabury, 1978), pp. 235–251.

7. Gary Schwartz, *Sect Ideologies and Social Status* (Chicago: University of Chicago Press, 1970), p. 242.

8. Thomas Robbins, Dick Anthony, and Thomas Curtis, "The Limits of Symbolic Realism: Problems of Empathic Field Observation in a Sectarian Context," *Journal for the Scientific Study of Religion* 12 (1973): 259–271.

INDEX